ALCOHOLISM AND HEALTH

reprinted from

**Family &
Community
Health**

edited by
Sharon V. Davidson

AN ASPEN PUBLICATION®
Aspen Systems Corporation
Germantown, Maryland
London, England
1980

Library of Congress Cataloging in Publication Data

Main entry under title:

Alcoholism and health.

"Reprinted from Family & community health."
Includes bibliographical references.
1. Alcoholism. I. Family & community health.
[DNLM: 1. Alcoholism—Collected works.
2. Health—Collected works. WM274 A3552]
RC565.A4454   616.86'1   80-12354
ISBN 0-89443-292-3

Copyright © 1980 by Aspen Systems Corporation

Library of Congress Catalog Card Number: 80-12354
ISBN: 0-89443-292-3

Printed in the United States of America

1 2 3 4 5

ALCOHOLISM AND HEALTH

Janelle C. Krueger, R.N., Ph.D., F.A.A.N.
Professor, School of Nursing
University of Colorado Medical Center
Denver, Colorado

Edward O. Moe, Ph.D.
Principal Sociologist and Coordinator for Rural
    Development
U.S. Department of Agriculture
Cooperative State Research Service
Washington, D.C.

Dorothy V. Moses, R.N., M.S.
Professor of Nursing
San Diego State University
San Diego, California

Martin Nacman, D.S.W.
Director, Social Work Division
Strong Memorial Hospital
University of Rochester School of Medicine and
    Dentistry
Rochester, New York

Robert D. Newcomb, O.D., M.P.H., F.A.A.O.
Assistant Professor of Optometry
School of Optometry
The Medical Center
University of Alabama in Birmingham
Birmingham, Alabama

Mary O'Hara-Devereaux, R.N., F.N.P.
Director, Family Nurse Practitioner Program
Department of Family Practice
University of California, Davis
Davis, California

Martha Compton Primeaux, R.N., M.S.N.
Associate Professor of Nursing
President
American Indian Nurses' Association
Oklahoma City, Oklahoma

Orlando A. Rivera, Ph.D.
Assistant Professor
Educational Psychology
Associate Vice President for Academic Affairs
University of Utah
Salt Lake City, Utah

Paulette Robischon, R.N., Ph.D.
Professor and Coordinator
Community Health Nursing
Department of Nursing
Herbert H. Lehman College
City University of New York
New York, New York

Sally E. Ruybal, R.N., Ph.D.
Associate Professor
Graduate Program
College of Nursing
University of New Mexico
Albuquerque, New Mexico

Jessie M. Scott, Ph.D.
Assistant Surgeon General
Director
Division of Nursing BHM/HRA
Department of Health, Education and Welfare
Hyattsville, Maryland

Jerome Shapiro, D.P.M.
Supervisory Podiatrist
District of Columbia Department of Human Resources
Washington, D.C.

Robert H. Sharpley, M.D.
President
Solomon Fuller Institute
Cambridge, Massachusetts

Anne R. Somers
Professor, Department of Community Medicine
    and Family Medicine
College of Medicine and Dentistry
New Jersey—Rutgers Medical School
Research Associate
Industrial Relations Section
Princeton University
Princeton, New Jersey

Lillian Gatlin Stokes, R.N., M.S.N.
Associate Professor
Indiana University School of Nursing
Indianapolis, Indiana

Jack L. Tedrow, M.D., J.D.
Associate Clinical Professor
Department of Psychiatry
University of Utah College of Medicine
Chairman, Utah State Board of Mental Health
Salt Lake City, Utah

Minnie H. Walton, B.S.N., M.S.
Director of Nursing
Cape Cod Hospital
Hyannis, Massachusetts

Donald M. Watkin, M.D., M.P.H., F.A.C.P.
Special Assistant to the Director
Office of State and Community Programs
Administration on Aging
Office of Human Development Services
Office of the Secretary
Department of Health, Education and Welfare
Washington, D.C.

Thelma J. Wells, R.N., Ph.D.
Assistant Professor (Gerontological Nursing)
University of Rochester School of Nursing
Rochester, New York

Lucille F. Whaley, R.N., M.S.
Associate Professor
Department of Nursing
San Jose State University
San Jose, California

Carolyn A. Williams, R.N., Ph.D., F.A.A.N.
Associate Professor of Nursing
School of Nursing
Assistant Professor of Epidemiology
School of Public Health
Department of Epidemiology
University of North Carolina
Chapel Hill, North Carolina

Sue Rodwell Williams, R.D., M.P.H., M.R.Ed., Ph.D.
Chief, Nutrition Program
Kaiser-Permanente Medical Center
Oakland, California
Clinical Faculty
Public Health Nutrition
University of California, Berkeley
Berkeley, California

Rowena A. Wilson, R.N., M.P.H.
Director, Professional Education
Community Cancer Control
President
Quality Care Associates
Los Angeles, California

From the editors . . .

ALCOHOLISM: THE NEGATION OF HEALTH

The extent of alcoholism, a negative addiction and a serious health and social problem, has recently been growing, affecting the health status and lives of an increasing number of Americans. Alcoholism is a primary, progressive, chronic and often fatal disease. It is now recognized as a treatable entity, and a number of important changes in the identification and treatment of alcoholism portend advances that are having a significant impact upon this major health problem.

For example, since the founding of the National Institute of Alcohol Abuse and Alcoholism in 1971, federal funds have been made available for increased research efforts to further the understanding of alcoholism as a health problem, to promote prevention and the early identification of problem drinking, to educate a growing number of alcoholism counselors and to improve and extend treatment efforts. Furthermore, it has recently been pointed out that:

> . . . employers in business and industry have been creating and implementing programs of early detection and intervention into alcohol (abuse) problems; third-party payments have been developed by health insurance companies for the treatment of alcoholism . . . and public awareness regarding

alcoholism has increased markedly through creative use of advertising media.[1]

There are an estimated 9.3 to 10 million problem drinkers and alcoholics in the adult population—seven percent of the 145 million adults in the United States.[2] A recent report indicates that in addition to adult problem drinkers, there are an estimated 3.3 million problem drinkers among youth in the 14–17 age range. This is 19 percent of the 17 million persons in this age group. (Youth problem drinking is defined differently than for adults, because youth problems tend to be acute rather than chronic.)[3]

It is estimated that alcohol-related deaths may run as high as 205,000 per year (11 percent of the 1.9 million deaths in 1975). Clinical studies consistently show that various types of alcohol problems in males are associated with mortality rates two to six times higher than rates in the general population.[4]

Alcohol abuse and alcoholism costs in the United States totalled nearly $43 billion in 1975; this includes $19.64 billion in lost production, $12.74 billion in health and medical costs, $5.14 billion in motor vehicle accidents, $2.86 billion in violent crimes, $1.94 billion in social responses and $0.43 in fire losses.[5]

The first issue on Alcoholism and Health contains basic information on alcoholics, i.e., the extent of the problem, stages of becoming an alcoholic, juvenile problem drinking, community treatment and a framework for conceptualizing negative and positive addictions. Alcoholism and Health—Part II will focus on physiological changes resulting from the disease process and on treatment problems posed by the alcoholic. FCH recognizes the need of health care providers for expanded knowledge and understanding concerning alcoholism, its recognition, treatment and rehabilitation.

The issue editor for FCH's two issues devoted to alcoholism is Sharon V. Davidson, R.N., B.S.N., M.Ed., Ob-Gyn Unit Coordinator, Memorial Hospital, and President, Continuing Professional Education and Nursing Review Programs Inc.,

Colorado Springs, Colorado. Our issue editor is well versed in the problems presented by the serious problem drinker and the alcoholic on both practical and theoretical levels.

This first issue on alcoholism contains five articles that are comprehensive in their assessment and description of this multifaceted, complex health problem.

Davidson, in "The Assessment of Alcoholism," recognizes that all members of the health care team must possess the ability to identify and assess alcoholics as well as potential problem drinkers. Often, upon a patient's admission to a hospital emergency room or on coming to a community clinic, the nurse may be the first professional to interact with the alcoholic and thus may be instrumental in identifying the patient's symptoms. The author presents a group of working definitions of alcoholism and describes the progressive symptoms of alcoholism (the preaddiction and addiction stages). Davidson describes a number of diagnostic and assessment techniques for alcoholism along with an assessment of their validity and reliability. She also includes several questionnaires that have been used to identify the alcoholic and a proposed nursing assessment tool for alcoholism, with the caveat that much more research needs to be completed in this important area.

"The Alcoholic Professional" by Sonya E. Schnurr, R.N. is a highly sensitive, personal and forthright account of the author's life experience as an alcoholic. Her eventual personal struggle with various treatment techniques and her determined self-cure are described in a moving and beautiful narrative. Any health care professional will gain a "gut-level" experience from this material that will increase the sensitivity to and understanding of the seriously addicted alcoholic and the battle to recover from the disease.

"Adolescent Alcoholism: Treatment and Rehabilitation," Bessie Fields, R.N., head nurse of the Alcoholism Unit at Talbot Hall, St. Anthony Hospital, Columbus, Ohio, notes the recent upsurge in alcohol abuse among teenagers; in many cases alcohol abuse may be conducive to polydrug use, although alcohol appears to be the drug of choice for a large number of teenagers because of its accessibility. To understand teenage alcoholism, the author emphasizes that the health professional must understand the disease as well as normal physiological and psychosocial adolescent development.

Fields provides a detailed account of the treatment model used with adolescent alcoholics, describing group therapy, individual counseling and recreational and occupational therapy. Defenses and personality dynamics of the teenage problem drinker are described, as are phases of group therapy. Ms. Fields points out that alcoholism is a family disease in that it affects communication patterns within the family and the family's lifestyle in a very profound manner. Thus the family must be intimately involved in the treatment process.

Alcoholism is not only a major killer in an individual and family context but it also has an immense impact upon the community. Arthur Knauert, M.D., emphasizes the costly impact of alcoholism upon community resources. Alcoholism increases demand on community-based facilities and emergency and inpatient hospital facilities, and it increases the incidence of criminal activities, injuries and fatalities resulting from drunken driving, wife beatings, rape, child abuse and numerous other crimes. Many community agencies throughout the United States devote costly treatment facilities, both publicly and privately funded, to health problems associated with alcohol abuse.

Knauert stresses that there are three basic types of alcoholic clients and that workers in a comprehensive treatment center should be able to make a differential diagnosis so that proper disposition and referral can be made.

In the final article, Gary G. Forrest, Ed.D., P.C., presents a unique framework for conceptualizing negative and positive addictions. His article provides the reader with an enlightening perspective on addictions.

It is our intention that this issue and the remaining issues of Volume 2 of FCH continue to meet your interests and needs as health care professionals.

—*Adina M. Reinhardt*
Editor
—*Mildred D. Quinn*
Associate Editor

REFERENCES

1. Estes, N. J. and Heinemann, M. E., eds. *Alcoholism: Development, Consequences and Interventions* (St. Louis: The C. V. Mosby Co. 1977) p. vii.
2. U. S. Department of Health, Education and Welfare. *The Third Special Report to the U.S. Congress on Alcohol and Health from the Secretary of HEW.* Preprint copy (Washington, D.C.: Government Printing Office, June 1978) p. 20.
3. Ibid., p. 21.
4. Ibid., p. v.
5. Ibid., p. 21.

APPROACHES TO TREATMENT OF ALCOHOL ABUSE

Alcoholism and Health—Part II focuses on the physiological changes which result from the alcohol disease process and on treatment problems posed by the alcohol- and/or chemical-addicted individual. The majority of the articles included in this issue are based on presentations given at the Fifth Annual Advanced Winter Workshop on "Treatment and Rehabilitation of the Alcoholic," sponsored by Psychotherapy Associates, P.C., and held last January in Colorado Springs, Colorado. This conference included many nationally recognized alcoholism counselors (physicians, psychologists and nurses) who have had extensive experience in working with the alcoholic patient.

Alcohol and chemical abuse is not a moral or character weakness. Rather, it is a health problem of major proportions that is subject to a variety of differential diagnoses and multiple treatment modalities.

Treatment of the alcohol- and chemical-addicted patient is complex, time consuming and frustrating. Such treatment can only be successful if the health care professional treating the addicted patient is knowledgeable, experienced, innovative and tolerant. Health care providers are usually reluctant to become involved in treating the alcoholic patient since the work is so demanding.

If patients are only treated until detoxification and the cessation of withdrawal symptoms occur, they will use medical facilities as a revolving door. Since the treatment of alcoholism roughly amounts to 15 percent of the nation's hospitalizations and its medically related complications (i.e., peptic ulcer disease, accident, trauma) and treatment accounts for 30 percent or more of inpatient beds, familiarity with the disease becomes a must for every health care professional, particularly for primary care physicians who work the front lines.[1]

The articles presented here cover a broad spectrum of issues and approaches to alcoholism and its treatment. Article topics range from the differential diagnosis of alcoholism to the "burnout syndrome," a condition often experienced by counselors working with alcoholics.

Arthur P. Knauert, M.D. postulates a system of classification of alcoholics into three major categories: (1) primary alcoholics, characterized by a background of inconsistent nurturing; (2) secondary alcoholics, individuals with underlying mental illness that must be treated first; and (3) reactive alcoholics, those having experienced a major situational life trauma.

A gastroenterologist, W. Jeff Wooddell, M.D., addresses two aspects of physiological phenomena often associated with alcoholism. In one article Dr. Wooddell discusses chronic liver disease in alcoholics; the second article reviews the alcohol withdrawal syndrome in a comprehensive manner.

Thomas E. Bratter, Ed.D., a practicing psychotherapist, contributes "The Psychotherapist as a Twelfth Step Worker in the Treatment of Alcoholism." This article describes the twelfth step worker model derived from the Alcoholics Anonymous (AA) concept. In addition, Glasser's Reality Therapy is explored as a psychological treatment method, evolved through clinical application for improved outcome.

Gary G. Forrest, Ed.D., P.C., in "Setting Alcoholic Patients up for Therapeutic Failure," vividly describes the counselor's role as rescuer of the alcoholic patient. The author believes this role may be the major cause of rehabilitative or therapeutic failure, and may sometimes lead to suicide by the patient. Eventually, counselors engaging in the rescuer role find themselves physically tired and generally depressed.

In "Maintaining the Sanity of Alcoholism Counselors," Knauert combines with issue editor Sharon V. Davidson, R.N., M.Ed. to present some methods to help professional alcoholism counselors avoid the "burnout syndrome." For example, counselors can delegate some of the nurturing of the alcoholic to organizations such as AA. Counselors need to reserve portions of their lives for meeting their own needs for relaxation and regeneration. Without such regeneration, counselors may become ineffective in their therapeutic roles.

A comprehensive review of significant research on the effectiveness of various methods of alcohol abuse treatment is the focus of our final article, by Chad D. Emrick, Ph.D. This previously unpublished study was prepared for HEW's Alcohol Program and Policy Review Project at the request of HEW Secretary Joseph Califano. Emrick's article is a review of current literature pertinent to alcohol treatment. The author categorizes and analyzes studies in regard to the effectiveness of treatment approaches to alcohol abuse. Emrick's extensive clinical background, experience and knowledge of alcohol abuse therapy qualifies him to report on the current "state of the art" of alcohol treatment research.

In these two issues devoted to alcoholism and health, we have endeavored to provide information and fresh perspectives on alcoholism—its definition, recognition and treatment. We hope that you, our readers, will find this information definitive, realistic and practical for your needs as health care providers.

REFERENCE

1. Fletcher, D. J. "EtOH Is No Longer Just a Chemical Formula in Med School." Editorial, *Medical News* 3:6 (March 12, 1979) p. 23.

—*Adina M. Reinhardt*
Editor
—*Mildred D. Quinn*
Associate Editor

The Assessment of Alcoholism

Sharon V. Davidson, R.N., M.Ed.
President
Continuing Professional Education and
  Nursing Review Programs, Inc.
Ob-Gyn Unit Coordinator
Memorial Hospital
Colorado Springs, Colorado

THE PROFESSIONAL NURSE is becoming increasingly aware of the danger of alcoholism to individuals and society. One index of the enormity of the alcohol problem comes from research measuring the number of people who require hospitalization as a consequence of their alcoholism. Most of the studies have shown that between 25 and 64 percent of admissions to medical wards in acute care facilities were related to alcoholism.[1] In addition, half of all highway fatalities and disabling injuries are associated with alcohol abuse.[2] In fact, alcoholism is presently considered this nation's third most serious health problem, following heart ailments and cancer.[3]

Identifying the potential alcohol abuser during admission to the hospital is a skill required of the professional nurse. Some alcoholics are admitted with a diagnosis of alcoholism; some present themselves for care while inebriated; but others receive care without any member

2

of the health team identifying the patient as an alcoholic. With nine million alcoholics in the United States, a vast majority of these are not currently in treatment.[4] The nurse may provide the first professional contact with the alcoholic, and, as such, may be instrumental in the identification of the alcohol problem, and may be extremely significant in determining the chances that the patient will follow through with treatment recommendations.

Therefore, the nurse must have an assessment tool for identifying potential problem drinkers. Of current nursing assessment tools, a few are practical methods for assessing the potential alcohol abuser, and none has been adequately validated. But before a nurse can help select or design an assessment tool and validate its effectiveness, the nurse must understand what alcoholism is, how it is diagnosed and how its progress is measured. Furthermore, the nurse should be familiar with the types of assessment questions currently used by psychiatric health professionals for identification of alcoholics.

ALCOHOLISM DEFINED

General Definition

There are hundreds of definitions of alcoholism. The World Health Organization defines alcoholism as follows:

Any form of drinking which in its extent goes beyond the traditional and customary 'dietary' use or the ordinary compliance with the social drinking customs of the whole community concerned, irrespective of the etiological factors leading to such behavior, and irrespective also of the extent to which such etiological factors are dependent upon heredity, constitution, or acquired physiopathological and metabolic influences.[5]

A second definition considers an alcoholic "one whose drinking interferes with his health, his job, his relations with his family, or his community relationships—and yet he continues to drink."[6] A still shorter description defines the alcoholic as "one who repeatedly seeks to change reality through the use of alcohol."[7]

Behavioral Definition

Another definition of alcoholism is based on measures of behavior:

1. Loss of control—victims find themselves drinking when they intend not to drink, or drinking more than they planned;
2. Presence of functional or structural damage—physiological, psychological, domestic, economic or social; and
3. Use of alcohol as a kind of universal therapy, as a psychopharmacologic substance through which people try to keep their lives from coming apart.[8]

Problem drinking is usually recognized whenever anyone drinks to such an excess that the person can no longer control actions or maintain a socially acceptable life adjustment. A problem drinker may exhibit the following behaviors:

1. Drinks in order to function or "cope with life;"
2. Frequently drinks to a state of intoxication (as defined by the drinker or family and friends);
3. Goes to work intoxicated;

4. Drives a car when intoxicated;
5. Sustains bodily injury requiring medical attention as a consequence of an intoxicated state;
6. Does something under the influence of alcohol that the drinker contends would never happen without alcohol;
7. Needs to drink before facing certain situations;
8. Engages in frequent drinking sprees;
9. Steadily increases alcoholic intake;
10. Drinks alone;
11. Drinks in the early morning; and
12. Experiences "blackouts." (For the heavy drinker, a blackout is not "passing out" but a period of time in which the drinker walks, talks and acts, but does not remember.)

PROGRESSIVE SYMPTOMS OF ALCOHOLISM

In addition to understanding what alcoholism is, the nurse should understand the progressive symptoms of alcoholism. The progression of alcoholism is sufficiently insidious and gradual to make it impossible to distinguish the alcoholic from the heavy drinker in the early stages. For the drinking population, alcoholic beverages are used primarily in social situations. Social drinkers may continue to use alcohol for the rest of their lives and suffer no more than an occasional hangover. However, incipient alcoholics march to the beat of a different drum—they respond more emotionally to alcohol than nonalcoholics and attach an

Incipient alcoholics respond more emotionally to alcohol than nonalcoholics and attach an inordinate significance to it, often at the time of the first drink.

inordinate significance to it, often at the time of the first drink.

The behavioral characteristics of alcoholics are as progressive as their tolerance to alcohol and the course of the disease itself. These progressive symptoms can be grouped as preaddiction, addiction and last stages.[10]

Preaddiction

This stage begins when drinking is no longer social but rather a means of psychological escape from tensions and inhibitions. Although the eventual problem drinkers are still in reasonable control, their habits begin to fall into a definite pattern.

Gross drinking behavior—They begin to drink more heavily and more often than their friends. Getting drunk becomes a habit. When drunk, they may develop an inflated self-image, recklessly spending money, boasting of real and fancied accomplishments.

Blackouts—A "blackout," temporary loss of memory, is not to be confused with "passing out," loss of consciousness. Drinkers are suffering from blackouts when they cannot remember things they said, things they did or places they visited while carousing the night before—or for longer periods. Even social drinkers can have a blackout. With prospective alco-

4

holics, blackouts are more frequent and develop into a pattern.

Gulping and sneaking drinks—Anxious to maintain a euphoric level, they begin to gulp drinks at parties and sneak extra ones when they think nobody is looking. They may also drink before going to a party to insure euphoria. They feel guilty about this behavior and nervously avoid talking about drinks or drinking.

Chronic hangovers—As they grow more and more reliant on alcohol as a shock absorber to daily living, hangovers become more frequent and increasingly painful.

Addiction

Until now problem drinkers have been imbibing heavily but not always conspicuously. More important, they have been

---

Until the addiction stage, problem drinkers have been imbibing heavily but not always conspicuously. More important, they have been able to stop drinking when they so chose.

---

able to stop drinking when they so chose. Beyond this point, they develop the symptoms of addiction with increased rapidity.

Loss of control—This is the most common symptom that a psychological habit has become an addiction. Problem drinkers may still refuse to accept a drink. But once they take a drink, they cannot stop. A single drink is likely to trigger a chain reaction that will continue without a break into a state of complete intoxication.

The alibi system—Their loss of control induces feelings of guilt and shame, so problem drinkers concoct an elaborate system of "reasons" for their drinking, such as—"I just completed my income tax" or "I failed to complete my income tax." They hope these reasons will justify their behavior in the eyes of their families and associates. In reality, the reasons are mostly to reassure the drinkers.

Morning drinks—Problem drinkers need a drink in the morning "to start the day right." Their "morning" may start at any hour of day or night, so a morning drink is in fact sedation to ease their jangled nerves, hangover or feelings of remorse after involuntary abstinence while sleeping. They cannot face the upcoming hours without alcohol.

Changing the pattern—By now problem drinkers are under pressure from their families, employers or both. They try to break the hold alcohol has on them. At first they may try changing what they drink, such as shifting from whiskey to beer. That does no good. Then they may set up rules as to when they will drink and what they will drink, such as, "only three martinis on weekends and, of course, holidays." They may even give up alcohol for a period. But when problem drinkers take one sip of alcohol, the chain reaction starts all over again.

Antisocial behavior—They prefer drinking alone or with other alcoholics, regardless of social level. They believe that only other alcoholics can understand them. Problem drinkers brood over imagined wrongs inflicted by nonalcoholic associates and think people are staring at them or talking about them. They are highly critical of others and may become violent or destructive.

Loss of friends and job—Their continuing antisocial behavior causes friends to avoid them. The aversion is now mutual. Members of the family may become so helplessly implicated that the spouse leaves "to awaken" the partner who is drinking. The same situation develops between problem drinkers, their employers and colleagues at work. Eventually problem drinkers lose their jobs.

Seeking medical aid—Physical and mental erosion caused by uncontrolled drinking leads problem drinkers to hospitals, doctors, psychiatrists and other health care sources. But because they will not admit the extent of their drinking, they seldom receive any lasting benefit. Even when they reveal some of their problem to doctors, the drinkers fail to follow the doctors' instructions, and the result is the same.

Last Stages

Until this point, alcoholics have had a choice: to drink or not to drink—that first drink. But in the last stages of alcoholism, they have no choice at all. They *must* drink.

Drinking sprees—They get blindly and helplessly drunk for days at a time, hopelessly searching for that feeling of alcoholic euphoria they once appreciated. They utterly disregard everything—family, job, food, even shelter. These periodic flights into oblivion might be called "drinking to escape the problems caused by drinking."

Tremors—In the past their hands may have trembled during hangovers. But now when they are forced to abstain, they get tremors, a serious nervous condition which racks the whole body. When combined with hallucinations, these tremors are known as delirium tremens (DTs) and are often fatal if medical help is not close at hand. During and immediately after an attack, problem drinkers will swear off liquor forever. Nevertheless, they return to alcohol.

Protecting the supply—Having an immediate supply of alcohol available becomes the most important thing in their lives—to avoid tremors, if nothing else. They will spend their last cent to get alcohol. Then they hide their bottles so there will always be a drink close at hand when they need it—which can be any hour of day or night.

Unreasonable resentments—They show hostility to others. This can be a conscious effort to protect their precious liquor supply. But hostility can also be outward evidence of an unconscious desire to punish themselves.

Nameless fears and anxieties—They become constantly fearful of things they cannot pin down or describe in words. It is a feeling of impending doom or destruction. This adds to their nervousness and further underscores the compulsion to drink. These fears frequently show up in the form of hallucinations, both auditory and visual.

Collapse of the alibi system—They finally realize that they can no longer make excuses or put the blame on others.

6

They have to admit that the fanciful "reasons" they have been fabricating to justify drinking are preposterous to others and now ridiculous to themselves. This may have occurred to them several times during the course of their alcoholic careers. But now the realization is final. They have to admit that they are licked, that their drinking is beyond their ability to control.

Surrender process—Now, if ever, they must give up the idea of ever drinking again and be willing to seek and accept help. If at this point the alcoholic is unable to surrender, all the signposts point to custodial care or death. If the person has not already suffered extensive and irreversible brain damage, there is a strong likelihood that some form of alcoholic psychosis will develop. The amnesia and confabulation of Korsakoff's syndrome and the convulsions and comas of Wernicke's disease are possibilities. Death may come in advanced cases of cirrhosis of the liver, pancreatitis or hemorrhaging varices of the esophagus. Or the alcoholic may commit suicide; the suicide rate among alcoholics is three times the normal rate of self-extermination.

Alcoholism and Behavioral Disorders

Addiction to alcohol is not a condition which is brought about rapidly. On the average it takes from 5 to 20 years for the male alcoholic to move from the heavy social-drinker status (five or more drinks per occasion, two or more times weekly) to the chronic-alcoholic status.[11] In women the process may take as little as four years.[12] In such instances, the telescoping of the drinking experience shortens the time and frequency between the disease's early symptoms and its active stage.

No proof exists that the disease is inherited. It appears to be a result of behavioral disorders that, given proper treatment at the proper time, can be corrected. Furthermore, there is no stage in the progression, not even the final stage of alcohol domination, at which rescue is impossible.

A knowledge of the psychological problems and attributes which are typical of many alcoholics can be of tremendous practical importance to anyone who wishes to help or identify the potential alcohol abuser. Psychological studies of alcoholics have shown them to have:

1. a high level of anxiety in interpersonal relationships;
2. emotional immaturity;
3. ambivalence toward authority;
4. low frustration tolerance;
5. grandiosity;
6. low self-esteem;
7. feelings of isolation;
8. perfectionism;
9. guilt; and
10. compulsiveness.

These psychological attributes are often present in enlarged proportions when the person is in the nightmare of active alcoholism. However, they are not entirely the result of prolonged excessive drinking. In fact, the attributes are present in many alcoholics before they begin excessive drinking and persist in diminished form long after sobriety has been achieved.[13]

DIAGNOSING ALCOHOLISM

Alcohol problems are often slow to be recognized by those who could treat them. Thus, the diagnosis of alcoholism is often made only when the illness is in its advanced stages—when the victim is unable to control drinking, may no longer have an established family life or a job, or

> *The diagnosis of alcoholism is often made only when the illness is in its advanced stages—when the victim is unable to control drinking, may no longer have an established family life or a job, or may already suffer from malnutrition or organic damage.*

may already suffer from malnutrition or organic damage.

Members of the health team must realize that since alcoholic individuals rarely admit, even to themselves, that they have drinking problems, a special effort must be made to discover the illness in its early stages.

Unfortunately, there is no simple diagnostic procedure for detecting alcoholism. Some of the factors involved in diagnosing an alcoholic person include:

1. *The quantity of alcohol consumed*—But quantity alone is an insufficient measure.
2. *The rate of consumption*—One pint of distilled spirits consumed during a ten-hour period causes different behavior than a pint consumed in one hour. Drunkenness depends on rate of consumption as well as quantity.
3. *Frequency of drinking episodes*—Someone who gets drunk three or four times a year is less liable to be labeled alcoholic than someone who gets drunk every week. Frequency of drunkenness is one factor indicating alcoholism.
4. *The effect of drunkenness upon self and others*—A man who commits deviant sex acts or beats his wife while drunk is more likely to be labeled alcoholic than a man who quietly gets drunk and leaves others alone. That is, the effect of drunkenness on others and the reaction of others to the drunkenness determines if and how the individual is labeled alcoholic.
5. *Visibility to labeling agents*—The police, court personnel, school personnel, welfare workers, employers, family friends, and helping agents—psychiatrists, physicians, nurses, lawyers—are the key sources of alcoholic labeling.
6. *The social situation of the person*—There are different standards set by each class and status group in our society. How a person does or does not conform to the standards of one's own group will determine whether that person will be labeled an alcoholic and, therefore, be reacted to as an alcoholic.[14]

NCA Criteria

Extensive treatment programs have developed for the alcoholic which have required the establishment of a set of criteria for the diagnosis of alcoholism. The National Council on Alcoholism

8

developed diagnostic criteria that could be used to ascertain the nature of the disease from a cluster of symptoms.[15] The criteria set has been applied to promote early detection, provide uniform nomenclature, prevent overdiagnosis and establish treatment purposes.

The criteria data are assembled in two "tracks": Track I—Physiological and Clinical, and Track II—Behavioral, Psychological and Attitudinal. (See Appendix A.) The Track II data are grouped together because behavioral manifestations, the easiest to determine and most objective to recognize, imply attitudinal and psychological manifestations.

There is no rigid uniformity in the progress of the disease, but, since early diagnosis seems to be helpful in treatment and recovery, manifestations are separated into "early," "middle" and "late." In addition to identifying early and late symptoms and signs, each datum was graded according to its degree of implication for the presence of alcoholism. Of course, some of the more definite signs occur later in the course of the illness. But this does not mean that people with earlier signs may not also have alcoholism.

The signs are graded on three diagnostic levels, with those symptoms weighted as "1" being the most significant.

- *Diagnostic level 1*—Classical, definite, obligatory. A person who fits this criterion must be diagnosed as being alcoholic.
- *Diagnostic level 2*—Probable, frequent, indicative. A person who satisfies this criterion is under strong suspicion of alcoholism; other corroborative evidence should be obtained.
- *Diagnostic level 3*—Potential, possible, incidental. These manifestations are common in people with alcoholism, but do not by themselves give a strong indication of its existence. They may arouse suspicion, but other significant evidence is needed before the diagnosis is made.

Using the NCA Criteria

The National Council on Alcoholism believes it is sufficient for the diagnosis of alcoholism if one or more of the major criteria are satisfied, or if several of the minor criteria in Tracks I and II are present. If a health care professional is making the diagnosis based upon major criteria in one of the tracks, the professional should also complete a strong search for evidence in the other track. A purely mechanical selection of items is not enough; the history, physical examination and other observations, and laboratory evidence, must fit into a consistent whole to ensure a proper diagnosis. Minor criteria in the physical and clinical track alone are not sufficient, nor are minor criteria in the behavioral and psychological track. There must be several criteria in *both* Track I and Track II areas.

Risk Factors

Persons at high risk of alcoholism have been identified from epidemiological and sociological studies as having certain traits. There is not complete agreement on the extent of risk for each factor, according to the National Council on Alcoholism. The risk factors include:

1. A family history of alcoholism, including parents, siblings, grandparents, uncles and aunts;
2. A history of total abstinence in the family, particularly where strong moral overtones were present and, most particularly, where the social environment of the patient has changed to associations in which drinking is encouraged or required;
3. A history of alcoholism or total abstinence in the spouse or the family of the spouse;
4. Coming from a broken home or home with much parental discord, particularly where the father was absent or rejecting but not punitive;
5. Being the last child of a large family or in the last half of a large family;
6. Belonging to a cultural group, such as the Irish and Scandinavians, with a higher incidence of alcoholism than other cultural groups, such as Jews, Chinese and Italians. (The health team, however, should be aware that alcoholism can occur in people of any cultural derivation);
7. Having female relatives of more than one generation who have had a high incidence of recurrent depressions;
8. Smoking heavily (Heavy drinking is often associated with heavy smoking, but the reverse need not be true).

Even if a nurse is familiar with risk factors involved in diagnosing alcoholism, and significant symptoms of alcoholism, the nurse still needs a simple procedure for identifying the alcohol abuser.

ASSESSMENT QUESTIONNAIRES

Patients with alcoholism present psychosocial and physiological problems that are complex and sometimes obscure. Questionnaires have been developed that reflect areas that are problems for alcoholic patients, such as drinking history, physical symptoms related to damage-prone systems, psychosocial status, use of other drugs and family, job or police difficulties. The length of the assessment tools varies from 10 items to more than

One of the major difficulties with assessment questionnaires is the lack of comprehensive validity.

100 items. One of the major difficulties with the tools is the lack of comprehensive validity.

Appendix B contains examples of three questionnaires, a nursing history tool, and descriptions of other assessment methods and the validity of each.

After reviewing this material, the nurse may be confused about the type of items critical for the identification of the potential alcohol abuser, and may have questions about the competency of the methods being used by the health professionals.

10 PROPOSED NURSING ASSESSMENT TOOL FOR ALCOHOLISM

In preparing an assessment tool for the professional nurse to use in the acute care facility for the identification of potential alcohol abusers, Memorial Hospital related the definition of alcoholism to the criteria for symptoms and finally to the types of questionnaires used for identifying alcoholics. Key points for assessment include information about blackouts, difficulty with family or job, driving while intoxicated, presence of DTs, frequency of drinking and ability to stop drinking. The result was assessment questions based on behaviors that could be applied to problem drinkers and questions taken from some type of validated study. The following questions were chosen.

1. Have you ever awakened in the morning, after some drinking the night before, and found that you could not remember part of the evening?
2. Can you stop drinking without a struggle after one or two drinks?
3. Have you ever attended a meeting of AA because of your drinking?
4. Do you ever drink before lunch?
5. Has drinking ever created problems between you and your wife, husband, parent or near relative?
6. Have you ever gotten into trouble at work because of your drinking?
7. Have you ever neglected your obligations, your family, or your work for two or more days in a row because you were drinking?
8. Have you ever had DTs?
9. Have you ever had severe shaking, heard voices or seen things that weren't there after heavy drinking?
10. Was drinking part of the problem that resulted in your hospitalization?
11. Have you ever been arrested, even for a few hours, because of drunken behavior? How many times?
12. Have you ever cut down on your drinking by switching to something else?
13. Do you get the inner shakes unless you continue drinking?
14. Do you prefer (or like) to drink alone?
15. Has drinking made you irritable?
16. Do you crave a drink at a definite time daily?
17. Does drinking cause you bodily complaints?

VALIDATION OF TOOL

The tool should be validated to be sure that it can distinguish the nonalcoholic from the potential alcoholic. The validation procedure could include the following steps:

1. Empirically determine appropriate items for the nursing assessment tool that will discriminate between alcoholic and nonalcoholic behaviors.
2. Establish criteria against which to measure discriminated behaviors.
3. Pretest the tool and revise it.
4. Administer the assessment tool to

two groups, one a known group of alcoholics and the second a group of nonalcoholics.

5. Analyze the results, and modify the assessment tool for the best item discrimination.

6. Readminister the assessment tool to two additional groups (control and alcoholic), and revise as appropriate.

7. Evaluate nursing assessment tool for face validity, construct validity, concurrent validity and predictive validity.

8. Standardize the tool to various populations.

9. Apply the tool in a clinical setting and evaluate results on a continuing basis.

Difficulty of Validation

Validation of the assessment tool may experience some difficulties with face validity. If the tool actually looks like it measures what it purports to measure, people could conceal a drinking problem.

Also, if the tool is validated on self-identified alcoholics who have nothing to lose by answering honestly, the validation may be less when used on future groups that are increasingly different from the original validation group.

Evaluation of the construct validity is important to establish that the assessment tool does relate to alcoholism and drinking behavior. Statistically an acceptable predictive validity will have to be established with controlled or limited rates of false positives and false negatives.

Need for Valid Questionnaire

The development of a valid assessment tool that can be used by the professional nurse for distinguishing between alcoholics and nonalcoholics is needed to enhance individual health care in hospitals. Even though many questionnaires have been developed and are in clinical use, their validity and reliability have not yet been established. Additional research is required.

REFERENCES

1. Stark, M. J. and Nichols, H. G. "Alcohol-Related Admissions to a General Hospital." *Alcohol, Health and Research World* (Summer 1977) p. 11–14.

2. McCarrol, J. R. and Haddon, W. "Controlled Study of Fatal Automobile Accidents in New York City." *The Journal of Chronic Diseases* 15 (1962) p. 811–826.

3. Ayerst Laboratories. *Medical Management of the Alcohol-Dependent Patient* (New York: Inter Medica, Inc. 1978).

4. Hall, L. C. *Facts about Alcohol and Alcoholism* (Rockville, Md.: National Institute on Alcohol Abuse and Alcoholism 1976) p. 5.

5. Ibid.

6. The Alcoholism Center, Baltimore City Health Department. *Handbook for the Alcoholism Counselor* (Rockville, Md.: National Institute on Alcohol Abuse and Alcoholism 1976) p. 5.

7. Ibid.

8. Hall. *Facts about Alcohol and Alcoholism* p. 15.

9. Ibid.

10. The Alcoholism Center. *Handbook for the Alcoholism Counselor* p. 10–11.

11. Dorris, R. T. and Lindley, D. F. *Counseling on Alcoholism and Related Disorders* (Beverly Hills: Glencoe Press 1969) p. 37.

12. Ibid.

12

13. Clinebell, H. J., Jr. *Understanding and Counseling the Alcoholic* (Nashville: Abingdon Press 1968).
14. The Alcoholism Center. *Handbook for the Alcoholism Counselor.*
15. Estes, N. J. and Heinemann, M. E. *Alcoholism: Development, Consequences and Intervention* (St. Louis: The C. V. Mosby Co. 1977) p. 47–58.

SUGGESTED READINGS

Corey, G. *Theory and Practice of Counseling and Psychotherapy* (Monterey, Cal.: Brooks/Cole Publishing Company 1977).

Coleman, J. C. *Abnormal Psychology and Modern Life* (Glenview, Ill.: Scott, Foresman and Company 1976).

Criteria Committee, National Council on Alcoholism. "Criteria for the Diagnosis of Alcoholism." *American Journal of Psychiatry* 129 (1972) p. 129–135.

Evenson, R. C. et al. "Factors in the Description and Grouping of Alcoholics." *American Journal of Psychiatry* 130 (1973) p. 49–54.

Evenson, R. C. et al. "Development of an Alcoholism Severity Scale Via an Iterative Computer Program for Item Analysis." *Quarterly Journal of Studies on Alcohol* 34 (1973) p. 1336–1341.

Forrest, G. G. *The Diagnosis and Treatment of Alcoholism* (Springfield, Ill.: Charles C Thomas 1975).

Goldfried, M. R. and Davison, G. C. *Clinical Behavior Therapy* (New York: Holt, Rinehart and Winston 1976).

Guze, S. B. and Goodwin, D. W. "Consistency of Drinking History and Diagnosis of Alcoholism." *Quarterly Journal of Studies on Alcohol* 33 (1972) p. 111–116.

Leitenberg, H. *Handbook of Behavior Modification and Behavior Therapy* (Englewood Cliffs, N.J.: Prentice-Hall 1976).

Miller, W. R. and Munoz, R. F. *How to Control Your Drinking* (Englewood Cliffs, N.J.: Prentice-Hall 1976).

National Institute on Alcohol Abuse and Alcoholism. *Alcoholism Treatment and Rehabilitation* (Rockville, Md.: NIAAA 1975).

O'Leary, D. K. and Wilson, G. T. *Behavior Therapy: Application and Outcome* (Englewood Cliffs, N.J.: Prentice-Hall 1975).

Major and Minor Criteria for Diagnosis of Alcoholism

Major Criteria	Diagnostic Level

Track I. Physiological and Clinical

A. Physiological dependence.

1. Physiological dependence as manifested by evidence of a *withdrawal syndrome* [1], when the intake of alcohol is interrupted or decreased without substitution of other sedation. It must be remembered that overuse of other sedative drugs can produce a similar withdrawal from alcohol.

	Diagnostic Level
a. Gross tremor (differentiated from other causes of tremor)	1
b. Hallucinosis (differentiated from schizophrenic hallucinations or other psychoses)	1
c. Withdrawal seizures (differentiated from epilepsy and other seizure disorders)	1
d. Delirium tremens (usually starts between the first and third day after withdrawal and minimally includes tremors, disorientation and hallucinations [1])	1

2. Evidence of *tolerance* to the effects of alcohol. (There may be a decrease in previously high levels of tolerance late in the course.) Although the degree of tolerance to alcohol in no way matches the degree of tolerance to other drugs, the behavioral effects of a given amount of alcohol vary greatly between alcoholic and nonalcoholic subjects.

	Diagnostic Level
a. A blood alcohol level of more than 150 mg without gross evidence of intoxication	1
b. The consumption of one-fifth of a gallon of whiskey or an equivalent amount of wine or beer daily, for more than one day by a 180-lb. individual	1

3. Alcoholic blackout periods. (Differential diagnosis from purely psychological fugue states and psychomotor seizures.)

B. Clinical signs—major alcohol-associated illnesses.

Alcoholism can be assumed to exist if major alcohol-associated illnesses develop in a person who drinks regularly. In such an individual evidence of physiological and psychological dependence should be searched for.

	Diagnostic Level
1. Fatty degeneration in absence of other known cause	2
2. Alcoholic hepatitis	1
3. Laennec's cirrhosis	2
4. Pancreatitis in the absence of cholelithiasis	2
5. Chronic gastritis	3
6. Hematological disorders:	
a. Anemia—hypochromic, normocytic, macrocytic, hemolytic with stomatocytosis, low folic acid	3
b. Clotting disorders—prothrombin elevation or thrombocytopenia	3
7. Wernicke-Korsakoff syndrome	2

14

Major Criteria	Diagnostic Level
8. Alcoholic cerebellar degeneration	1
9. Cerebral degeneration in absence of Alzheimer's disease or arteriosclerosis	2
10. Central pontine myelinolysis (diagnosis only possible postmortem)	
11. Marchiafava-Bignami disease (diagnosis only possible postmortem)	2
12. Peripheral neuropathy (see also beriberi)	2
13. Toxic amblyopia	3
14. Alcohol myopathy	2
15. Alcoholic cardiomyopathy	2
16. Beriberi	3
17. Pellagra	3

Track II. Behavioral, Psychological and Attitudinal

All chronic conditions of psychological dependence occur in dynamic equilibrium with intrapsychic and interpersonal consequences. Similarly, in alcoholism there are varied effects on character and family. Like other chronic relapsing diseases, alcoholism produces vocational, social and physical impairments. Therefore, the implications of these disruptions must be evaluated and related to the individual and his pattern of alcoholism. The following behavior patterns show psychological dependence on alcohol in alcoholism.

	Diagnostic Level
A. Drinking despite strong medical contraindication known to patient	1
B. Drinking despite strong, identified contraindication known to patient (intoxication, marriage disruption because of drinking, arrest for intoxication, driving while intoxicated)	1
C. Patient's subjective complaint of loss of control of alcohol consumption	2

Minor Criteria	Diagnostic Level
Track I. Physiological and Clinical	
A. Direct effects (ascertained by examination)	
1. Early	
Odor of alcohol on breath at time of medical appointment	2
2. Middle	
a. Alcoholic facies	2
b. Vascular engorgement of face	2
c. Toxic amblyopia	3
d. Increased incidence of infections	3
e. Cardiac arrhythmias	3
f. Peripheral neuropathy (see also major criteria, Track I, B)	2
3. Late (see major criteria, Track I, B)	

Minor Criteria	Diagnostic Level
B. Indirect effects	
1. Early	
a. Tachycardia	3
b. Flushed face	3
c. Nocturnal diaphoresis	3
2. Middle	
a. Ecchymosis on lower extremities, arms or chest	3
b. Cigarette or other burns on hands or chest	3
c. Hyperreflexia or, if drinking heavily, hyporeflexia (permanent hyporeflexia may be a residuum of alcoholic polyneuritis)	3
3. Late	
Decreased tolerance	3
C. Laboratory tests	
1. Direct	
Blood alcohol level at any time of more than 300 mg/100 ml or level of more than 100 mg/100 ml in routine examination	1
2. Indirect	
a. Serum osmolality (reflects blood alcohol levels)—every 22.4 increase over 200 mOsm/litre reflects 50 gm/100 ml alcohol	2
b. Results of alcohol ingestion	
(1) Hypoglycemia	3
(2) Hypochloremic alkalosis	3
(3) Low magnesium level	2
(4) Lactic acid elevation	3
(5) Transient uric acid elevation	3
(6) Potassium depletion	3
c. Indications of liver abnormality	
(1) SGPT elevation	2
(2) SGOT elevation	3
(3) BSP elevation	2
(4) Bilirubin elevation	2
(5) Urinary urobilinogen elevation	2
(6) Serum A/G ratio reversal	2
d. Blood and blood clotting	
(1) Anemia—hypochromic, normocytic, macrocytic, hemolytic with stomatocytosis, low folic acid	3
(2) Clotting disorders—prothrombin elevation, thrombocytopenia	3

Minor Criteria	Diagnostic Level
e. ECG abnormalities	
(1) Cardiac arrhythmias: tachycardia; T waves dimpled, cloven or spinous; atrial fibrillation, ventricular premature contractions; abnormal P waves	2
f. EEG abnormalities:	
(1) Decreased or increased REM sleep, depending on phase	3
(2) Loss of delta sleep	3
(3) Other reported findings	3
g. Decreased immune response	3
h. Decreased response to Synacthen test	3
i. Chromosomal damage from alcoholism	3

Track II. Behavioral, Psychological and Attitudinal

A. Behavioral

  1. Direct effects

a. Early	
(1) Gulping drinks	3
(2) Surreptitious drinking	2
(3) Morning drinking (assess nature of peer group behavior)	2
b. Middle	
Repeated conscious attempts at abstinence	2
c. Late	
(1) Blatant indiscriminant use of alcohol	1
(2) Skid Row or equivalent social level	2

  2. Indirect effects

a. Early	
(1) Medical excuses from work for variety of reasons	2
(2) Shifting from one alcoholic beverage to another	2
(3) Preference for drinking companions, bars and taverns	2
(4) Loss of interest in activities not directly associated with drinking	2
b. Late	
(1) Chooses employment that facilitates drinking	3
(2) Frequent automobile accidents	3
(3) History of family members undergoing psychiatric treatments; school and behavioral problems of children	3
(4) Frequent change of residence for poorly defined reasons	3

	Diagnostic Level
Minor Criteria	

    (5) Anxiety-relieving mechanisms, such as telephone calls inappropriate in time, distance, person or motive (telephonitis)   **2**

    (6) Outbursts of rage and suicidal gestures while drinking   **2**

B. Psychological and Attitudinal

  1. Direct effects

    a. Early

    When talking freely, makes frequent reference to drinking alcohol, people being "bombed," "stoned," or admits drinking more than peer group   **2**

    b. Middle

    Drinking to relieve anger, insomnia, fatigue, depression, social discomfort   **2**

    c. Late

    Psychological symptoms consistent with permanent organic brain syndrome (see also major criteria, Track I, B)   **2**

  2. Indirect effects

    a. Early

    (1) Unexplained changes in family, social and business relationships; complaints about wife, job and friends   **3**

    (2) Spouse makes complaints about drinking behavior, reported by patient or spouse   **2**

    (3) Major family disruptions; separation, divorce, threats of divorce   **3**

    (4) Job loss (owing to increasing interpersonal difficulties), frequent job changes, financial difficulties   **3**

    b. Late

    (1) Overt expression of more regressive defense mechanisms, such as denial, projection   **3**

    (2) Resentment, jealousy, paranoid attitudes   **3**

    (3) Symptoms of depression—isolation, crying, suicidal preoccupation   **3**

    (4) Feelings that patient is "losing his mind"   **2**

Appendix B

Diagnostic and Assessment Techniques
for Alcoholism

[Source: Jacobson, G.R. *Diagnosis and Assessment of Alcohol Abuse and Alcoholism*
(Rockville, Md.: National Institute on Alcohol Abuse and Alcoholism 1975)]

Title of Test	Description and Validity
Alcadd Test	Developed in 1949. Sixty scorable items and five fillers stated in simple language (e.g., "I would rather drink alone than with others," "I drink because it takes away my shyness"). Given individually or in groups. Used for rapid screening in busy outpatient facilities.
	Questionable, and serious confusion about the use. Alcadd test is not valid when used with people who wish to conceal a drinking problem, because test has high face validity and the test was developed, standardized and validated with known, self-identified alcoholics. Also, the five "clusters" of personality factors used in the test have never been shown to be valid, and there is no evidence that items in any of the clusters really belong together. Author's sampling methods were faulty, and scores are strongly related to age.
Alcoholism Assessment Interview	Developed in 1965. Focuses on interrelated areas of information and behavior, including demographic, physical, psychological, family and occupational. Is a mimeographed format for a structured interview to be conducted on an individual basis. Thirty-nine items are expressed as questions to interviewer (e.g., "How drunk does he believe he gets during interims between bouts?") A judgment sheet is provided for interviewer's recording. Not enough information is available to allow a final analysis, and more research is needed.
Alcohol Use Questionnaire	Developed from 1961 to 1964. Theory underlying development is that alcoholism is not a unitary, clinical entity or a simple disease that always progresses in an unvarying fashion, but a group of disorders or multiple syndromes that have many different appearances and manifestations and in many patterns. One hundred sixty-one items that require a yes or no response (e.g., "Does drinking help you to be more alert mentally?") provided in reusable test booklet. Test given individually or in groups. The test should not be used as a screening device or for identification or detection of alcoholics, since it was standardized and developed with populations of known alcoholics. Test is useful for measuring alcoholics on various dimensions and developing treatment plans.
	Authors utilized apparently appropriate and sophisticated methods and factor analyses, and presented generally acceptable reliability and validity information. Some questions remain: (1) test distributed commercially but no reports about it in the literature, (2) testing situations questionable, (3) very little information about concurrent validity and (4) strong face validity. More research on validity and reliability is needed.
Bell Alcoholism Scale of Adjustment (BASA)	Developed in 1968. The BASA is a series of 40 statements (e.g., "I can stop drinking any time I want to," "It makes me feel anxious when the subject of alcoholism is discussed"). Subject responds by indicating any one of six possible replies. Given to individuals or groups. Not in widespread or general use and should be considered an experimental test. There is not sufficient information available to determine the BASA's reliability or validity, and further research is needed.
Drinking Behavior Interview (DBI)	Developed in 1969. Consists of 31 empirically selected items in a structured interview-questionnaire format covering type of drinking and some related behaviors (e.g., "Any use of nonbeverage alcohol?"), effects on family and social life (e.g., "Number of quarrels with spouse or family members, drinking-provided, dur-

Title of Test	Description and Validity
Drinking Behavior Interview (DBI) (continued)	ing the past two months?'') and effects on job (e.g., ''Any reprimands from employer or superior?''). DBI does not seem to have any widespread or general utilization. There is not sufficient information available to make a judgment about the validity or reliability of the DBI.
Essential-Reactive Alcoholism Dimension (ERA)	The theory underlying the development is the psychoanalytic hypothesis that alcoholics are relatively passive, dependent and emotionally immature persons who use alcohol excessively as a means of coping with stress. Consists of 69 questions (55 are scorable, 14 are ''fillers'') to be asked in a structured interview, organized around eight basic areas of behavior: economic dependence, emotional dependence, persistent application to reality tasks, age at onset of drinking and possible causes, relationships with friends, character traits, presence of gastrointestinal symptoms and multiform oral gratifications, willingness to imbibe anything that has the desired pharmacological effect. Requires 20–30 minutes for administration. Test is classified as an experimental technique, and should not be used for detection or identification of alcoholics, but for the purpose of differential diagnosis after the presence of alcoholism or problem drinking has been determined.

The reliability and validity of the ERA interview has not been firmly established, and users are cautioned to interpret the results of testing as conservatively as possible. |
| Iowa Alcoholic Intake Schedule (IAIS) | Developed from 1958 to 1964. Based on the theory that the way people think about an object and the way they define an object will be consistent with the way they act toward that object. In other words, attitudes and actions will be equivalent and related, so that if a person thinks of alcohol as a means of making himself a more likeable person, then that person will use alcohol for that purpose. Consists of 200 discrete items covering 10 basic areas: identifying information, job status, family status, drinking pattern, attitude toward alcohol, recognition of a drinking problem and actions taken to deal with it, relationships with other people, drinking and driving, and use of other medicines and drugs. Given individually in form of an interview and requires about 45 minutes.

Scales can be used for broad and general type of household survey aimed at determining the epidemiology of alcoholism, its prevalence and incidence, or at detecting actual and potential problem drinkers and alcoholics. Scales were standardized on populations that were predominantly white and middle class, both urban and rural.

The four principal aspects of the IAIS have been extensively used in large-scale and well-conducted studies over a period of several years and can be accepted with a fair degree of confidence. There may be problems with face validity since the nature of the scale items is so obvious. Questions about validity also raised because the language of some of the scale items may be inappropriate, false-positive identifications may be obtained, and attitudes toward alcohol may not necessarily correspond to overt behavior.

Nevertheless, this is probably the best tool available. |
| MacAndrew Alcoholism Scale | Developed in 1965. The scale is comprised of 49 objective statements (e.g., ''I like to cook,'' ''I have never been in trouble with the law'') which the respondent answers true or false. All statements are included in the 566-item Minnesota Multiphasic Personality Inventory (MMPI). The scale is intended for use only as a detection or identification technique and does not provide any sort of differential diagnosis. No applications to treatment planning have been adequately documented. |

Title of Test	Description and Validity
MacAndrew Alcoholism Scale (continued)	The validity and reliability of the test have not been unequivocally established, and some problems and criticisms remain unanswered, including no construct validity; it simply has no bearing on alcoholism and has nothing to do with drinking behavior. Classificatory accuracy or predictive validity has been unacceptably low, and rates of false positives and false negatives are unacceptably high. Most studies that could relate to the validity of the test are confusing, based on conflicting methodologies and full of inconsistent or inadequate external criteria to diagnose alcoholism. The reliability has not been actively or directly studied.
	Even though further research is needed on validity and reliability of this test, the MacAndrew Scale seems to be one of the best of its kind and can be cautiously applied where a screening device is necessary.
Manson Evaluation	Developed in 1948. The test was developed as a means of screening alcoholics in a variety of populations and settings, understanding the personality of alcoholics and clarifying the psychodynamics of alcoholism. The test consists of an objective pencil-and-paper measure consisting of 72 items (e.g., "I was often unhappy because of sadness," "My life is quiet and peaceful") which require only a yes or no response. Given individually or in groups in about 10–15 minutes.
	Very little published information is available on the reliability and validity of the test, and much of that is erroneous and unfavorable. The test is incapable of distinguishing between alcoholics and nonalcoholic deviants (neurotics and psychopaths).
Michigan Alcoholism Screening Test (MAST)	Developed in 1972. Not related to any particular theoretic orientation, but arose out of the author's experience with medical students and his perception of their need for a simple, quick and consistently effective means of identifying alcoholics. Conducted by interviewing potential alcoholics and/or members of their families. Test consists of a list of 25 questions (e.g., "Do you ever drink before noon?" "Have you gotten into fights when drinking?") to be answered yes or no. Requires 10–15 minutes for administration. Widespread use as an inexpensive screening device.
	Most of the published research indicates an acceptable level of validity and reliability. Some particular problems include: no explanation of discriminant analysis techniques used in development of present scoring, an overly sensitive format which may result in unacceptably high rates of false-positive identification, and high face validity. Another serious question about MAST's validity must be raised because the security of the test has been greatly compromised. The *Chicago Tribune* (October 3, 1973) distributed hundreds of thousands of copies of the test in an article that revealed the complete content, the alcoholic and nonalcoholic responses, the scoring weights for each item and the cutoff points. Also, there are almost no data available regarding reliability.
Mortimer-Filkins Test	This test is also called the Court Procedures for Identifying Problem Drinkers or the HSRI. It is one of the best-developed and most extensively field-tested diagnostic approaches available. The first part of the test consists of an empirically derived, 58-item questionnaire to which the respondent replies yes-no, true-false or supplies a brief response (e.g., "Do you think that creditors are much too quick to bother you for payment?" "I have long periods of such great restlessness that I cannot sit long in a chair"). First part is self-report questionnaire requiring 10–15 minutes for administration. The second part of the test is the interview, which consists of approximately 70 discrete items (plus subparts for some questions), and requires about 30 minutes for completion. The materials have been specifically designed for, and used in, settings where one must separate problem drinkers from other drinkers involved in alcohol-related traffic offenses.

Title of Test	Description and Validity
Mortimer-Filkins Test (continued)	Validity and reliability, for the most part, are acceptable but with a few problems. For example, favorable outcome of the initial validation and cross-validation studies did not derive entirely from field-tests; external criterion variables may not have been as valid as assumed; and educated persons are able to fake, falsify or deny in order to avoid a diagnosis of problem drinking.
(NCA) Criteria for the Diagnosis of Alcoholism	Developed from 1971 to 1972 in response to recurrent social and medico-legal problems arising out of the absence of any clear-cut or widely accepted diagnostic definition of alcoholism. Consists of a three-page chart of symptoms, divided and subdivided into several levels. (See Appendix A.) The NCA criteria are valid because, in effect, the medical profession has unanimously decided that, based on their collective knowledge, experience and expertise, the symptoms listed are definitive and diagnostic of alcoholism at some stage and to some degree of certainty. Also, the results are replicable; any competent physician should be able to arrive at the same conclusion or diagnosis as any other physician if the NCA criteria are correctly and uniformly applied.
Alcohol History Form—Alcoholism Severity Scale (AHF)	Developed from 1968 to 1969. Consists of a standardized 34-item multiple-choice questionnaire which requires the patient to describe his or her drinking and related behavior by circling one or more appropriate statements. The AHF is essentially self-administering, individually or in groups, and requires 15–20 minutes. Scoring is not always relevant except for special purposes.

The scale is currently in use throughout Missouri, and its primary application seems to be inpatient-hospital settings. No definitive statement is possible about reliability and validity because of lack of data. The AHF does have face validity. The instrument should be viewed as an experimental measure. |

Questionnaire # 1
Are You an Alcoholic?
(Source: Alcoholics Anonymous)

1. Do you require a drink the next morning?

2. Do you prefer (or like) to drink alone?

3. Do you lose time from work due to drinking?

4. Is your drinking harming your family in any way?

5. Do you crave a drink at a definite time daily?

6. Do you get the inner shakes unless you continue drinking?

7. Has drinking made you irritable?

8. Does drinking make you careless of your family's welfare?

9. Have you thought less of your husband or wife since drinking?

10. Has drinking changed your personality?

11. Does drinking cause you bodily complaints?

12. Does drinking cause you to have difficulty in sleeping?

13. Has drinking made you more impulsive?

14. Have you less self-control since drinking?

15. Has your initiative decreased since drinking?

16. Has your ambition decreased since drinking?

17. Do you drink to obtain social ease? (Are you a shy, self-conscious person?)

18. Is drinking clouding your reputation?

19. Has your sexual potency suffered since drinking?

20. Do you show marked dislikes and hatreds since drinking?

21. Has your jealousy, in general, increased since drinking?

22. Do you show marked emotion or moodiness as a result of drinking?

23. Has your efficiency decreased since drinking?

24. Are you harder to get along with since drinking?

25. Do you turn to an inferior environment since drinking?

26. Is drinking endangering your health?

27. Is drinking affecting your peace of mind?

28. Is drinking jeopardizing your business?

29. Do you drink for self-encouragement or to relieve marked feelings of inadequacy? (Are you a person with feelings of inferiority?)

30. Have you ever had a complete loss of memory while, or after, drinking? (Blackouts)

If your answers are YES to three or more of the above, there is definite warning that you may be an alcoholic.

Questionnaire #2
Twenty Questions from Youth Information Branch of ACGLA

(Source: Alcoholism Council of Greater Los Angeles
2001 Beverly Blvd., Los Angeles 90057)

1. Do you lose time from school due to drinking?

2. Do you drink because you are shy with other people?

3. Do you drink to build up your self-confidence?

4. Do you drink alone?

5. Is drinking affecting your reputation—or do you care?

6. Do you drink to escape from study or home worries?

7. Do you feel guilty or bummed out after drinking?

8. Does it bother you if somebody says that maybe you drink too much?

9. Do you have to take a drink when you go out on a date?

10. Do you make-out (in general) better when you have a drink?

11. Do you get into financial troubles over buying liquor?

12. Do you feel a sense of power when you drink?

13. Have you lost friends since you've started drinking?

14. Have you started hanging out with a crowd where stuff is easy to get?

15. Do your friends drink less than you do?

16. Do you drink until the bottle is gone?

17. Have you ever had a complete loss of memory from drinking?

18. Have you ever been to a hospital or been busted due to drunk driving?

19. Do you turn off to any studies or lectures about drinking?

20. Do you THINK you have a problem with liquor?

Based on a similar test used by Johns Hopkins University Hospital, Baltimore, Md., you can utilize the following guidelines in determining whether or not you are an alcoholic: If you answered YES to any one of the questions, there is a definite warning that you may be alcoholic. If you answered YES to any two, the chances are that you ARE an alcoholic. If you answered YES to three or more, you are definitely an alcoholic.

Questionnaire #3
The Rap Ratings
(Source: The Monterey County Alcoholism Program,
Monterey County Health Department
The California State Department of Rehabilitation)

PART I

Check each statement under "yes" or "no," using firm pressure so that the results will be recorded on the following page. Please speak to the examiner if any question is not clear or if it is difficult for you to answer with a straight "yes" or "no." There is no time limit, but we suggest that you answer rapidly without long pondering of the question.

1. I have a strong and clear faith in life.

2. Many times I feel uneasy or blue.

3. My home life is as happy as it should be.

4. Some days I feel I am not my real self.

5. I feel sorry for myself and frequently indulge in self-pity.

6. I am moderate in my habits.

7. I often feel guilty or apologetic without knowing why.

8. I am pretty much like everyone else I know.

9. Sometimes I go out of my way to avoid people I dislike.

10. It seems to me I'm going nowhere in my life.

11. I feel there is a barrier between me and the world.

12. My interest or enthusiasm fades quickly.

13. I keep thinking about things I fear.

14. I'm inclined to be serene and relaxed.

15. I feel all alone in the world.

16. My moods change rapidly.

PART II

1. Discussions about my drinking (or drug use) make me nervous.

2. I am a shaky, jittery person.

3. I have had trouble remembering what I did while drinking.

4. My drinking (or drug use) has caused me legal, family, health, job, or social problems.

5. I consume more alcohol (or drugs) than most of my friends do.

6. I have sensations of numbness or tingling in my fingers or toes.

7. I often want more drinks after the party is over.

8. I feel guilty about my drinking (or drug use).

Nursing History Tool for Use
with Patients with Alcohol Problems

[Reprinted with permission from: Estes, N. J. and Heinemann, M. E. "Assessing Alcoholic Patients." *American Journal of Nursing* 76:5 (May 1976) p. 785-789.]

Place of interview _____Date _____

Name of interviewer _____

Patient's name _____

Ethnic group _____ Age _____ Sex _____

Birthplace _____ Occupation _____

Last grade attended _____

1. For what reason did you come to this agency?

2. What do you most want help with at the present time?

Drinking History

3. How old were you when you started drinking alcohol regularly?

4. How long have you had problems with alcohol?

5. How often do you drink alcoholic beverages?

6. What kinds of alcoholic beverages do you drink?

7. How much of each alcoholic beverage do you drink?

*8. When did you have your last drink?

*9. When did you start your last drinking bout?

*10. What have you been drinking during this last drinking episode?

*11. How much alcohol did you consume each day during your last drinking episode?

*12. Has your drinking created problems for you in any of the following areas?
    with spouse _____ on the job _____
    with family _____ with children _____ with friends _____

13. Have you ever been injured because of drinking?
    Yes _____ No _____
    in fights _____ auto accident _____ accidental fall _____
    other _____

14. Have you ever been arrested because of drinking?
Yes _____ No _____
On what charge: DWI _____ drunk in public _____
fights _____
other (specify) _____

15. Have you ever been in prison or jail because of drinking?
Yes _____ No _____

16. What previous treatments have you had for alcohol problems?

Date   Place

_____

_____

Symptoms Relating to Gastrointestinal System

*17. What have you been eating during this most recent drinking bout?

*18. What is your usual eating pattern?
(a) When not drinking:
(b) When drinking:

19. Have you had recent changes in appetite?

20. Have you had any recent weight changes?

21. Are you on a special diet?

22. What fluids do you drink other than alcohol?
Kind of fluid and amount per day:
regular coffee _____ tea _____
water _____ decaffeinated coffee _____
juices _____ milk _____

23. Do you have frequent irritation of your mouth and throat?

24. Are you having pain in your stomach?

25. Are you bothered by heartburn or gas?

*26. Are you nauseated?

*27. Are you vomiting or having dry heaves?

*28. Have you ever vomited blood? If yes, when?

*29. Have you ever had stomach ulcers or other stomach problems?

30. How frequently and for what reason do you use aspirin?

31. What medications do you use to relieve stomach pain?

32. Are you having pain in your abdomen?

33. Are you having diarrhea or constipation?

34. Do you have hemorrhoids?

35. Have you had bleeding from your bowels?

36. Have you noted a change in the color of your stool?
    clay colored _____ black _____
    bright red _____

37. What problems have you had in the past with your bowels?

38. What medications do you use to relieve abdominal or bowel pains?

39. Have you ever had problems with your pancreas?

*40. Has your skin or the whites of your eyes ever turned yellow?

*41. Have you ever had problems with your liver?

*42. Do you have diabetes? If yes, what medication do you take?

Symptoms Relating to Neurological System

43. Have you noticed any change in the amount of alcohol it takes to get the effect you desire? If yes, describe the change.

*44. What reactions occur when you stop drinking?
    tremors _____ DTs _____ seizures _____
    hear or see things _____ other _____

*45. Have you ever taken Dilantin or any other drug for seizures?

46. Have you ever experienced a period of time you don't remember when drinking?

47. Have you experienced tingling, pain or numbness in hands or feet?

48. Have you experienced muscle pain in your legs or arms?

*49. Are you experiencing any difficulty in keeping your balance?

*50. Are you experiencing any difficulty with your vision?

51. Do you have problems with your sleep? If yes, describe.

52. How many hours do you usually sleep?
    when sober _____ when drinking _____

53. Do you feel rested after a night's sleep?

54. What do you do when you are unable to sleep?

55. Have you noticed any recent changes in your sex life? If yes, describe.

Symptoms Relating to Cardiovascular and Pulmonary Systems

*56. Do you have heart trouble? If yes, describe.

*57. Do you have swelling of the hands and feet?

*58. Do you have shortness of breath?

*59. Do you have chest pain?

*60. Are you taking any medication for heart disease?

61. Have you had pneumonia?

62. Have you ever had tuberculosis? If yes, are you taking any medication for it?

63. Do you have frequent infections (e.g., colds, flu, boils, sores that don't heal quickly)?

64. Do you have a chronic cough? If yes, describe.

65. Have you ever coughed up blood or phlegm?

66. Describe any other lung problems you have had.

67. Do you smoke? If yes, how many packs a day?

Psychosocial Status

68. What is your marital status?

69. With whom do you live?

70. Does this person have alcoholism or use alcohol regularly?
    Yes _____ No _____

71. To whom do you feel close?

72. Do your neighbors, relatives and/or friends use alcohol regularly?
    Yes _____ No _____

73. How many children do you have?

74. How often do you see your children?

75. Describe the place you live.
    type of residence (i.e., house, apartment, room); cooking facilities; number of stairs; availability and type of transportation.

76. Have you had mental or emotional problems?
    depression _____ suicide attempt _____
    nervousness (anxiety) _____
    loneliness _____ other _____

77. Are you currently involved in a counseling program?

*78. Are you currently taking medication for emotional problems?
    If yes, describe.

79. Are you actively affiliated with a religious group?

80. What is your current employment status?

81. Do you have some special job skills?

82. If employed, how does this period of treatment affect your employment?

83. If unemployed, what is your current source of income?

84. What hobbies or special interests do you have?

85. How do you spend a typical day at home?

Drug Taking Other Than Alcohol

*86. What drugs do you take that you haven't mentioned?
    prescribed drugs _____

    over-the-counter drugs _____

    drugs obtained on the street _____

*87. What is your usual manner of taking drugs?
    as directed _____ more than directed _____
    less than directed _____

*88. Are you allergic to any drugs?

32 **Final Questions**

89. What are your ideas for managing your drinking when you leave this agency?

90. Are there any questions you would like to ask?

Write a summary of the nursing history interview

1. Describe your overall impressions of the client (mood, attitude, intelligence, ability to relate, social skills, general physical and emotional health, level of orientation, reliability of information given).

2. List all the problems identified in order of priority.

3. Suggest a plan of action for each problem identified.

---

*Indicates questions providing important information for a quick survey of intoxicated patients.

The Alcoholic Professional

Sonya E. Schnurr, R.N.
Coordinator
Patient Care Services
Talbot Hall
St. Anthony Hospital
Columbus, Ohio

THE BEGINNING

IN THE MID-50s I was a student nurse in Chicago. It was there that I turned "legal" and celebrated the fact with my first drink, which I chug-a-lugged. The fellow who bought me my first drink drank his straight down. Because I wanted very much to be grown up and sophisticated, I followed suit.

I still am able to recall the sensations and feelings that followed. My head had separated from my neck; I turned it, it seemed to keep right on revolving. That was followed a short time later by a very giddy and animated sensation which made me feel larger than life, on top of the world, clever. It all wore off and the following morning I was no worse for the wear.

It was not a very exciting beginning except for one very important thing. It had been a positive, pleasant experience with no resultant pain. I stored that

34

information in my head and continued on my way.

I recall only one other contact with alcohol during training and that was in my senior year. A group of us went out for pizza and wine after work one night. My memory of that evening is blurred but I do remember being startled by the speed at which the wine kept disappearing. We would order a bottle of wine and turn around and it was gone. At that time I had no idea that my time perception had been altered; it was almost magical to me that the wine kept disappearing.

The following day, however, brought NLN exams, which were given nation-wide to senior nursing students. Once again I felt no aftereffects from drinking, even though I had consumed rather large quantities. I took the examination eagerly and did very well.

However, in looking around the examination room I discovered a very strange thing. My buddies from the night before looked like whipped puppies, rubbing their heads and eyes; some actually looked green. I couldn't understand it; I felt fine. So I learned that not only did alcohol work, but it always worked for me. Feeling a certain amount of pride and power, I thought I could handle it better than other people.

Between those two isolated drinking experiences I learned other important lessons regarding pills and their wonderful problem-solving qualities. In my junior year when I was on my obstetric rotation, I worked nights in the newborn nursery. It was 80 degrees, very warm, very late and I was very drowsy. I used to put a baby on the table, cradling it with my left arm and holding its bottle in my right hand. That way, if I fell asleep I would not drop the infant. While I continued to struggle against drowsiness, it was a losing battle, and more than once I nodded off to sleep.

Nurseries have glass windows along one wall for easy viewing, so my losing battle with fatigue was known to all the OB staff. One night I was awakened abruptly by someone tapping on the window. It was the Ob-Gyn resident who did two things. He sympathized with me and he handed me the cure—speed.

On speed, I could stay awake all day and work all night. In addition, speed provided a synthetic ambition. I saw and did countless little things I had never noticed or done before. The shifts passed quickly and I was very pleased with my superwoman performance.

In speed I found another reliable drug with truly magical properties, and I tucked that information away in my head. I also learned something else. Because I was a student nurse I had access to interns and residents, and we shared a common ground that made it very easy to get samples or prescriptions from some of them.

When I came off the night shift, I came off speed. I used it a couple of times to stay up all night to cram for an occasional test, but that was all.

I graduated in September 1957 clean and sober. It never occurred to me then that I was clean and sober since that was my normal state. I was 20 years old, had my education behind me, was bright, pretty and in love with life in general and one guy in particular. I had the world by the tail.

Two weeks after the state boards, I

married and moved to Ohio. I had many of the dreams that many brides share. Ours was going to be a close, meaningful and "successful" marriage—meaning my marriage would not end in divorce.

I had many unrealistic expectations for myself, some of which I hung on to with varying success for the next 15 years. I was to "present" well at all times. That meant I should look sharp, display good manners and be considerate to others. The children and house were also required to pass inspection. Differences within the family were a state secret— what would other people say? I was so consumed with secretiveness and the way others viewed me that eventually I was proud of the fact that I registered no facial reaction to anything. Good or bad did not matter; I used the same solemn look (had I kept that up I might have been wrinkle free today!).

During the first three months of the marriage, I stayed home and was able to fulfill my expectations fairly easily. But soon after I started full-time work I began feeling really frantic. I could handle working, but trying to keep up with meals, dishes, shopping, washing, ironing, and cleaning in the evenings and on weekends was impossible. Remember that everything was to be perfect, including me. I was an obsessive who ironed everything so it would look nice on the shelf or in the drawer. Every shelf had to be lined, the medicine chest had to be emptied and cleaned weekly, etc.

I was beginning to feel bad about myself and my "poor" performance, and I remembered the answer: the wonder drug, the clock expander, the cure was speed. I got a prescription from a sympa-

I was beginning to feel bad about myself and my "poor" performance, and I remembered the answer: the wonder drug, the clock expander, the cure was speed.

thetic anesthesiologist for amphetamine Spansules®, refillable p.r.n. Since I am 5'7" and at that time weighed 120 pounds, appetite control was not my aim. But no one questioned me and I certainly didn't. I thought the pills contained the answer to my problem. I had no idea there were side effects or what they were. I did not know the pills were addictive or that I had a disease that made addiction inevitable.

My life moved along right on schedule the first few years. I became pregnant and we bought a nice little house. During that period I took the amphetamines when I needed them. I do not believe I exceeded one pill per day, and I did not experience any difficulty falling asleep at night.

After my daughter was born I stopped working for a while, which meant I was cut off from my source of supply. But I turned to my Ob-Gyn for pills and found him very obliging.

During the next couple of years it started to become evident even to me that my husband and I were mismatched. The idea of this was abhorrent and I tried hard for many years to overlook the facts. When I said "Till death do us part," I meant it literally.

Around that time I decided the problems in the marriage were probably my fault. I felt if I performed better my husband would like me better, so I redoubled my efforts to be a fastidious housekeeper, gracious hostess, devoted wife, untiring church worker, a superior nurse, etc. Now of course I did not do that alone. I had the help of speed every obsessive step of the way.

Conversation between my husband and me lessened, except that he criticized me and compared me to other wives who were doing thus and so, and why wasn't I? Correspondingly, I concentrated my efforts and energies on my activities in a desperate attempt to prove that I was worth something.

In early 1962, I became pregnant again. Around the end of the second trimester I started experiencing insomnia and since my little blue prenatal instruction book said this was a reportable symptom, I reported it. At this point a whole new dimension was added to my world—the sleeping pill. My specific variety was glutethimide (Doriden®), which immediately became my favorite. It was a synthetic and therefore not addictive like barbiturates were, or so I reasoned.

As we explore these years of my life, remember that I knew nothing about alcoholism. It was not discussed or taught during my nurses training. I had had no exposure to it among my family, friends or patients.

One thing I had been taught was that physicians were superhuman beings. I was a very compliant, passive, docile young woman, and I felt that "if the doctor says so, it is so." My physician was prescribing both amphetamines and sleeping pills right along with my MOL-IRON®, afternoon naps and eight glasses of H_2O a day. Since I was a very good patient I took everything.

Now it is a great help to decide when you are going to fall asleep and when you are going to wake up and be alert and ready to go. I wanted to manage every minute of every day in the most efficient and productive way, and I planned and executed my days accordingly. Soon after my son was born I started to set my alarm 30 minutes early. That way I could take my speed, sleep another 30 minutes and wake up the second time in gear and ready to go. Waiting around for the pill to take effect was an unnecessary waste of time. I felt a continuous sense of urgency due partly to myself and partly to speed.

About this time one pill no longer lasted 12 hours but began wearing off by midday, so I took a second one. I was starting to develop a tolerance to the drug, but I did not know that. So I took more and more pills to speed up and correspondingly a larger number at night to slow down. Eventually I was to take four amphetamine pills a day, and four or five sleeping pills at night as a regular practice. Special occasions and stress called for more.

This presented a new problem. I kept running out of pills. I solved it by having five or six different prescriptions, all refillable, at five or six different drugstores, all available at the same time. This was very easy to do; I got all the prescriptions from one obstetrician. On one or two occasions he did question me about my continued use of the medications but I pleaded my need for them and he continued to give me prescriptions. In addition, at work I could help myself to a variety of drugs. I seized both the opportunity and the drugs.

At times my husband questioned my lethargy and lack of coordination, but I explained this easily. I had a sinus problem and my antihistamines caused those side effects. He bought this for years. He had no idea of the type or quantity of drugs that I was taking. Neither did I. The amounts I say I took are what I *remember* taking. Often I was not able to remember if I had taken anything or not, so I took some more.

As a result of my increasing dependency on drugs, I hid my supply, I lied to my physician and my husband and I stole medicine from my patients and my employers. This behavior would have been unthinkable five years earlier, but chemicals had become the prime focus of my life.

At this time I drank alcohol in moderate amounts. No one told me not to and I was not abusing it. However, I was unaware of a problem called synergistic effect. That means when you add one pill and one drink you do not get two but instead get the effect of four or five, because alcohol affects the action of the pill.

DEPENDENCY AND OTHER SYMPTOMS DEVELOP

Around 1965 I experienced my first blackout. A blackout is a period of amnesia associated with the use of alcohol. My first one lasted about nine hours and I was terrified. My husband and I had gone square dancing with another couple. My last recollection of the evening was doing a do-si-do. My next awareness was six o'clock in the morning when I awoke, fully dressed, in my own living room. What had happened? Had I fainted? Had I made a scene? Was I in disgrace? I had no idea. I undressed hurriedly and got into bed.

In the morning I watched my husband very carefully for some reaction. Concern, anger, anything that would tell me what had happened the night before.

In the morning I watched my husband very carefully for some reaction. Concern, anger, anything that would tell me what had happened the night before.

There was nothing. I was baffled. Surely if something unusual had happened he would say something or communicate it in his behaivor. Instead, he acted like nothing out of the ordinary had happened.

When my husband left for work, I called the friend we had gone with the evening before to get her reaction. She was very friendly and pleasant and said what a good time we had had and invited us to go again. She said nothing unusual.

I did not understand what had happened during that nine-hour interval and I will never know. I certainly was not going to ask them or let them know that I could not remember. I did not connect that with the use of alcohol in any way, either on that occasion or when it

38

happened later. It was not until 1972 when I was in treatment that I learned what a blackout was and I understood what had been happening. Even so, I have never found out what happened during the blackouts simply because I never told anyone I was having them.

I started withdrawing from friends and activities outside the home for several reasons. I was losing interest, more and more, in anything outside myself. I was enormously preoccupied with drugs. Did I have enough of a supply? When could I take another dose? Where would I get the money for the next purchase? Which pharmacy had I called last? As my tolerance grew, so did my deviousness. I kept a written record of drugstores, dates refilled, prescription numbers and next dates of refills, as I could no longer trust my memory.

I also learned a new way to obtain drugs. I would call different pharmacies saying I was Doctor so-and-so's nurse calling in a prescription for a patient. Need I say that I was that patient? This was a real stroke of genius! I could bypass the physician entirely, could order whatever I needed and of course make all prescriptions refillable p.r.n.

The situation at home deteriorated gradually but inexorably. By now my husband and I were arguing openly. Without the artificial courage provided either by alcohol or pills, I lacked the courage to fight, and besides, that was "unladylike" behavior. But now I became very sarcastic if I responded at all, or I was disinterested and apathetic. The more he yelled, the more I yelled back, followed by a quick trip to the closet for

pills or the laundry room for a drink. He threatened divorce; I threatened suicide. More and more I left the children with babysitters because I did not trust myself to remain conscious all day.

In the fall of 1967 I drove the children with me to the grocery store where I passed out on the floor. Apparently this was from a cumulative effect of drugs since I had not had any for several hours before leaving the house. The store manager called my husband, who came to claim his unconscious wife and three very frightened children.

Several hours elapsed and I did not regain consciousness, so he took me to the emergency room of a local psychiatric hospital. When I regained consciousness and the physician explained what had happened, I was very frightened and ashamed. What if I had passed out driving the car with the children in it? The physician suggested I stay there awhile; maybe they could help me. I readily agreed.

My first experience in a psychiatric facility was not a happy one. The doors were locked. The staff had keys; I did not. The staff wore uniforms; I wore pajamas. They told me what to do; I did it. I found the total role reversal humiliating. As soon as the drugs wore off, of course, I made sense.

They declared I was well enough to return home in two weeks and that is when I received a terrible shock: my husband refused. He did not really care where I went but it was not going to be home. Today his behavior makes sense to me. He did not know what was happening any more than I did, and he was protecting himself and the children the only way he knew how. But I did not understand it then, and was very hurt and at a loss for what to do and where to go.

After much persuasion, I convinced a friend of mine to let me live with her for a while. It was against her better judgment and she made that abundantly clear when she finally consented.

The day I was discharged my husband picked me up and dropped me off at the house so I could pack and move in with my friend. He went to work. I immediately took three sleeping pills. Then I packed. Then I went to the liquor store and got my friend a fifth of gin as a "hostess gift" for her. But I was really establishing a supply in a new place.

I was doing private duty nursing at the time. I worked nights so I could be alone during the day to sleep (take drugs). I called the registry and accepted a case for the second night. I fiddled around my friend's apartment, vacuumed, fixed dinner and took a nap—chemically induced. When she got home from work we had a couple of drinks, ate dinner and watched TV. I decided I was "too nervous" so I went to the bathroom and took several more pills to "relax" me. I was so relaxed, in fact, that on the way to work I totaled a parked car and was back in an emergency room for a bloody nose and skull films. The police officer who came to the scene said my seat belt was the only thing that prevented my head from going through the windshield.

Let's digress for a moment and look at one of the symptoms of alcoholism, namely, the compulsive urge to drink. Another, better understood word for this

Many times during the course of these years I had made a conscious and deliberate decision to stop using drugs, not because I had a realistic idea of what was happening to myself; I had some vague concern that in the future drug use **might** *become a problem.*

is *addiction.* When one is addicted, the object of the addiction becomes of paramount importance. It is stronger than the desire to procreate, stronger than the need to eat or survive. Many times during the course of these years I had made a conscious and deliberate decision to stop using drugs, not because I had a realistic idea of what was happening to myself or my family. I did not. Drugs, by design, seriously impair judgment. I had decided to stop because I had some vague concern that in the future drug use *might* become a problem. I firmly believed the automobile accident was the result of poor visibility. But the addiction, or urge to intoxicate, caused me to return to using pills immediately upon discharge from the hospital.

After two or three uneventful weeks with my friend, I was invited to return home with the proviso that I "be good" (not take drugs) and in November 1967, just like a repentant little girl, I did so.

In December my husband and I traveled to the east coast; he on a work assignment, I on a vacation. He spent the week working while I spent it in a motel room drinking. The singleness of purpose of a person with alcoholism is truly

40

remarkable. I never drank or took drugs openly. It requires tremendous will and effort to remain drunk and look and smell sober, to remain incandescent and still function. A simple thing like driving to the pharmacy or liquor store became a major undertaking. I saw two of everything, and I had to drive with one eye closed. My perception of time and space was altered, so there was a great chance for an accident. Consequently I drove very slowly.

I had become paranoid and thought people in the liquor store knew I was an alcoholic. I also thought grocers and merchants knew, as well as people in church on Sunday. More and more I stopped leaving the house. I started to deal only with pharmacies that delivered.

But in February 1968 two men from the vice squad came to my door looking for me. They had discovered my clever way of procuring drugs by calling in phony prescriptions. This constitutes a felony in Ohio, and I was eligible to go to the Women's Reformatory. I was terrified of being imprisoned; my supply of pills was cut off and if my husband found out, I would be out on the street again. I was so out of touch with reality that I believed I could keep this a secret. I was booked and fingerprinted during the day and released on recognizance bond. I was home by the time the kids were out of school. I saw a criminal attorney and extracted a promise from him that he would not tell my husband.

The whole thing exploded a few weeks later. Normally alcohol is an anesthetic, so that a person who drinks too much and passes out is responding normally. Alcoholics, on the other hand, are turned on by alcohol and pills and become gregarious and energetic. Even with three, four or five sleeping pills at night, I did not sleep.

One night I refilled my lighter and in the process spilled fluid over my hand. When I lighted a cigarette my whole left hand went up in flames. I ran screaming to the bathroom to stick it under a faucet and my husband awakened.

By that time my husband had watched a long series of accidents, numerous overdoses and trips to local hospitals to have stitches put in or my stomach pumped out. This was the final straw. He made arrangements to have me committed.

However, I was unwilling to be "put away," as I viewed it, and consulted my attorney. I was greatly relieved to learn that it was legally impossible for my husband to bring it off. The attorney pointed out, however, that I had a serious problem with drugs and that my chances in court would improve if I did something constructive about that before my hearing. We agreed that I would make a voluntary commitment to the state hospital for 60 days.

I felt humiliated and degraded. Something very positive came out of it, however. I said goodbye to drugs—forever. My psychiatrist explained the necessity of that if I were ever going to get better and stay better. I certainly wanted that. Unfortunately, a major piece of information was not given to me. But over the next seven years I would learn the very hardest way possible that alcohol is a drug, just like amphetamines or sleeping pills or any of the other mood changers.

I START OVER AGAIN

When I was released from the state hospital, I had no home, no car and no job. I interviewed for a job and was hired, but their orientation did not start for another month. During that month my drug case came up. The charge was reduced to a misdemeanor and I paid a $100 fine.

I got a small apartment and went to work full time at a local hospital on the kidney transplant floor. I did well and learned quickly. Within two months I was selected to learn to operate the dialysis machine. That was quite an honor. I was only the sixth nurse in the county at that time able to do this. The patients were terrific, and I enjoyed the work a great deal and took considerable pride in my performance. Nursing has always been important to me and was later to prove a very significant factor in my recovery.

The hospital was seriously understaffed, and I worked a "deal" with my supervisor. I worked six shifts every week and was scheduled to be off on Saturdays so I could see my children and have them stay with me overnight.

I was no longer taking any drugs and had not rediscovered the magical properties of alcohol, and for four months I did exceedingly well. I bought a car and could take any route to and from the hospital. But I soon came home via the liquor store. I began drinking moderately,

soon I was drinking more. Because of my high tolerance, I metabolized alcohol quickly, so I awakened each day clear-headed and ready for work.

My husband was encouraged by my performance and again invited me home. Of course he did not know I was drinking daily, and I did not tell him. We bought a new home in a new neighborhood and were going to "start over." This is known as a "geographical cure." But it didn't work because my disease moved right along with me. But off we went, optimistic about the future.

My preoccupation with chemicals was back and my main problem on moving day was to insure a supply at both houses. I was successful and kept myself fortified all day.

Although alcohol is a legal drug some problems are associated with its use. First, you can smell it and so can others. Second, nobody delivers it to your door, so you must get dressed and make the hazardous journey to and from the liquor store. In addition, bottles are difficult to hide.

Alcohol gave me diarrhea so I was concerned about a constant supply of Paregoric. The alcohol would not always stay down and a large amount was lost in vomiting. In blackouts I hid bottles and forgot where they were and spent days frantically searching for them. I could not get through the night without getting up to drink.

In the mornings I was shaking so badly I could not make coffee, let alone drink it. I would race to the laundry room and down a large amount of alcohol, only to

42

I was hospitalized for a week so that a melanoma could be removed. I remember only bits and pieces of that week, however, as I was going through withdrawal unaided by any medication or knowledgeable care of the withdrawal symptoms.

have it come right back up. I'd try again. Usually the third try succeeded. Then I would start breakfast. Soon I quit eating—it interfered with the alcohol and food no longer stayed down.

In the fall of 1969 I became concerned about a mole on my left foot. It turned out to be a melanoma. I was hospitalized for a week so that it could be removed and skin grafted from my hip. I remember only bits and pieces of that week, however, as I was going through withdrawal unaided by any medication or knowledgeable care of the withdrawal symptoms.

Nurses should realize that patients with alcoholism often do not know they have alcoholism. When they see a patient with shakes and/or memory lapses and hallucinations, they should be alert to what is going on. They should talk to the physician and the family who are apt to be more candid than the patient. The presence of the disease must be established so that treatment can be instituted and health restored to the entire family. Healing is much slower in active alcoholics, and anesthesia can prove fatal. But I did not know that and apparently neither did those caring for me. Fortunately my cancer was treated in time, and I had no untoward reactions to the anesthetic.

In August 1970, I gave birth to our fourth child, a third son. Again the time spent in the hospital was largely a blank because I was in withdrawal. When I returned home I immediately went back to alcohol. My husband noticed a profound change. I was no longer able to keep up with the children and the house, and I seemed very withdrawn. He hauled me off to still another psychiatrist.

I remember being in his office, but I do not remember the trip to or from. (That is the way this whole ten-year period was for me; parts of it are fairly clear, while other parts are gone forever.) The decision made that day by my husband and the physician was that I should be hospitalized and be given shock treatments.

This was my third psychiatric admission. Since no one knew about my alcoholism, it remained untreated. I was given a new psychiatric label and treatment for a disease I did not have. In defense of the physicians, I was not honest with them. In defense of myself, I was unable to be honest because of the very disease I had. The alcohol was the only thing I had left. I knew if I told anyone it would be taken away. That thought was terrifying, so I kept my secret.

After two weeks and six shock treatments I was released as "cured." However, this time I did not leave with a clear head and quick responses. I did all right with current questions and tasks but I could not remember anything from the past. I still recall my feelings of panic. I would struggle hard for an answer, but it just would not come. My confidence had left me with the shock treatments.

I was transported, along with my newborn and four-year-old son to my parents while my husband "decided what he was going to do." That had a very ominous ring to it.

After three weeks my husband returned to render his verdict. He had decided that if I was willing to return to work full time I would be allowed to return home. My working was equated with being straight to him. For my part, although I felt humiliated that terms and conditions were attached to my returning to my own home, I was nonetheless grateful that I had a place to go.

Now ponder for a moment the insanity of this action. Here is a woman going off to care for others when her own brain is in hock. Unable to make quick decisions or recall vital information, she is going to drive on the freeway to and from work. Then, in her spare time, she is going to care for four young children, a large house and, incidentally, it seems, herself.

To compound the situation, some of those days I was required to work from noon to 8:30 PM, alone and solely responsible for unconscious patients in a recovery room for four hours. I was frightened all the time and kept comparing myself to others and double-checking everything I did, but the evening I was alone I was petrified. I was so afraid of making a mistake I hesitated to do anything at all.

By the time I reached home at the end of the day I was literally shaking all over, partly from tension and partly due to the lack of alcohol for ten hours. My first action upon arriving home was to go to

My first action upon arriving home was to go to the laundry room and have at least two very tall drinks. I am sure we had the cleanest clothes in the city.

the laundry room and have at least two very tall drinks. Ostensibly I was down there washing and as long as I was there, I did start a load. I am sure we had the cleanest clothes in the city. I was in that room so much that, since I had to have a cover for being there, when I ran out of dirty clothes many times I rewashed the clean ones.

I was soon in such poor physical shape that it was an extreme effort to haul myself in to work, let alone stay there unmedicated for up to ten hours. One day when I had had just enough alcohol "to steady my nerves," I started off to work. I was involved in another automobile accident. Unlike the first accident when I was on pills, the officer knew immediately what was the matter. I was put in a paddy wagon and hauled off to the workhouse, where they took an alcohol level. In Ohio 0.1 mg. is legally drunk and 0.4 is fatal. My level was 0.29, and I was on my way to work! At the very least I should have been unconscious.

Over a year later, when I finally was being treated, I would maintain steadfastly that I never mixed chemistry and nursing. My profession was and remains so important to me that I was unwilling to face the fact that my disease had affected my performance. I was in treatment some six months before I got brutally honest

44

and could recall my blood alcohol level on the day of that accident.

TO THE BOTTOM

From there I went steadily downhill until I could no longer make it to work and finally I quit over the phone. My husband became increasingly disgusted and began to get physical to get his way. For example, when I refused to get out of bed, he threw me out; if I talked back, he slapped me.

In June 1971 my mother-in-law had a stroke and my husband asked me if I would go home and care for her (his folks lived across the street from mine in a neighboring state). Taking the request at face value and being genuinely fond of his mother, I was happy to do so. Once I had arrived on my parents' doorstep, I was informed that I could stay there, he did not want me.

Now, objectively and from the distance permitted by the passage of seven years, I can understand his actions. At that time, however, I was frantic; I was very ill physically, extremely nervous and felt totally alone and vulnerable. I could not understand being "dumped" and resorted to harder ammunition. I cried on my brother-in-law's shoulder, complained about how badly my husband treated me and even had a black eye to show as evidence. It worked. Some of his siblings talked to him and about a week later he apologized, which was something new, and I was again on my way home.

After my return to Ohio I had to appear in court on a drunk driving charge. My attorney, however, had it

reduced to reckless operation, which is a lesser charge and a small fine. This is a common practice in our traffic court and I believe is a mistake. However, they did attach two other provisions that I agreed with and I think were productive in my case. They lifted my license for 30 days and put me on probation for a year. I was required to report monthly to a probation officer.

In August 1971 I awakened in a psychiatric emergency room. To this day I have no idea what happened that caused my husband to come home from work in the middle of the day and take me in. I was in a blackout. My first memory is opening my eyes in a little room and seeing my husband and daughter sitting there looking at me. Nobody said anything. We were all silent, looking at each other. I was thoroughly frightened. After a while an attendant came in and wheeled me up to the psych unit.

I spent three weeks on the unit and met still another psychiatrist. There were no shock treatments this time; instead we had daily lengthy conversations. I soon came to trust the psychiatrist, and I started to talk more and more to him, which was new for me.

On arrival, I had the usual admission physical which revealed a very significant finding. My liver was four times its normal size. They called in a "liver physician," and the immediate suspicion was that the cancer had metastasized. The specialist told me later that in 20 years of practice he had never encountered such a large liver. That necessitated a needle biopsy to rule out or confirm the diagnosis. They were amazed and I was relieved to learn that the size was caused by fatty metamorphosis (precirrhosis) of the liver, which is caused by the excessive use of alcohol.

So we talked about quantities and reasons for the quantities. I could explain that. If the physician was married to the man I was married to, he would drink too. It was all externally caused. He had several conferences with my husband and found himself agreeing with me. He decided it was a situational reaction, a way of coping with stress caused by someone else. He even went so far as to say I was *not* alcoholic but that I did have a very sensitive liver and for that reason should not drink. My liver simply would not withstand any further insult.

While I was in the hospital a sheriff served me with divorce papers. The physician had tried to prepare me for this, but I had refused to believe it would happen.

The physician said when I was discharged I must not return home. The stress would be too great, especially now with a divorce pending. My attorney, however, said I should return for legal reasons. He was concerned that I would be accused of desertion. My husband said he would not permit my return. I informed him of my legal rights and intention to return. He said simply that he would throw me out bodily. I pondered that for a few days and finally decided discretion was the better part of valor. I would go somewhere else. But where?

During the course of that three-week stay I made a very interesting observation about myself. I was very distrustful and suspicious of the nurses. I was a nurse and at the same time their patient. I felt

competitive with them and at the same time very embarrassed that I was a psych patient. I did not have that problem when I was hospitalized for surgery or delivery. It boils down to the fact that I put a value on different diseases. Cancer and babies are OK conditions to have; mental illness is not. That was a reflection of my attitude at the time, and I invite each of you to examine yours. Do you feel that some patients are less worthwhile than others, depending on their diagnosis?

Several relatives came to visit me during my stay, and one of them invited me to come to live with her. I felt it was an imposition, but at the same time I knew of no alternative. I set about making myself valuable to her, partly out of gratitude and guilt and partly out of a longstanding genuine affection for her. I babysat with her little boy, did household chores, shopped and sometimes helped with dinner. I visited my psychiatrist weekly and did well for a couple of months.

Then one day, as on numerous previous occasions, I got an overwhelming desire to drink and I was off and running once again. My usefulness stopped abruptly, and I became a very real liability. I had blackouts, fell and passed out. It was not safe for her to trust me with her son any more than it had been safe for my husband to trust me with our own children. She and her husband asked me to leave. I did not leave as much as I fled. I took my purse, got in my car and drove off.

I holed up in a motel for a couple of days and walked to a carryout for my supply as I no longer trusted myself to

46 drive. My niece called my husband and told him what had happened and he came looking for me. I refused to see him.

The next thing I remember is the phone ringing in the motel room and when I answered I was amazed to hear my father's voice. He inquired if I was all right and was there anything he could do. Absurdly, I declared myself to be fine, thank you very much, everything was under control. It was total denial of my desperate situation.

After I hung up, I started to sob. I felt so little and dirty and frightened and I wanted nothing so much as to "go home" with all that implies. So I called him back and asked him to come.

I want to explode another myth right here. A lot of people believe that if you drink vodka no one else can smell it. That's wrong. If you drink enough of anything eventually you can become so saturated that you exhale it through your lungs and perspire it through your pores. For years, however, I had believed the myth and so my drug of choice was vodka.

I had, however, reached the saturation point and even I could smell it emanating from my body. I took a shower, washed my hair, brushed my teeth and still I smelled like a brewery.

Then I did a truly remarkable thing: I hid the bottle so my parents would not know I had been drinking! Unbelievable. As I sit here today, six and a half years later, I am filled with an unspeakable sadness for myself. My trip through the disease was a very solitary and terrifying one. I floundered many times, not because of a lack of will to recover but because I did not know the way. I did not, at this time, even know the name of the disease I had.

My kind parents came for me one more time and carried me home. I felt that day that I had reached the bottom, there was no way up, I was totally defeated.

Upon arrival in Michigan, I took another bath to try to wash away the smell. I was not a pretty picture; alcoholism is a very unlovely disease. My parents encouraged me to eat some nourishing food. I nearly threw up. There is nothing so revolting as the smell or sight of food when a person first starts to sober up. Liquids are tolerable. So I lived on liquids for a couple of days and as the alcohol wore off, my appetite returned.

I was 34 years old and, as in former instances, I soon brightened up once the drug was gone. The depression lifted and was replaced by anger and determination. The anger, of course, was "other" directed. I was an innocent victim. And of course I was, but so was my husband a victim of the disease, yet I directed all my anger at him. Had he not deserted me in the time of my need? The fact that I had also deserted him, in a very real sense if not literally, did not occur to me for some time.

In January 1972 I returned to Ohio to get a job and an apartment near my children. I came in the west side of town and got a job on my way through. Easy. Then I proceeded to the east side, got a motel room and did it again. I went to the liquor store. After two months without a drink I was off again. I stayed about a week, taking cabs to the liquor store and back.

Living at a first-rate motel is very expensive, especially since I was unemployed. I found a former neighbor who was willing to take me in. I took the bus to her house, sobered up and two days later returned for my car. I went to settle accounts with the motel manager only to learn I had already paid the bill—apparently in a blackout, since I have no recollection of having done so. I looked at my checkbook and found some indecipherable entries.

I secured another job and an apartment. I moved in and had the children over. After I returned them safely home I went out and got a bottle. It was less than a day before I found myself unable to drive again and I was reduced to buying watered down, fruit-flavored vodka at a neighborhood carryout. I was afraid my husband would show up, throw it out and take my money, so I hid the drinks, only to discover a few hours later that I could not remember where. I literally spent hours looking for things I had hidden. The day for me to start orientation at the hospital came and went. I called in sick.

I had now reached the point in my disease where I could not get drunk, which I equated with passing out, and I could not stay sober. I could no longer sleep or eat. I spent about a week in this state, drinking all the while. At odd hours, so I would not meet my landlady in

---

I had now reached the point in my disease where I could not get drunk, which I equated with passing out, and I could not stay sober.

---

the hallway, I would carefully pick my way to and from the carryout. I lived in fear of falling on the ice and being taken to an emergency room. I was totally consumed with what others thought of me during those years. All my values came from the outside—or not at all.

AT LAST, THE CORRECT DIAGNOSIS

On February 18, 1972 my phone rang. My brother, visiting from another city, wanted to see me. I had reached the point where I no longer opened the door to anyone, so it was fortunate that he called ahead. He and I had always been close, and I trusted him. He arrived, carrying milk and groceries. He asked me if I had called Alcoholics Anonymous (AA). I said I had, although I had not. I do not remember whether or not he asked me what was wrong but I do remember telling him, loud and long and tearfully. It was that rat I was married to. He had done thus and so and I was driven to drink as a result. I believed what I was saying. My brother was very kind, and he listened. When he left he promised to find me some help and return the following morning. I was filled with a terror I still cannot name. I felt that something terrible would happen if he left me alone. I begged him to stay, but he refused. I have learned since that this unreasonable, unexplainable fear is a fairly common experience with practicing alcoholics. I did not know that then, however, nor would the information have eased the feeling.

Sure enough, my brother called again

48 in the morning and outlined what was going to happen. I would be taken to a local hospital until I felt better and was stronger and then I would go to a treatment center he knew about. There is no doubt in my mind that if my husband had said the same thing I would have refused. My brother, however, was the right person, at the right time, with the right words. I was more than willing to have him direct me.

I had thrown away my bottles the night before, prior to his arrival, so by the time he came for me I was very shaky. I set about, almost in slow motion, getting packed and bathed. It seemed to me that I no sooner hung up the phone than he was at the door. I accused him of calling from across the street. In actuality, my time perception was so altered that minutes seemed like seconds.

We waited an interminable length of time in the emergency room to be admitted to the hospital. I could barely stand and he would literally lean me against a wall or a post for support. When our turn came, my brother had to sign me in because I was having such severe tremors. He even had to hold my hand to make an X.

Once I had been taken to my room he left; he and his family were returning home. A nurse came in and suggested I take a bath before I climbed into bed. My translation: I stink. I am sure I did but I had just had a bath. I felt terribly judged by her.

Remember that attitudes are sensed by patients without any words from nurses. I was very quiet and ashamed and made an important decision about that nurse: she was my enemy and I did not trust her.

A couple of hours later I started to hallucinate, which is the second stage of withdrawal. I saw faces on the wall, and the television was on another wall! I was sufficiently cognizant to know the faces could not be there and yet there they were. Because of my distrust of the nurse, however, I decided to keep the faces a secret. I was afraid she might have me locked up. When she came to see how I was and inquired about my withdrawal, I maintained that I was just fine.

This is very serious, because I could easily have proceeded to the third stage of withdrawal, grand mal seizures, without the proper medication. I did not know this. All I knew was this nurse was judgmental and I was not going to trust her.

Had she explained the reason for asking what I was experiencing or reassured me by telling me what she was going to do with the information (medicate me versus locking me up), I probably would have told her. It is very important to be factual with alcoholic patients and to let them know that you have seen withdrawal symptoms before and are comfortable with them. The patients must know that it is for their protection and comfort that questions are being asked and that only if they are honest can they be helped with their withdrawal. The nurse's interest must not arise from curiosity but from concern.

I was fortunate; I did not convulse. I dried out, albeit very "nervously," had all the usual tests and recovered my appetite. The diarrhea stopped. The bile-colored urine started to clear. I got so I could get to the bathroom and back without hanging onto furniture. The smell dissipated.

Insomnia persisted for about another three weeks and I learned, to my surprise, that insomnia is not a fatal condition.

ENTERING TREATMENT

About five days later, I was sent to the treatment center for a preadmission interview. On the way over, my husband informed me that this center did not take just anybody and that I had better "behave and give the right answers." I had no idea what that meant either then or now but I was very tense and nervous.

We were greeted at the door by a woman with a face I recognized. She went to our church, and she stood with her arms out to me. I'll never forget that. I do not remember the questions or my answers but apparently they had little doubt that I qualified as an alcoholic for admission. The following day, February 24, I entered treatment. The contract called for a minimum 120-day stay but other than that I really had no conception of all the things that would happen to me.

When I entered treatment that day I was unconsciously a very dishonest person in several ways: I lied, I stole and I was phony. I felt like a little girl at the mercy of big people. I felt dirty, despised and alone. I did not trust myself or others. I was silent and compliant, unwilling to think, say or do anything for fear of criticism. What other people thought of me always came first. I had been ejected from my family. I had removed myself from my church and my friends. I was out of work and had lost all hope.

I had received moderate doses of tranquilizers while at the hospital. These were stopped soon after my arrival at the center. I felt a great deal of anxiety about this and was sure I would never relax or be able to sleep without them. After about two weeks, however, I started to fall asleep, like everyone else, at the end of the day. I awakened much more refreshed than I ever had when sleep was chemically induced. Over two or three months, my responses became quicker

While at the hospital, I was sure I would never relax or be able to sleep without tranquilizers. After about two weeks, however, I started to fall asleep, like everyone else, at the end of the day.

and I learned that I could again trust my own memory, that without pills or booze I was able to remember things again. I was greatly relieved and felt that my brain was still intact.

My days were planned. I was told where to be and when, what to do and how to do it. My brain was still "in hock" to some degree and I was required to rely on other people in the beginning for decision making. I was very comfortable with that as it fit right into my own unwillingness to make my own decisions.

I was taken to my first meeting of AA. It was a discussion meeting and opened with everyone saying their first name, followed by the words, "I am an alcoholic." I still was far from convinced on that score, but I would have said anything rather than draw attention to myself, so I said the words. My voice sounded like

50 someone else's and I felt like I was in a foreign land.

Sick as I was, though, I was impressed by several things: these people were sincere; they believed in something and said so; they were attractive, clean and smelled good; and they seemed to be genuinely happy without alcohol. I was amazed. The idea of facing a lifetime without the help of pills or alcohol was inconceivable to me. I felt like a woman facing a lifetime sentence as I peered ahead down an unlighted tunnel. And yet I had just met 18 or 20 people who were doing it. Amazing!

My time was filled with the study of the 12 steps of AA, attending three AA meetings a week, hearing lectures, seeing films, listening to tapes of AA leads and doing household chores. I soon realized that no one in this place was going to eat me for lunch and I settled into the routine and plodded along, sheeplike, from one day to the next.

After about two months, I was invited into the director's office for a visit. I am sure many things were discussed but the only one I remember was his question to me. "What are you doing about your own recovery?" I was dumbfounded. I was there, wasn't I? I was doing everything they told me to. It was their job to make me better. It was my job to submit to treatment. I firmly believed that at the end of 120 days I would be "all better." That's what the treatment was supposed to accomplish. No one had suggested, before this, that I had to *do* anything. What on earth was this man talking about? I was bewildered and indignant about the whole exchange and I had no

answer for him. I did, however, carry the question out of his office with me and asked it to myself over and over.

What he was talking about was responsibility. My recovery was *my* responsibility. I would either get better or I wouldn't, depending on what I did. There was no magical cure coming from outside, not from him, not from any other staff member, not even from the fellowship of AA. I was responsible, and until I shouldered that responsibility and accepted it as my own nothing was going to happen to me. When I finally understood, I heard the same old things in an entirely new way. I also decided that I had been gathering dust the first two months, accomplishing precious little.

I learned the other half of the importance of the word *responsible* from the nurse in her lectures about the disease of alcoholism. I learned I was not responsible for getting the disease. I had it before I ever took my first drink. I did not get it from drinking, any more than a diabetic gets his disease from eating sugar. It is not a disease visited by God upon the weak-willed, "bad" people of this world.

After a while it became apparent to me that the fact that I had alcoholism was not the important issue. What was important was what I *did* about it. I was powerless over the disease; I had it. When I drank I was powerless over everything, but sober I had choices and power. Whether or not I recovered was squarely in my lap. I could look at people who were not making it and say, "See, it's hopeless." Or I could look at people who *were* making it and say, "Why not me?" That was a very conscious, deliberate decision on my part and I remember the day and the place I made it.

A woman there said over and over, "Stick with the winners." She meant that any one of us can go either way, at any time. But if we stick with the winners we have control over our own direction. Imagine that! I had control over something. I found that feeling to be new, heady and very scary. The word *responsible* had come to mean a great deal more to me over the years and I will explore that as I go along.

I was in treatment a full three months before I stopped blaming other people for my being there. I would recite, over and over, 27 good and valid reasons for how I had ended up in treatment and they all had to do with other people. I had been "done unto" and was the innocent victim of others.

At the treatment center we had a psychiatrist whom we were required to see at regular intervals. It was during one of these visits with her that it finally occurred to me that I *had allowed* others to use me, walk on me, etc. By accepting responsibility for allowing that to happen in the past, I took the first faltering step toward the prevention of it in the future. Manipulation is like the tango—it takes two people. It is impossible for you to manipulate me unless I allow you to do so. That was a whole new perception for me and a very important one.

I learned in my classes about the disease, that there is a phenomenon among alcoholics known as cross-tolerance. I was not only addicted to alcohol but also to all other mood-changing pills: uppers, downers, tranquilizers, etc.

One woman exactly my own age wound up in the morgue. That's when I came to believe that alcoholism is a fatal disease.

Through my own experience with these drugs I had no difficulty believing this. Others frequently did and ran into all kinds of difficulties as a result. They would give up alcohol and at the same time reserve the right to hang on to sleeping pills or tranquilizers once they left treatment. Inevitably these people returned to alcohol and wound up in treatment again, or in jail or the state hospital. One woman exactly my own age wound up in the morgue. That's when I came to believe that alcoholism is a fatal disease.

I discovered a great many new and exciting things while I was in treatment. They did not come all at once, like a bolt of lightning. They came as tiny little insights or discoveries, seemingly unrelated and sometimes a long way apart. They all had to do with me, however, and how I operated, and it was a composite of these learnings that I used to change and fashion the "old" me into the "new" me. (I hasten to point out that I am not a finished project but rather an ongoing one. I am still learning and changing and thereby growing.)

Prior to treatment I had required perfection of myself, an impossible goal. I used each failure as a bat to beat myself. I did that silently, inside my head. I would berate myself and call myself names and insist that I do better. It was unheard of

52

for me to accept less than excellent performance.

I received permission, again from the nurse, to make a mistake and still like myself. She behaved toward me like I had some intrinsic worth, even when I made a mistake. What she gave me was unconditional love. I took permission from her to do that for myself and I can make a mistake now and giggle. I take delight in being human and find it an infinitely easier place to be than perfection ever was. It is also more attainable. On the other side of the coin, I'm allowed to pat myself on the back when I do a creditable job.

At first I bought the myth "Only an alcoholic can help an alcoholic." I took a look at my own recovery and discovered that the three most helpful people, to me, were all nonalcoholic. I am not discounting the considerable assistance I received from alcoholics, but I am discounting the idea that usefulness can be separated by diseases. Imagine where I would be today if I had insisted that my cancer surgeon had been through the same thing I had before I permitted him to operate. I believe that statement is a con perpetrated on nonalcoholics to make them keep their distance. If that myth is not confronted, 90 percent of the helping population is discounted. The ability of someone to assist has to do with their honesty and openness and feelings, not their catalogue of diseases.

AN END AND A BEGINNING

After I had been in treatment for three months, the day of my divorce hearing arrived, the most painful experience I have ever faced cold sober. I had resigned myself to the divorce itself. Indeed, I took great relief from the mere prospect.

The terrible hurt came from two areas. First, the loss of my four children was for me an indescribable experience. People who had been through a similar situation or who had witnessed it seemed to believe this was a permanent arrangement and the sooner I reconciled myself to the fact, the better off I would be. I was unwilling to accept this as final. As the next months and years passed, I gradually reconstructed myself and my life with the belief that some day the children would at least have their own choice in the matter.

Second, when I saw the people who were testifying for my husband I felt great pain. Friends and relatives that I dearly loved were "on the other side." Now that was a logical and reasonable place for them to be, under the circumstances. I know that, in my head, and I knew it then. However, the pain I felt did not arise from my head.

AA has a Serenity Prayer:

God grant me the serenity to accept the things I cannot change, courage to change the things I can and wisdom to know the difference.

I clung to that prayer in the months to come and used it as a yardstick to determine my own direction. I could not, at the moment, have my children. I could rant and rave and throw a fit or I could use the same energy to change me and do what I could so that some day perhaps I would have my children. I chose the latter course.

One of the requirements for going back

to work imposed upon us by the staff was that we complete the first five steps of AA. I had completed the first three but procrastinated about steps four and five. Step 4 says we "made a searching and fearless moral inventory of ourselves" and Step 5 says we "admitted to God, to ourselves, and to another human being the exact nature of our wrongs." I was not fond of doing such tough stuff. I did, however, want very much to return to work and get on with my life, so I undertook the steps in July 1972. After I had successfully completed them I was allowed to seek employment.

I went immediately to the hospital where I had interviewed and been hired (but failed to report) the preceding February. I was in infinitely better shape for the second interview. I was hired and started to work on August 7, 1972, a very important day for me. One of my AA friends took me shopping, and we had a great time finding uniforms and shoes for my big day. I worked full time on a surgical floor and I loved it. I was also good at it.

In October of that year I was invited to join the staff at the treatment center and provide emergency night coverage. Occasionally residents became ill at night; also new residents needed close observation the first week or so. I received room and board in exchange. I began to view myself as a responsible adult instead of the dependent little girl who had entered treatment six months earlier. This was reinforced by the staff and also my co-workers at the hospital. I worked hard and enjoyed my work. I saw my children every other weekend.

Another very important lesson oc-

curred about this time. I learned how to say no. Simple word. Two letters I had never used. In the past, when someone from the PTA or church called and asked me to bake six dozen cupcakes, I had always said yes and then proceeded to resent the person who had asked me. It would not have occurred to me to refuse. "Nice girls" and "good mothers" always said yes to these requests. I equated standing up for myself as bad and I really believed that if I refused anything I wouldn't be liked and might even be hit. However, I learned in treatment that all my meek, submissive behavior was an excuse for not making decisions.

I still remember the first time I tried saying no. It was over the telephone, said very cautiously, and it elicited from my caller a loud "What?" He also was not used to my use of the word. I stood my ground, however, and repeated, "No." Afterwards I felt high as a kite, swollen up and proud of myself. I tried it again and again. It worked. People did indeed accept the word when I used it. I no longer found myself doing things I hated and wondering how I had gotten pushed into them. I simply said no when I meant no.

Another significant word to me was *options*. I could explain to you what it meant but I never had applied it to myself. I used to sit enviously, watch assertive people and think, "Wouldn't it be nice if I could do that?" I found that I could do a vast number of things but only if I were willing to try them.

Once, if you told me to turn right, I turned. Today if you told me to turn right, I know I have other choices—left, backward, forward, up and down. And I

54 will decide my own direction, thank you.

Many times, though, I am on unfamiliar turf (I have become quite adventuresome) and I am unaware of my options. I simply open my mouth and ask. I am amazed by some of the choices presented to me by others when I ask them.

In June 1973 I was approached by the evening supervisor and asked if I would consider the head nurse position on the floor on which I was currently working. I also inquired about other possibilities. Well, there was also an evening supervisor position available. I retired back to the treatment center to try these choices on for size. I also sounded out the staff to see if they thought I was ready. We all agreed I was. The head nurse position was an honor, but I viewed the supervisor job with more excitement and communicated my choice to my boss. Two or three days later she returned with the verdict. I was to be the new evening supervisor!

I felt obligated to inform my employer about my disease and drug arrest record. They were entitled to know these things if they were preparing to entrust their hospital to my care for eight hours a day. I was very nervous about doing this, being afraid they would retract their offer.

I was appointed evening supervisor. Part of my job involved having keys to the pharmacy where all kinds of marvelous medicines were available. But the trust that my superiors showed me was a very precious gift and one that I would never violate.

Even more uncomfortable, though, was the thought that they would find out later and dismiss me. So I made an appointment and told them my history. They had known for some time and were still willing to put their money on me! What a relief not only that I still had the job but that everything was out in the open. This was very significant since part of my job involved having keys to the pharmacy where all kinds of marvelous medicines were available. But the trust that my superiors showed me was a very precious gift and one that I would never violate.

In October of 1973 I decided the time had come for me to go back out into the world all the way. So I rented a townhouse in the childrens' school district and moved out of the treatment center. My daughter was, at this time, just 14 and by law was now allowed to choose who she would live with. I created a home for myself and for her, contacted an attorney and got a custody hearing date for February 1974.

At this point it was necessary for me to move to the day shift in order to be home with my daughter in the evenings. She had repeatedly expressed a desire to be with me and the only impediment to that was the judge's permission. I talked to the director of nursing about the possibility of a transfer to the day shift and was in for another pleasant surprise. The hospital was preparing to open an alcoholism treatment unit the following summer and was looking for a head nurse for that unit. There was a price attached, however. She had an immediate need of a head nurse for a urology floor, and if I would do that now I could have the other later. It was a good trade and one that benefited us both. She got her unit covered and I was able to go on the day shift. I accepted.

The day for the custody hearing arrived. My attorney had repeatedly warned me about being too optimistic. I had been sober then just 16 days short of two years. I was required to produce witnesses who could vouch for my recovery. I chose the nurse and psychiatrist from the treatment center and the evening supervisor with whom I had worked for nearly a year. At last my daughter was called and stated her desire to live with me. I was delirious! We went and picked out sheets and drapes and a spread for her new room, picked up a week's supply of clothing from her house and went together to meet my friend for dinner at what is still my daughter's favorite restaurant.

In April the prospective director of the new unit came from Cleveland to meet with the board of Trustees, and I met him for the first time. I was very interested in finding out what he was like since he would be the person who decided policy and philosophy. I listened carefully, said little and was satisfied with what I heard.

Shortly after this, I learned of an opportunity to attend the Rutgers University Summer School of Alcohol Studies. Using my newly found skills of researching options, I set off to track this down. The hospital was willing to pay my salary for the three weeks I was gone; the state of Ohio was willing to pay my air fare and Rutgers was willing to give me a scholarship. It turned out my toughest obstacle was presented by my daughter.

She was very unhappy about having to spend the three weeks with her father and carried out a really impressive campaign to pull my guilt string. She pouted, she whined, she was silent, all with a notable lack of success.

The week before I was due to leave for Rutgers, the hospital sent me to Cleveland for three days to visit an already established alcoholism treatment unit; it was the one where our new director still worked. I remember how daring and adventurous I felt driving off by myself to find a hospital in downtown Cleveland. That was a pretty big trip for a woman who two years before had barely been able to make it to the liquor store and back!

On the way, however, I started to experience some very real qualms about this whole new venture. I thought the nurses on the unit should be involved in therapy; what if the new director did not and viewed us merely as pill pushers? I got angry just thinking about it and decided that that was the first thing I would ask when I got there. If that was going to be the case, I would want nothing to do with the unit. So I set about analyzing this man.

I was both delighted and relieved by what I found. He was open, warm and caring. He was willing to listen to my suggestions and consider them. I observed him at work and play and was greatly impressed. At the end of the three days I said goodbye and started home. As I drove up the entrance ramp to the freeway I was amazed to find myself crying. I didn't want to leave him. What was happening to me?

56   Two days later I flew off to New Jersey. The three weeks I spent there were the longest three weeks of my life. I felt obligated to concentrate and learn a lot and yet my heart was back in Ohio. But I was sure that my feelings for this man were one sided and that I was setting myself up for still more pain. I tried desperately to talk myself out of it, advancing all kinds of logical arguments to dissuade myself. After about two weeks I relaxed and realized that I felt what I felt. I was in love with him. The future would bring what it would bring. I stopped struggling against it.

In spite of the 90-degree heat and my own distractions, I learned some things and even had some good times. I spent an enormous amount of the time, however, daydreaming and writing letters. I claimed to myself and him that I was writing a daily diary of my experiences so that we could use them when we started work on the unit upon my return. I did not fool either one of us.

When I returned from Rutgers and he moved from Cleveland, we began preparation for the new unit. There was an enormous amount of work to be done before it opened, and I loved every minute of it. I was sorry when the day ended and he went his way and I went mine. I felt in a sense like a pioneer, very adventurous and excited. We waded through policies, procedures, philosophy, interviews and plans for staff orientation.

We held six inservice presentations for the general hospital staff. There was a great deal of resistance, in the beginning, to having "those drunks in our hospital." To a lesser extent that still remains.

Many health care professionals have attitude problems and view alcoholism as a sin rather than as a disease.

Opening day finally came, and we received seven patients. I still remember all their names. For the first year and a half I did group therapy daily, along with the other day nurses and found that this was truly the most rewarding kind of nursing that I had ever done. Out in the general hospital I was always battling the clock and doing things to parts of people: a dressing here, an IV there. But on the treatment unit I got to know each of the patients and to follow their remarkable growth and changes over a three-week period.

From the patients I learned more about responsibility. I had been attending AA for nearly three years and had never led a meeting. I was too scared. The other person could get up and do it, but not me because "I'm so shy, you understand."

One day I finally heard myself saying those things and realized what a cop-out that was. I took from the program all the time, and I was giving nothing back. I looked at some of the patients who were making some really gutsy changes and asked myself, "Why not me?" I really believed that I would die of fright or be

I reached the point where I can enjoy myself and the audience when I lead an AA meeting. That only came about because I was willing to face my fright rather than back out or run away as I would have done in past years.

struck dumb, but I survived and did a fair job. The second time I was still scared, but less so, and I actually have reached the point now, three years later, where I can enjoy myself and the audience when I lead a meeting. That only came about because I was willing to face my fright rather than back out or run away as I would have done in past years.

I tried daily to communicate to the patients a concept that is very significant to me. I wrote it on the board every morning for months and one day when I came to work I saw a beautiful banner hanging in the hall with "my words" on it. The director had had it made as a surprise gift to me. It reads:

I am responsible for my own changes (recovery).

If I don't make any changes I am responsible for that, too.

That was important to me because it was not until after I had grasped that idea that I started to get better. It remains important to me because "getting better" is an ongoing process. If I see something in myself I dislike or am dissatisfied with, I am able to change it. The choice to make a change is mine alone.

A WHOLE NEW DIMENSION

God, as I understand Him, has been infinitely good to me. The man that I had come to know and love even better also loves me. At first that was too much for me to accept. I was afraid something terrible would happen. It was too good to be true. I certainly did not deserve him. I tortured myself for months with threats that something would happen and I would

once again be alone. I'm happy to say that he is still alive and well.

We were to be married in October 1975. The summer before, my second child, a son, expressed his desire to come and live with me. My fianceé and I discussed it at length. I was concerned that this was more children than he had bargained for and was an imposition on him. Not so. He was especially fond of my son and urged me to go ahead with the custody change. So in September my son came, just in time to help with the move and to start in a new school.

My brother came from Nebraska and my parents came from Colorado to stay with the children while we went off to Maine for three glorious weeks. The wedding was not the end to a romantic courtship but rather the beginning of a very special marriage. The courtship continues, as does the friendship and sharing and growth on both our parts. He is for me a permission giver, and I take on bigger and bigger things, reassured by the knowledge that he is always in my corner. Sometimes I am amazed at how brave I have become; he never is. He sees things in me long before I acknowledge they are there.

Once again I have let the little kid inside me out and I giggle, sing, skip and goof off if I want to, doing things I had given up as "unladylike" in my serious, somber drug-filled years.

The children at various times found themselves squarely in the middle. They remained loyal and loving throughout the drinking years, however, and continue so. When I entered treatment, my daughter was 11 and was very serious and quiet.

58 She kept to herself, withdrawing from school as she took on more and more responsibilities at home. In a very real sense, we reversed roles. She became the parent and I the child.

As I made changes and started resuming my responsibilities following treatment, we got into a real tug of war. She viewed disciplining her three younger brothers as her job; I viewed it as mine. Realizing what was happening, I put into words the fact that I was the mother, she was the child. She wasn't happy about relinquishing the power she had acquired over the years. I insisted, and just as I frequently take permission from my husband to try new things, she has taken permission from my changes to make some neat ones of her own. Her sense of humor has returned and she has a lightness again that was missing for a long while. To a large extent she has given up measuring herself by how others will view her and is content to follow her own way. She also has learned a great deal about alcoholism and is proud of my recovery.

Her oldest brother has also made significant changes. Although he was barely nine when I stopped drinking, he remembers a great deal. When he joined his "new" family two and a half years ago he was different than he is today. He has always been a strong outspoken individual. He is much more trusting and open than he was. He is less critical and is giving up comparisons and competition and is replacing them with affection and acceptance—of himself as well as others. His word is important to him now that he can trust ours. He has come to believe that his new father and I love him because he's himself, not because he performs or doesn't, and he has relaxed noticeably in the last couple of years. He has learned a few facts about alcoholism but is primarily bored by the subject and takes my sobriety for granted, much as he does my recovery from cancer or his recovery from a broken arm. They were crises once but are now ancient history.

I am very glad that my children have an opportunity to be a part of a family where there is respect and concern. If their only view of marriage had been the one they were exposed to earlier, they might well have been content to settle for far less themselves.

TODAY

I have become very greedy over the years. If I see a quality in someone else that I admire, I go after it for myself. I heard a woman tell a group of people how neat she was and why. I learned something from her—it is alright for me to pat myself on the back. I no longer sit back and gather dust and hope that I will be noticed. I pat my own back or open my mouth and tell you what I've done or both.

I learned from my husband that it's alright for me to ask for what I want. In the old days I sat around hoping someone would figure it out and offer it to me. Now I ask for it. Sometimes I get, sometimes I don't. That's OK too.

I have a new independence. I also guard that independence fiercely. I no longer allow others to explain how I feel or decide what I want or need. It took me

35 years to learn how, and I object loud and long if anyone attempts to tamper with that.

There is a vast difference between being merely dry and being sober. Dryness denotes absence of the chemical. Period. I was dry when I entered treatment, viewing life without alcohol and pills. Sober means a positive change in a person and a joy and lightness without chemicals. It's like walking down a dark, rainy side of the street versus crossing over into the brightness and the warmth of the sunshine. I have gradually crossed the street and I have been fortunate enough to see my children follow.

Today I live in the present and get as much out of each day as I can. I have let go of the past and no longer dread the future. Instead I welcome it! Every morning is like a new adventure for me, and I enjoy being a part of that adventure. I have come full circle. Six years ago I dreaded each day and viewed life as an overwhelming effort. I am now delighted to be alive and want more and more of life. In fact, I have decided to live to be 101, fully and one day at a time!

Adolescent Alcoholism: Treatment and Rehabilitation

Bessie L. Fields, R.N.
Head Nurse
Department of Talbot Hall
St. Anthony Hospital
Columbus, Ohio

Beg

TEENAGE DRINKING is not a new phenomenon. However, there has been a recent upsurge in alcohol abuse among this country's teenagers. Alcohol—because of its accessibility—seems to have become their drug of choice, although almost every teenager who drinks also uses another drug.

The National Institute on Alcohol Abuse and Alcoholism (NIAAA) reports that 1.3 million Americans between the ages of 12 and 17 have a serious drinking problem. Health care providers are faced with the question of how to treat these young alcoholics. The first requirement for providing treatment is a working knowledge both of the disease itself and of normal adolescent development.

WHAT IS ALCOHOLISM?

According to the NIAAA, alcoholism ranks fourth among major health problems in this country; only heart disease, cancer and mental illness affect more

61

Beg.

62   people. Alcoholism is the third leading cause of death in this country. It is a primary, progressive, chronic fatal disease. *It is also a treatable disease.* Alcoholism is characterized by significant impairment directly associated with persistent and excessive use of alcohol. Impairment may involve physiological, psychological or social dysfunction.

Alcoholism also manifests itself as a type of drug dependence, of pathological extent and pattern, which usually interferes seriously with the patient's mental and physical health and adaptation to the environment. Such dependence is of the sedative-hypnotic type. Cross tolerance of alcohol with barbiturates and other sedative drugs is common. Thus alcoholism is conducive to polydrug use in the perpetuation of dependence.

The most noticeable effects of alcohol are upon the central nervous system. Changes occur earliest in the emotional and autonomic functions; judgment, memory, learning ability and other intellectual phenomena are adversely affected as intoxication progresses. Adolescent alcoholics experience tremendous mood changes. It is not uncommon for their parents to report that these teenagers are hard to live with, cannot make up their minds and act like split personalities.

The effects of alcohol upon the liver are complex and not well defined. However, in an adolescent with a history of long-term alcohol abuse, physical examination may show liver enlargement and/or tenderness. Such an examination also not uncommonly reveals cardiac arrhythmias, slight tremors, tachycardia and hypertension.

Aspects of Alcoholism

Four characteristics of alcoholism provide particular insight into the nature of the disease:

1. Alcoholics experience a profound and recurring urge to intoxication to change the way they feel. The urge comes and goes, but when it comes it is stronger than any other feeling or need—whether instinctual (sex, hunger, life) or learned. This is what makes some alcoholics think they are crazy. But what is involved is addiction, not mental illness.

2. The urge becomes automatic. Once individuals are "hooked" on the experience of intoxication, their drinking becomes a self-generating process. The urge to drink becomes,

---

The urge to intoxication is incurable. The condition of alcoholism may be cured, but not the underlying urge.

---

in effect, an instinct like any other. It does not have to be provoked. It comes and goes by itself. The instinct takes over. It is automatic.

3. The urge to intoxication is incurable. The condition of alcoholism may be cured, but not the underlying urge. The urge remains, so powerful and meaningful that it can never be forgotten.

4. The persisting urge to intoxication must be kept in awareness and dealt with as real. To deny its presence and reality is to deny the disease itself. Such denial is characteristic

of alcoholics, who often describe themselves as social drinkers.

In many cases, young alcoholics are misdiagnosed as being mentally ill and undergo extensive psychiatric care without any signs of improvement. Their alcoholism problem may be compounded by the drugs sometimes administered as part of such care. Thus accurate diagnosis is extremely important.

Identifying Alcoholism in Adolescents

Alcoholism is most clearly recognizable not by how much or how often individuals drink, but by the *way* in which they use alcohol. There are at least nine signs or indications of possible trouble.

1. *Preoccupation with the Use of Alcohol.* Drinking feels good; adolescents fall in love with its effect and look forward increasingly to the next time they can become intoxicated. Individuals who are anticipating the next opportunity to drink when they should be thinking about something else are psychologically dependent on alcohol.
2. *Rapid Intake.* The goal in using the drug is to get it into the drinker's system fast enough to alter the emotional state and produce a "high."
3. *Using the Drug Alone.*
4. *Unplanned Use.* This means that individuals cannot control their use of alcohol predictably.
5. *Protecting the Supply.* Alcoholics are afraid of being caught without anything to drink and therefore will usually ensure that they have extra "just in case."

6. *Alcohol as Magic.* Drinkers begin to think of alcohol as a panacea. Having a drink becomes the first thing they think of when depressed, anxious, frightened, angry or glad.
7. *Increased Tolerance.* There is an increase in the intake of sedatives, and drinkers remain completely efficient in routine activities. Pride in the amount of drink individuals can "hold" may reflect the increased chemical tolerance characteristic of alcoholism.
8. *Blackouts.* Chemically dependent persons have difficulty remembering everything they do while drinking. The morning after finds them with holes in their memory.
9. *Stop-Start.* Chemically dependent persons are always swearing off alcohol or promising to cut down.

A person with four or more of these nine signs is an alcoholic.

The physical symptoms characteristic of chronic adult alcoholics, such as cirrhosis and Korsakoff's psychosis, are not always as apparent in alcoholic teenagers. Therefore, a thorough patient history must be obtained from all significant persons in an adolescent's life (e.g., parents, family physician, school nurse, etc.) before a diagnosis of chemical dependency or alcoholism can be made.

MEDICAL TREATMENT

Detoxification

Alcoholism among teenagers is a serious medical problem warranting serious treatment. At St. Anthony Hospital in Columbus, Ohio, a special unit (the

63

64   Adolescent Alcoholism Unit) has been established for this purpose. Because of the increased tendency of young people toward multiple drug use, the first step in treating adolescent patients is to admit them to the acute care unit for safe withdrawal from chemicals and for observation. A thorough drug history is obtained from the adolescent in addition to the information required for the routine nursing data base. The drug history is a helpful assessment tool for medical and nursing staff and directs their attention to possible withdrawal signs.

The goals of detoxification are: to assure safe and complete withdrawal from alcohol or other mood-changing chemicals; to obtain a complete history and physical examination; to initiate physician's orders; and to accomplish routine laboratory workup. Its short-term goals include providing a well-lighted environment, hydrating the patient with high carbohydrate fruit juices, monitoring vital signs and medicating as necessary and observing for behavior indicative of any stage of drug withdrawal.

Nursing Assessment

The Nursing Assessment Process for the alcoholic patient at St. Anthony includes:

Physical Assessment
- vital signs;
- stage of withdrawal;
- nutritional status;
- personal hygiene.

Psychological Assessment
- level of orientation and alertness;
- level of knowledge about chemical dependency;
- motivation for treatment.

Social Assessment
- identification of existing or potential problems;
- need for referral;
- family stability;
- vocational status.

Length of Stay-Discharge

The individual response of adolescents to detoxification treatment determines their length of stay in the unit. Generally, the initial withdrawal can be completed in 24 to 48 hours. Discharge planning begins at the time of admission. Parental participation in this process is required, with parents being informed that adolescent alcoholic patients are subject to rules of behavior necessary for safety and treatment. Violation of these rules results in consequences to the patient. The consequences of repeated or severe violations may be discharge from the hospital. In the event of such a discharge, parents are notified as soon as practicable. Patients are not informed about the discharge until parents arrive at the hospital to assume custody. In such instances, parents put in writing their plans for continued care for the adolescent alcoholic.

Concerned Person Information

Because alcoholism is a disease of denial, it is not unusual for adolescent alcoholics, like their adult counterparts, to minimize or rationalize their use of alcohol. Consequently, family members or persons close to the patient are requested to complete a "Concerned Person Information Sheet." This may provide more data on the patient's drinking habits; it also gives the treatment team a chance to know the patient from another viewpoint, thus enhancing comprehensive, quality diagnosis and treatment. Some of the questions asked are:

1. What events led them to seek admission for the patient?
2. What drugs do they know the patient uses (alcohol, marijuana, volatiles, amphetamines, barbiturates, tranquilizers, hallucinogens and psychedelics, cocaine, Class A narcotics)?
3. How long has the patient been using the drug(s)?
4. What is the frequency of use?
5. What is the pattern of use (alone, with others, daily use, using during school, weekend use)?
6. What other drugs does the concerned person suspect the patient may be using?
7. Does the patient use drugs openly in the presence of the concerned person? If so, what drugs?
8. Has the patient experienced any legal consequences as a result of his or her drug use (e.g., arrests, juvenile court involvement, etc.)?
9. How has the patient's drug use interfered in family life? (Example: worries, verbal or physical abuse, broken promises, arguments, dishonesty, irresponsibility, changing relationships.)
10. Have there been changes in the patient's physical appearance, habits or general health?

Analysis of family dynamics can help identify the extent of emotional or physiological addiction.

Questioning the Adolescent Alcoholic

It is also important to understand the adolescent alcoholic's own views and feelings about his or her situation. Answers to the following questions provide the clinician with a measure of the patient's alcoholism; answering them also gives the adolescent alcoholic an opportunity to think about drinking and its consequences:

1. Have you lost time from school due to drug use or drinking?
2. Do you use drugs to feel more comfortable?
3. Do you use drugs to build self-confidence?
4. Is using drugs (alcohol included) affecting your reputation?
5. Do you use drugs to escape from study or home worries?
6. Do you feel guilty or "bummed out" after using?
7. Does it bother you if someone says you use too much?
8. Do you feel more at ease on a date when using drugs?
9. Have you gotten into trouble at home because of your drug usage?
10. Do you borrow money or do without other things to buy alcohol or other drugs?

Analysis of family dynamics can help identify the extent of emotional or physiological addiction. It is also important to understand the adolescent alcoholic's own views and feelings.

---

11. Do you feel more powerful when you use drugs?
12. Have you lost friends since starting to drink or use drugs?
13. Have you ever woken up and wondered what happened the night before?

ONGOING TREATMENT

Treatment for adolescent alcoholics at St. Anthony consists of five weeks' hospitalization. The treatment program is intense, running seven days a week and including group therapy, recreational therapy, occupational therapy, individual counseling and lectures. Treatment is based on Alcoholics Anonymous (AA) philosophy and built around AA's 12 steps to sobriety. Attending AA meetings is part of the treatment. The first seven days of hospitalization constitute the Evaluation Phase; this is followed, for selected patients, by an Advanced Treatment Phase lasting four weeks.

Evaluation

In more detail, the course of treatment is generally as follows. After successful completion of detoxification, each patient is interviewed by a counselor from the adolescent unit evaluation team who decides whether or not that patient should be admitted to ongoing treatment. Consideration is given to the extent and history of the patient's drinking behavior, his or her relapse record, failure to meet academic obligations because of alcohol abuse, etc.

During the Evaluation Phase, the adolescent is interviewed by a social worker for the purpose of developing a personal treatment plan. Treatment planning is an ongoing, dynamic process that starts in the Evaluation Phase and continues through discharge and follow-up. Continuing review, assessment and modification of the plan and its goals are inherent in this process.

The Evaluation Phase has the following goals: first, and most important, to assist patients in identifying their relationship to mood-altering chemicals; second, to enable the staff to identify and evaluate this relationship; and third, to introduce patients to the group process so that they may begin to experience themselves and others as feeling people.

These goals are achieved in four ways:

1. *Lectures and Films.* These introduce patients to the disease concept of alcoholism/chemical dependency, the nature of the disease and the ways in which mood-altering chemicals affect the feeling life of alcoholics and the feelings of those around them. There are also special lectures designed to acquaint patients with the group process.

2. *Group Therapy.* Patients are confronted by staff members with hard data regarding their alcohol-related behavior. The purpose of this is to break through the alcoholic's powerful denial system. Group therapy in the Evaluation Phase of treatment differs from group therapy in the advanced phase. While in evaluation, patients are encouraged to share experiences and past behaviors, whereas advanced group ther-

apy emphasizes dealing with here-and-now feelings.

3. *Values Clarification.* The chemically dependent alcoholic experiences a conflict between values and behavior. Dealing with this conflict is particularly difficult for adolescents because they tend to lack concrete value systems. Values clarification assists adolescent alcoholics to delineate their value systems and to recognize that their alcoholic behavior goes against their values. Values clarification groups have proved to be an effective diagnostic tool for both patients and staff at St. Anthony.

4. *One-to-One Counseling and Intervention.* Individual counseling is available to the adolescent patient in addition to the regularly scheduled group therapy and is provided on a p.r.n. (whenever needed) basis. It has been our experience that adolescents tend to be more open when they do not have to concern themselves with self-image in the presence of peers. In instances where neither group nor individual therapy appears to be helping a patient, an "intervention" is made.

To intervene is to "stick one's nose" into the life and affairs of another, to impose one's knowledge and values on an unaware or reluctant individual. In our context, the act of intervention is deliberately calculated to induce change in the perceptions or behavior of adolescents who are deluded about the role of alcohol in their lives. The persons involved in such an intervention are instructed to write down as many incidents as they can recall related to the patient's alcohol-induced behavior. The written-list approach helps keep the confrontation factual and reduces the judgmental aspect.

Transition

Before moving from evaluation to the advanced phase of treatment, the adolescent has a transition meeting with staff members and peers to answer the following questions:

1. What do you (the patient) want to have happen as a result of treatment?
2. What are your goals?
3. What do you see as your needs (problems), interests and strengths?
4. Do you have any ideas, questions or concerns about entering treatment?

At this time, patients also sign a treatment contract, which will be used, along with their personal treatment plan, midway through the advanced phase treatment in the "14th day evaluation conference." The purpose of this conference is to assess the patient's status and review treatment goals with the patient. Both nursing and counseling staff participate. The patient is asked the following questions:

1. What aspects of treatment do you think are more or less important, and why?
2. Do you have goals to suggest that are important to you?
3. Do you have questions or recommendations regarding your treatment plan?

68

4. Do you have any reactions or questions regarding staff recommendations or viewpoints?
5. Do you think you are making progress? If so, in what way?

Advanced Treatment

Group therapy is an important part of the advanced phase of treatment—each patient spends four hours a week (two two-hour sessions) in group therapy. Its

---

At St. Anthony, group therapy is an important part of the advanced phase of treatment—each patient spends four hours a week in group therapy.

---

primary goal is for patients to discover themselves and others as feeling persons and to identify the defenses that block this discovery. One of the advantages of treating adolescents in group is that they rely on group pressures and experiences to grow. Often the therapist is seen as an extension of an adolescent's parents and meets resistance accordingly. But the same adolescent finds it harder to deny the sincerity of a group of peers pointing out his or her denials and defenses. The interaction of adolescents in a group allows them to make interpretations to each other in their own language. The group also provides them with support; this is important since many adolescents are struggling with dependency needs they often deny.

GROUND RULES FOR EFFECTIVE GROUP THERAPY

1. Only one person talks at a time.
2. Patients are to listen and respond on a *feeling* level in group.
3. What is said in group should be directed to the entire group—no side conversations.
4. Each person should speak for himself or herself.
5. What is said in group stays in group; trust is essential.
6. There is to be no violence or threat of violence.
7. Each patient is responsible for his or her own group experience.

GROUP TERMINOLOGY AND PROCESSES

- *Confronting* is "presenting" a person with himself or herself as perceived by another (i.e., the confronter).
- *Leveling* is responding openly to being confronted. A group member levels when he or she takes the risk of being known by spontaneously reporting feelings.
- *Hiding* is responding without naming a feeling.
- *Defenses* are blocks used to avoid naming the feelings a person experiences in the here and now. Common defenses are:

      rationalizing
      justifying
      projecting
      blaming, accusing
      judging, moralizing
      intellectualizing
      analyzing
      explaining

questioning
minimizing
evading, dodging
defying
attacking, aggressing
withdrawing
silence
joking
agreeing
smiling, laughing

PSYCHODRAMA

Psychodrama is a structured group process designed to improve the patient's self-understanding. It aims specifically to increase the patient's spontaneous ventilation of suppressed or repressed feelings. The principles of psychodrama are the following: (1) therapy takes place in action and (2) past events are used only to set the scene and to warm up the "actors"; scenes are enacted in the here and now.

The persons needed for a formal psychodrama session are the chief therapist (the director), a subject (the protagonist), persons to play other roles (auxiliary egos) and other members of the therapeutic group. A psychodrama session has three distinct parts: warm-up, enactment and sharing.

The session begins with a warming-up process whereby the director and members of the group prepare for therapeutic work. During warm-up, one protagonist emerges from the group, usually with a particular life problem for which he or she is seeking help. The director interviews the protagonist briefly to establish the nature of the problem.

Moving from a verbal statement of the problem to action (enactment) is accomplished by a variety of techniques. Usually the protagonist is asked for specific examples of settings in which the problem manifests itself. One of these is chosen for enactment, and the protagonist is asked to move about the stage and set it up—placing windows and doors of a room, arranging chairs to represent its furniture and describing its colors and the feelings it evokes. The protagonist may be asked to take the role of some object in the room—a picture or a door—and speak from that object's "point of view" about the room.

Auxiliary egos are chosen from the group to play the important others in the scene. They may be prepared for their roles by having the protagonist play them first and establish the important features of each person. Such role reversal intensifies feelings and develops insight. It is important for quiet to be maintained during this stage so that voice tones and inflections may be picked up. With the setting established and the auxiliaries in place, the scene is begun. If the auxiliaries are in error, the protagonist may correct them or reverse roles again.

After the enactment, both participants and other members of the group are encouraged to share the personal feelings, responses and experiences it has activated. Sharing sometimes includes embraces or handshakes. Sharing is very meaningful to the protagonist in establishing a trusting relationship. It is very important that adolescents know it is possible to share their feelings without

70 being rejected, and that they know they are not alone in their experiences. One of the greatest concerns of this age group is fear of rejection. This is overcome effectively through psychodrama. A very special function of a formal psychodrama is preparing the adolescent alcoholic to face pending court hearings. Preparation for other difficult life events such as returning to school and facing peers (particularly those with whom the patient used drugs) can be handled in psychodrama as a sort of "rehearsal for life."

SERENITY GROUP

Many adolescents, as part of their movement toward independence, feel they must examine and reconstruct the religious beliefs given them by their families; some teenagers, on the other hand, have not been given any beliefs. The goal of Serenity Group is to encourage adolescent alcoholics to become aware and examine in an experiential way what their beliefs are through open discussion, and to provide them with spiritual values.

Serenity Group seeks to:

1. renew a level of basic trust, to provide an experience of belonging;
2. identify the distorted values of alcohol addiction;
3. teach the dynamics of forgiveness—a way to move from guilt, which blocks spiritual growth, to forgiveness and reconciliation;
4. expand inner space and make it more enjoyable.

AA INVOLVEMENT

The philosophy of AA is an integral part of the treatment of adolescent alco-

The philosophy of AA is an integral part of the treatment of adolescent alcoholics at St. Anthony. Each patient is required to work through the first four of AA's 12 steps to living.

holics at St. Anthony. Each patient is required to complete reading assignments from AA literature, and to work through the first four of AA's 12 steps to living. Step 1: *"Admitted that we were powerless over alcohol—that our lives had become unmanageable."*

At the first step, patients must give examples of their powerlessness over alcohol and make a written list of destructive behaviors caused by this lack of control—e.g., odd and insane behavior, loss of memory and blackouts while intoxicated, destructive behavior against self and others, accidents caused and dangerous situations produced. They are also asked to describe the ways in which their drinking has made their lives unmanageable through its effects on: their medical or physical condition, emotional life, social and family life, spiritual life, school and/or work.

Once this step is completed, the adolescent shares the results with peers in his or her therapy group.

Step 1 brings out what is wrong with the alcoholic's present life; Step 2 offers hope that a better life is possible in the future. Step 2: *"Came to believe that a power greater than ourselves COULD RESTORE US TO SANITY."*

To help adolescents toward personal acceptance of Step 2, they are asked to discuss the following questions in writing:

1. What keeps you from believing in a greater or higher power? How open are you to belief in such a power?
2. How have you been insane (e.g., through continuing use of drugs, avoiding responsibility for self, emotional instability, "messed up" thinking and decisions, deep resentments, fits of anger, planned or attempted suicide, delusions and paranoia)?
3. What is your higher power?
4. How did you come to believe in that power?
5. How can it "restore you to sanity?"
6. If the therapy group is your higher power, what benefits do you look to get from it, and how are you using the group to get those benefits?

Step 3: *"Made a decision to turn our will and our lives over to the care of God as we understood him."* To help patients toward the active faith of Step 3, they are asked to work through the following:

1. How have you been separated from God, as you understand him?
2. Discuss your relationship to your higher power.
3. Why is it important to turn your *will* and *life* over to God as you understand him? What keeps you from doing this?
4. Why is it important to turn *all* of your life and will over to God's care?
5. When can you make the decision that is imperative to turning over

your intellect, emotions and desires to the higher power?
6. Describe three parts of Step 3 and discuss what each part means.
7. What have you done and what will you do to turn your will and life over to God as you understand him? How will you plan to use your higher power in the future?

Step 4: *"Made a searching and fearless moral inventory of ourselves."* The goal of this step, which involves a detailed written inventory (See Appendix D), is to have the patient discover his or her liabilities through renewing relationships and behaviors.

In addition to their work with the first four steps to living, adolescent alcoholic patients also attend several outside meetings of AA.

FAMILY INVOLVEMENT IN TREATMENT

The last Sunday before discharge patients are given a six-hour pass to visit at home. This eases their reentry into family and community. It also gives adolescents an opportunity to become aware of stressful situations that will be encountered in the "outside" world and to work these through in group before discharge.

Research has shown that the results of therapy depend more on an improved relationship between adolescents and their parents than on the relationship between adolescents and the treating facility. Rarely do adolescent alcoholics improve much while there is a continuing state of insecurity at home, no matter how good the therapist. Consequently, it is best to concentrate first on the alcoholic

72 condition itself, next on the disturbed family unit and third on the individual personality maladjustments that may have resulted.

Because alcoholism is a *family* disease, the disease nature of the condition should be understood not only by the adolescent patient but by family members as well. Family involvement in modes of treatment such as Al-Anon family groups has been shown to enhance the results of treatment enormously. It is absolutely essential for successful treatment to involve parents; thus their participation is mandatory in the St. Anthony treatment program. The goals of this participation are as follows:

1. for parents or significant others to become aware of the effects of addiction on the adolescent alcoholic's life;
2. for parents to become aware of the disease concept of alcoholism;
3. for parents to become aware of themselves on a feeling level;
4. for parents or significant others to observe the changes in their loved ones as they progress through treatment;
5. for parents to increase levels of communication within the family.

While the adolescents are in treatment, parents are required to be involved in the Family Group two days a week. They are also encouraged to attend Al-Anon meetings. Family Group examines the family lifestyle and how it has been damaged by alcoholism. The major problem is the inability of the family to separate itself from the alcoholism within it. The entire family's responses—within itself and toward the outside world—revolve around the addicted person whose life revolves around alcohol. Almost everything the family does is in response to ongoing feelings of tension, anxiety and hopelessness. Its tensions are not relieved by the adolescent's periods of abstinence.

Another problem is the family's total inability to communicate in healthy ways. Direct and honest communication is driven underground in frustration. Family members also act inconsistently and irrationally in response to their frustrations and feelings of helplessness. One day a family member may be silent, the next day the same person may be screaming and yelling. The entire family is sick and is reacting to a chronic, progressive disease in an unhealthy, confusing and destructive way.

AFTER-CARE

Following discharge, both patients and their families are expected to participate in two-hour after-care family sessions once a week for 12 weeks. In addition to the 12 weeks, the adolescent returns for weekly sessions with peers only. The goal of after-care is to readjust interpersonal relationships that have turned bitter with alcohol abuse and to become aware of

---

The goal of after-care is to readjust interpersonal relationships that have turned bitter with alcohol abuse and to become aware of feelings and constructive ways of dealing with them.

feelings and constructive ways of dealing with them. (After-care does not lessen the need for the patient to go to AA, the parents to Al-Anon and the other siblings to Alateen.) The after-care group assignment is made during the last week of regular treatment in order to ease the transition.

Each patient completes an after-care contract effective for three months after discharge. After this period, a further evaluation is made for meeting the adolescent's needs in the best possible way. Contract goals are: to support the gains made by the patient during the primary treatment process, to deal with problems not resolved during the primary treatment process and to establish a link with other support systems to maintain sobriety.

In addition to the after-care contract, each patient is given a copy of the Discharge Planning Sheet. (See Appendix E.)

SUGGESTED READINGS

Alibrandi, T. *Young Alcoholics* (Minneapolis: Comp Care Publications 1978).

American Medical Association. *Manual of Alcoholism* 3rd ed. (Chicago: AMA 1977).

Bier, W.C. *Problems in Addiction: Alcohol and Drug Addiction* (New York: Fordham University Press 1962).

Blume, S.B. "Psychodrama in the Treatment of Alcoholism" in Estes, N. and Heinemann, M.E., eds. *Alcoholism Development, Consequences, and Interventions* (St. Louis: The C.V. Mosby Co. 1977).

Burkhalter, P.K. *Nursing Care of the Alcoholic and Drug Abuser* (New York: McGraw-Hill Book Co. 1975).

Cahn, S. *The Treatment of Alcoholics: An Evaluation Study* (New York: Oxford University Press 1970).

Johnson, V.E. *I'll Quit Tomorrow* (New York: Harper & Row Publishers 1973).

Schnurr, R.R. "Alcoholism—What is it? How is it diagnosed? How is it treated?" Pamphlet. Available on request from Talbot Hall, St. Anthony Hospital, Columbus, Ohio.

Appendix A
Routine Admission Order
Talbot Hall, St. Anthony Hospital

74

FAMILY NAME	FIRST NAME	ATTENDING PHYSICIAN	ROOM NO.	HOSP. NO.	STAMP BEFORE CHART INSERTION

Date / Time	ORDERS— (ANOTHER BRAND OF GENERICALLY EQUIVALENT PRODUCT, IDENTICAL IN DOSAGE FORM AND CONTENT OF ACTIVE INGREDIENT(S), MAY BE ADMINISTERED UNLESS CHECKED)	
	1. Ambulation according to physical condition.	
	2. Urinalysis for S & A on admission & on 3rd day and a routine UA in A.M.	
	3. EKG in A.M.	
	4. CBC and VDRL the day of admission. Fasting SMA$_{12}$ and Electrolytes in A.M.	
	5. PA and lateral chest X-ray when feasible.	
	6. Force fluids, juices at bedside.	
	7. Diet as tolerated. Special diets as indicated.	
	8. ADULTS: Vital Signs q 2-4h PRN in detox. Daily BP for 3 days after detox; then, if still elevated above 150/90, continue until stable and/or PRN.	
	ADOLESCENTS: Vital signs q 2-4h PRN in detox. V.S. BID after evaluation.	ADDRESSOGRAPH INFORMATION
	9. ADULTS: Surbex-T 1 tab on admission, then BID PO.	
	ADOLESCENTS: Surbex-T tabs 1 daily x 5 days then DC.	
	10. ADULTS: Mysoline 250 mg PO on admission and TID x 3 days, 250 mg BID x 2 days, then DC unless staying for treatment. Then Mysoline 250 mg PO BID x 2 more days, 250 mg PO daily x 4 days, then DC.	
	11. Sodium Amytal 250-500 mg IM or PO on adm. (Give only if patient has had mood-changing chemicals during preceding 72 hours and vital signs warrant), and q 2-4h PRN the first 72 hours. Then Sodium Amytal 250 mg q 2-4h IM or PO, PRN while in detox. Thereafter, Sodium Amytal tablets 65-130 mg QID PRN. Discontinue after the 5th day. If patient is anxious or tremulous, check BP and P q 1h. If pulse rate continues increasing and diastolic BP continues rising, give Sodium Amytal, 250 mg IM q 2-4h UNTIL ASLEEP. Then q 4h to maintain sleep for 12 hours. If patient has been on drugs in addition to alcohol, check with the DOD for withdrawal program. IF NECESSARY TO USE 500 MG. BEYOND THE FIRST 24 HOURS, NOTIFY PHYSICIAN.	
	ADOLESCENTS: On 5th day, if hallucinating and VS are stable, give Haldol 2 mg. PO. Repeat in 2-4h. Thereafter, q 2-4h PRN. Have DOD re-evaluate daily.	
	12. Thiamine HCl 100 mg PO on admission and daily x 2 days.	
	13. Craniotomy checks on admission and QID x 2 days, then daily until discharge from detox and/or evaluation unit. REPORT EYE CHANGES TO DOD STAT.	
	14. May shampoo hair or go to the beauty shop at discretion of charge nurse.	
	15. Tylenol gr X PO q 4h PRN.	
	16. Maalox 30cc PO q 4h PRN.	
	17. Milk of Magnesia 30cc PO PRN.	
	18. Chloraseptic Mouthwash at bedside, if transferred to treatment.	
	19. Endotussin tsp. 1 PO q4h PRN for consistent coughing.	
	20. Bentyl 10 mg q4h PRN for diarrhea.	
	21. ADULTS: For polydrug abuse, Whirlpool BID PRN for 10-14 days.	
	ADOLESCENTS: For polydrug abuse, Whirlpool BID x 6 days, then daily x 6 days, then DC.	
	22. On admission to the general hospital, notify Coordinator, Patient Care Services or Head Nurse on W-2 (Ext. 432), to have Talbot Hall DOD see patient daily.	
	23. Alcohol/Drug Studies on all admissions and PRN.	
	24. OUTPATIENT MEDICATION: Patients may return weekly, PRN, for IM Vit B$_{12}$ 1000 mcg/cc.	

SIGN YOUR NAME X _____

PHYSICIAN'S ORDERS

Appendix B

Introductory Interview
Talbot Hall, St. Anthony Hospital

NAME _____ Adm. Date _____
     (Last)   (First)   (Middle)

Case No. _____Phone No. _____

Residence _____

Age _____ Marital Status _____

Number of Children _____ Age(s) _____

Religious Preference _____

Occupation _____

Education _____

Presenting Situation

1. What events led to your coming to Talbot Hall? _____

_____

_____

2. How do you feel about the treatment program so far? _____

_____

Self-Evaluation

1. When did you first notice that you were using mood-changing chemicals differently than you would like to?

_____

2. Does your behavior change when you use mood-changing chemicals? _____

   How? _____

_____

3. How do you feel about your drinking and drug taking? _____

_____

4. How serious do you think your problem is? _____

_____

5. Do you want to stop using alcohol and drugs? _____

   Why or why not? _____

_____

6. Is there anyone who knows how you really feel inside? _____

   Who? _____

7. Do you tell them or expect them to know? _____

Family Relationships

76

1. How is your relationship with your parents? _____

_____

2. Have your parents ever talked to you about your use of mood-changing chemicals? _____ What
have they said *to you*? _____

_____

_____

3. Tell me something about your present family situation. _____

_____

_____

4. Are you satisfied with it? _____

5. Does anybody in your home drink to excess? _____

6. Does anybody in your home take any medication for nerves, medication to sleep or street drugs? _____

Peer Relationships

1. Do you have many close friends? _____

2. Do you have any friends who don't take drugs or drink? _____

3. Tell me something about your relationships with your friends. _____

_____

_____

4. Are you satisfied with them? _____

Special Interests

1. What do you do in your spare time? _____

_____

2. Is it different from what you would like to do? _____

Expectations of the Program

1. What do you think your problem is? _____

_____

2. What do you want to get from this program? _____

_____

3. What are you willing to do to meet these goals? _____

_____

Interviewer's Evaluation

A. The information obtained indicates that the resident is in the beginning _____, advanced _____, critical _____stage of alcoholism.

B. Problems which may contribute to this alcoholism are (check those that apply and explain):

1. physical disabilities _____

_____

2. psychiatric problems _____

_____

3. vocational/educational problems _____

_____

_____

4. family problems _____

_____

5. housing _____

_____

6. legal problems _____

_____

7. financial problems _____

_____

_____

8. other _____

_____

_____

_____

_____

_____

_____

Counselor

Appendix C

Sample Client Treatment Plan
Talbot Hall, St. Anthony Hospital

78

NAME J. Doe

Sex Male   Age 17

Medical Evaluation: Completed (   )
                    Needed   (   )

Client / Family Problem Identification and Treatment Goals:

Counselor: _____ Date: _____

Staff Conference Date: _____ Attendance: _____

Date	Areas of Concern	Treatment Objectives	Method	Progress (Date & Sign)
	Self-Expression			
	1. Pt appears unsure and uneasy about himself.	Acceptance of self	Group milieu Step 2	
	2. Pt appears to have difficulty expressing what he is feeling.	Tools for effective communication	Group didactics	
	3. At times pt appears somewhat withdrawn.	Opening of self	Group milieu	
	4. Pt appears restless (probably because he had just been disciplined).	Acceptance of consequences and tools for coping with them	Group	
	5. Pt expresses feelings of guilt and remorse for the hurt he has caused family members.	Reduction of guilt	Serenity group	
	6. Pt appears to be rather paranoid.	Establishment of trust level	Group milieu AA	
	7. Pt appears somewhat defensive at times.	Acceptance of situation	Group didactics	
	Self-Impression			
	Pt feels unwanted and unaccepted much of the time.	Improvement of self-image	Milieu AA group	
	Parental			
	1. One of pt's biggest concerns is a desire to be closer with father.	Family involvement in treatment program	Milieu AA group	
	2. Pt feels bad about what he has put his mother through.	Acceptance of responsibility for effective change	Group psychodrama	
	3. Patient feels father wishes he were like an older brother.	Family involvement	Al-Anon, AA, family group	

Date	Areas of Concern	Treatment Objectives	Method	Progress (Date & Sign)
	Educational			
	Pt doesn't want to finish school, is uncertain about life plans.	Honest reflection and goal orientation	Step 4, group	
	Social Environment			
	1. Pt has no friends who don't take drugs of some kind.	Establishment of relationship with nondrinkers	AA, family group, after-care	
	2. Pt doesn't trust peers, is afraid of being used.	Building of trust level	Group, step 5, AA	
	3. Pt "feels people are always talking about him."	Improvement in self-image; sharing of feelings more openly	Group	

Step 4 (like each of the steps) marks the beginning of a new way of life. It says that "today I will begin to take a realistic assessment of myself." This guide can help you begin to learn to know yourself.

ATTITUDES

These attitudes are important: to be searching, fearless and moral.

1. Are you searching? Are you really digging into your own self-awareness and describing your behavior as it really is?
2. Are you fearless? It takes courage to see yourself in terms of what has really been going on in your life.
3. Are you moral? Take a good look at the "good–bad" implications of your behavior. How does that behavior size up with your own values?

Take a searching, fearless and moral inventory, but don't be moralistic. You know your behavior has good and bad aspects. That is a fact of life. Look at it. Own your own behavior. But don't punish yourself. Our goal is to know ourselves and to accept ourselves. Only then can we begin to change and grow.

Give examples of your behavior that specifically describe your reality. Put this in writing, in black and white, on paper, with specific searching and fearless examples.

Many have found it helpful to reserve a special section for facing things they have

never shared before, the "what bugs me the most" behavior, what they least like to face in themselves, what they would find difficult to share with another person.

Step 4 is a simple and direct beginning to an ongoing task of life, a direction to walk toward self-awareness, a way to go today and each day from now on. The moral inventory becomes a way of life based on the courage to be honest with ourselves.

You may experience some distress while writing the Step 4. This is normal. You may find yourself growing resentful, becoming depressed, feeling guilty, afraid of failure. You may find yourself putting off the job until tomorrow! Share these thoughts and feelings with your counselor or chaplain, and make what you discover about yourself part of your inventory.

This self-assessment may very well be the most courageous act of your life. If you need encouragement, support and help, ask for it!

SELF-ASSESSMENT

False Pride is excessive pride, being so thin-skinned that we have trouble admitting any human weaknesses at all. Another word for this kind of pride is grandiosity. Describe how your pride has kept you from looking at your own behavior. The desire never to be wrong is one example. Write your examples.

Acceptance. As acceptance of ourselves grows, so does our acceptance of the world around us. We don't have to be so afraid, fearful and defensive, but there is always a lot to worry about. The point is what good does the worry do? We know that we can only do our best, and after that what will be will be. Are you learning to trust yourself and others? Do you find yourself being less afraid? Write specific examples.

Taking Things for Granted. Many of us tend to take things for granted when things are going well with us. We sometimes forget the effort, the action and the discipline which finally got things straightened out for us. Complacency and boredom are real dangers to our new ways of living. Can you recall instances when complacency or boredom caused you to slip back into irresponsible ways of behaving? Write specific examples.

Being Grateful. How do you feel about your new way of life? Do you show your gratitude to those who helped you build a new life? What are some ways you could express your gratitude right now? Can you see how feeling grateful can influence you in a positive way and help you avoid the pitfalls of complacency, boredom and depression? Write specific examples.

Admitting Mistakes. Most of us have not had much experience in admitting mistakes, admitting when we are wrong. We seem to give ourselves only two choices: being absolutely perfect or being totally worthless. What a relief it is when we can admit mistakes—admit that we're human. Can you think of examples of your being in the wrong and admitting it? Is it OK to make mistakes? Is it OK to say so

or do we stay silent? Write specific examples.

Being Phony. Being phony and cunning becomes part of our way of life when we are not being honest. We seem to have to look good to others, and being ourselves just doesn't seem to be enough sometimes. How have you been phony in the past? How are you being phony right now? Write specific examples.

Self-Pity. This is hard to recognize, and it's something no one likes to admit. It's a matter of feeling sorry for ourselves, maybe because we feel people just don't understand us, or maybe we feel that people don't respect us or don't love us enough. It sometimes means feeling hopeless, feeling like a victim of circumstances. Have you ever felt self-pity? Do you feel sorry for yourself right now? Write specific examples.

Feeling Good about Yourself. When we are working toward personal growth we can begin to see the true meaning of "Love Thy neighbor as thyself." It doesn't mean "more than" and it doesn't mean "less than" thyself. If we're able to respect ourselves, we are able to give love to others; that's a basic part of feeling worthwhile. Are you able to see yourself as being worthwhile? Able to feel good about yourself? Try to illustrate this feeling with examples from your recent experience. Be specific.

Forgiveness and Understanding. Learning how to accept situations we cannot change and how to understand those people we think have wronged us are marks of personal growth. What do you

82 know about forgiveness and understanding? Has the ability to accept the things you cannot change become a part of your life now? Write specific examples.

Resentment. Resentful people hang onto angry feelings—angry feelings about our families, angry feelings about how we live, where and when. Hanging onto bad feelings can really make us miserable. Resentments are always good excuses for our irresponsible behavior. Talk about resentments you have right now. Do you hang onto angry feelings because you think your anger is justified? Write specific examples.

Tolerance. As you learn to accept responsibility for your own feelings, do you find that you are more tolerant? Tolerant of yourself? Tolerant of others? Are you able to see the needs of others more clearly and to accept people as fellow human beings and to understand them? Are you able to accept yourself now? Write specific examples.

Intolerance. Intolerance can grow from self-pity and resentment. Once we learn how, it becomes easy to blame others for the way we feel. Being intolerant is especially easy when others have different ways of thinking or living. However, it's also easy to be intolerant of those people who are close to us and who are important in our personal lives. How were you intolerant of others in the past? Think hard about this one: Are you still intolerant of others? Write specific examples.

Alibis. How much have we invested in justifying our behavior to others by explaining for ourselves? Sometimes the explanations are true, sometimes they are partly true, often they are purely fiction. Can you think of ways you alibied for yourself? How did you feel about yourself when you did alibi? Do you catch yourself making up alibis now? Write specific examples.

Being Honest. What do you think of yourself now that you are trying to be open and honest? Do you feel more comfortable? Is it a relief not having to explain for yourself? Is it easier to be with other people? Write specific examples.

Being Yourself. Today you're doing something important: you're being honest and responsible. At last, you're just being yourself. Does it feel good? Are you giving yourself enough credit for this? Giving yourself a pat on the back? How does your new feeling about yourself affect your relationship with others? Write specific examples.

Selfishness. "I want what I want when I want it." Think about that. Do you spend a lot of time worrying about all the energy you put into trying, one way or another, to please yourself, to get your own way? How have you hurt others by putting your own needs first? When's the last time you did something for others? Write specific examples.

Humility. Now that you are learning that it is safe to admit your powerlessness and unmanageability, do you find it easier just to be human? Being humble doesn't mean being weak. It means accepting ourselves—our strengths as well as our weaknesses. Do you know something now about what humility really means? Are you able to be less defensive? To enjoy the peace that comes with genuine humility? Explain. Write specific examples.

Perfectionism. Too often we are unwilling to accept human mistakes, our own or those of others. When we are afraid of criticism, we set unrealistic standards for ourselves, and we are frustrated if we can't meet them. When we're feeling this way, we are impatient with family members and friends and coworkers when they are imperfect too. How has your need to be perfect hurt you? How have you made others unhappy by insisting that they be perfect too?

Dishonest Thinking happens when we begin making alibis to ourselves and believing them, when we really begin to believe our resentments, and when we actually feel abused and misunderstood. The danger is that we will lose all contact with reality. How have you deceivied yourself in the past? How could you deceive yourself now about important matters in your life? Write specific examples.

Honest Thinking. Being honest with ourselves is the most difficult form of honesty. As we learn how to accept ourselves as we really are, we can begin to laugh at ourselves for sometimes trying to be something else. Are you able to laugh at yourself in this way now? Be specific.

Putting Things Off. Often we put things off until we get the right inspiration, until everything is just right. And the right time almost never comes. When pressure builds to get a job done, we tend to react by becoming impatient and irresponsible.

List examples of projects you have put off while you have waited for just the right time. How did you feel when pressure built up to finish your work? How did you behave? Be specific.

Sharing. When we're feeling good about ourselves, we begin to care about the welfare and happiness of others too. Have you learned how to hear other people, to see them, to know them? Do you know how to respond to the needs of others, to give yourself? Have you learned how to share with others, to care about them? How does it feel? Write specific examples.

Impatience. When impatience gets the better of us, not only do we want what we want, but we want it right now. When we're feeling like this and things don't work out the way they should and on just the time table we set, our blood pressure rises and we can be really miserable. Describe some situations in which your impatience caused damage to you, to others. How does your impatience get in your way right now? Write specific examples.

Patience is an elusive goal; it's something we need to work on daily. Maybe we will never become truly patient people, but it is vital that we are not driven constantly by our impatience. As you work on your perfectionism problems, do you find that you are more patient with yourself and with others? Are you learning how to take it easy? Write specific examples.

Getting the Job Done. Have you learned how good it feels to complete a job, not because someone is breathing down your

84

neck about it, but because you want to finish it? How does it feel? Give some examples of things you have done recently that have helped you feel good about yourself. How do you feel about the job of putting your life together again? Be specific.

Guilt Feelings. Sometimes we hang onto bad feelings about ourselves in just the same way we hang on to our resentments against others. Feeling guilty can become an important part of our lifestyle, always there to give us another excuse for feeling miserable and behaving irresponsibly. So?

Freedom from Guilt. Are you able to let go of the guilt? Are you learning how important it is not to hate yourself but begin respecting yourself? Can you see that respect for yourself is really a basic part of personal growth? So?

Fear. Sometimes we're afraid of specific things—afraid someone will reject us, afraid a plan won't succeed, afraid someone will find us out—and sometimes we're afraid in some vague general way that we are bound to fail, that nothing will work out, that everything is going wrong. Talk about your own fears, the fears that you have right now, the fears that destroy your peace of mind. Be specific.

A PLAN FOR LIVING

Having completed your Step 4 inventory, where are you now in terms of self-awareness and self-acceptance? What is your attitude toward change and growth? Are you committed to making some changes? How do you see Step 4 now as part of a 12-step program?

To help you get at these important questions, we encourage you to begin making your own plan for living. As a suggestion, try listing some of your defects and the attitudes and behaviors that are causing you the most trouble, and make some plans to deal with these defects. List some of your assets and incorporate them into your plan for personal growth. Perhaps you have hit upon certain daily disciplines that are helpful. What about your new personal program of spirituality?

Write this material down. Try to be as specific in making your plan for living as you were in making your personal inventory.

THEN LIVE IT.

Appendix E

Discharge Planning
Talbot Hall, St. Anthony Hospital

PATIENT NAME _____

WORK PHONE _____ HOME PHONE _____

PRIVATE PHYSICIAN'S NAME _____

CITY _____

A. HEALTH STATUS:

1. PHYSICAL STATUS _____

2. EXERCISE _____

3. DIET _____

4. VITAMINS _____

5. SPECIAL INSTRUCTIONS: _____
    _____
    _____

6. Do you want a summary of your medical treatment here sent to your
    private physician? _____ Yes _____ No

7. Do you want a letter sent to your private physician from the Talbot
    Hall physician? _____ Yes _____ No

B. UNDERSTANDING ALCOHOLISM:

    Do you think alcoholism is a disease? _____ Yes _____ No

    Do you think you have alcoholism? _____ Yes _____ No

    Do you think you must maintain absolute and permanent sobriety from
    alcohol and all mood changing chemicals? _____ Yes _____ No

    Do you intend to do this? _____ Yes _____ No

    How will you do this? _____
    _____
    _____

    What convinces you that you have alcoholism? What symptoms do you
    have? _____
    _____
    _____
    _____

Appendix E—page 2

Does your family believe you have alcoholism?_____ Yes _____ No

How do you know this? _____

_____

_____

Have you talked with them about your disease?_____ Yes_____ No

If not, will you?_____ Yes_____ No

Do you know what or whom you blamed for your alcoholism?_____ Yes _____ No

Explain: _____

_____

_____

What do you intend to do about that? _____

_____

_____

Does your employer know you have alcoholism? _____ Yes _____ No

Do you intend to tell your employer?_____ Yes _____ No

UNDERSTANDING OF TREATMENT:

Did you do anything here to help yourself? _____Yes _____ No

What? _____

_____

_____

Did you do anything here to help others? _____Yes _____ No

What? _____

_____

_____

Are your feelings about yourself different than when you entered treat-

ment? _____Yes _____ No

How? _____

_____

_____

Appendix E—page 3

Are your feelings about others different now than when you entered
treatment? _____ Yes _____ No

How? _____

_____

_____

What in the Program here was the most helpful to you? _____

_____

_____

Was there anything not helpful to you? _____

_____

_____

What in treatment was the most difficult for you? _____

_____

_____

How do you plan to use what you learned here? _____

_____

_____

_____

UNDERSTANDING OF AFTERCARE PROGRAM:

Do you know what the Talbot Hall Aftercare Program is? _____ Yes _____ No

Explain _____

_____

_____

Do you plan to attend the 12 aftercare sessions? _____ Yes _____ No

Explain _____

Do you know that the weekly charge of $5.00 per session per family is
generally not included in your insurance coverage? _____ Yes _____ No

Have you talked with your family about attendance at aftercare?

_____ Yes _____ No

If you do not plan to attend the 12 weekly Talbot Hall sessions, where do
you plan to participate in aftercare? _____

_____

UNDERSTANDING OF A.A.

Have you read any of the A.A. literature in your book-kit? _____ Yes _____ No

Which? _____

Appendix E—page 4

Do you plan to attend A.A. meetings? _____ Yes _____ No

If yes, briefly describe your plans for participation. _____

_____

Do you have an A.A. advisor to call? _____ Yes _____ No

Name _____ Phone # _____

Will you telephone that person within the first week after discharge and

plan to attend a meeting? _____ Yes _____ No

Have you talked about A.A. Meetings with your family? _____ Yes _____ No

Do you think you "are powerless over alcohol and that your life has

become unmanageable?" _____ Yes _____ No

Have you taken the "fourth step inventory" of your self? _____ Yes _____ No

Have you received a schedule of A.A. meetings? _____ Yes _____ No

EMPLOYMENT PLANS:

1.   Date you plan to return to work _____

FINAL NOTES:

1.   May we contact you at 3 mo., 6 mo., 9 mo., & 1 yr. after discharge
     for the purpose of follow-up? _____ Yes _____ No.

2.   If you have any questions regarding any prescribed medications,
     telephone the Talbot Hall Nurse at 253-8877, Ext. 432.

3.   The telephone number of the A.A. Central Office nearest you is

     _____

PATIENT SIGNATURE: _____

R.N. SIGNATURE: _____

ATTENDING PHYSICIAN
SIGNATURE: _____

Appendix F

Adolescent's Treatment Schedule
Talbot Hall, St. Anthony Hospital

Time	Monday	Tuesday	Wednesday	Thursday	Friday	Saturday	Sunday
6:45	Wake up, clean rooms	Wake up, clean rooms	Wake up, clean rooms	Wake up, clean rooms	Wake up, clean rooms	Wake up	Wake up
7:30	Physical exercise	Physical exercise	Physical exercise	Physical exercise	Physical exercise	Community jobs	Mass (optional)
8:00	Breakfast	Breakfast	Breakfast	Breakfast	Breakfast	Breakfast	Breakfast
8:30	Step lecture 24-hr reading	Step lecture 24-hr reading	Step lecture 24-hr reading	Step lecture 24-hr reading	Step lecture 24-hr reading	Unstructured	Contemporary worship service
9:00	Community meeting	Psychodrama	Group therapy	Psychodrama		Men's/women's group	
9:30	Group therapy			Psychodrama	Group therapy	Men's/women's group	
11:00		Recreation	Physician's lecture	Soft recreation			
11:30	Soft recreation				Soft recreation	Soft recreation	Community meeting
12:00	Quiet time — on unit	Quiet time — on unit	Quiet time	Quiet time	Quiet time	Community meeting	
12:30							Introduction to AA
1:00	Lunch	Lunch	Lunch	Lunch	Lunch	Lunch	Lunch
1:30	Occupational therapy	Occupational therapy	Occupational therapy	Occupational therapy	Occupational therapy	Gym recreation	
2:30		Step study				Family lecture, discussion—film	
2:45	Gym recreation						
3:00	Unstructured	Group therapy	Film	Recreation	Steps study		Group therapy
3:45	Time—on unit		Lecture	Community meeting			
4:30	Dinner	Lecture/film	Steps study	Gym recreation	Gym recreation	Dinner	
5:30		Soft recreation					
6:30	Family group	Dinner	Dinner	Dinner	Dinner	Soft recreation	Dinner
7:30	AA meeting		Gym recreation	Unstructured time	Film	Swimming	
8:30				AA meeting	AA meeting	Men's/women's group	
9:00		Gym recreation				AA meeting	AA meeting
10:00	Unstructured time		Unstructured time				
11:30	Lights out	Lights out	Lights out	Lights out	Lights out	Lights out	Lights out

Appendix F cont'd

90   Recreation is an integral part of the adolescent treatment program. The objective is to provide scheduled recreational activities and relaxation as alternatives to alcohol and/or other chemical use. All patients are expected to participate in these activities; refusal to participate results in loss of privileges. However, patients with medical excuses are exempted from active participation.

Education is also considered an important part of treatment. Accordingly, the treatment staff assists in the process and coordinates education into the total treatment plan of each patient. Educational services are provided by the Special Education Department of the Columbus Public School System.

The Treatment of Alcoholism in a Community Setting

Arthur Knauert, M.D.
Private Practitioner
New York, New York
Medical Director of Transitional
  Services and Alcoholism Services
Guidance Clinic
Catholic Welfare Bureau
Trenton, New Jersey

MOST RECENT ESTIMATES place the number of alcoholics in the United States at approximately nine million.[1] That is, almost one out of ten adults in this country has an alcohol consumption problem that interferes with physical well-being, emotional growth and development, or, in the very least, ability to be a fully functional member of the community. Alcoholism is a disease whose impact upon the community is immense, and the magnitude of this problem gives it high priority in the allocation of community resources.

Alcoholism adversely affects a community in a number of ways. First, excessive alcohol intake is responsible for a significant proportion of physical illness. Emergency rooms, inpatient hospital facilities and other community-based health facilities constantly come in contact with the physical results of the disease process of alcoholism. Trauma cases, including automobile accidents, muggings and falls, are examples. In addition, liver disease,

92

gastrointestinal disturbances, pancreatitis and a variety of other syndromes are associated with chronic alcohol intake.

Alcoholism also takes its toll on the community in the form of increased criminal activities. Drunk driving, of course, is the most visible example, but numerous violent crimes of passion as well as a significant proportion of crimes that are secondary to impaired judgment (such as robberies of local establishments where the perpetrators are well known) are also alcohol related. It is impossible to say exactly what percentage of wife beatings, child abuse, rapes or homicides are directly related to the excess consumption of alcohol, but surely the percentage is significant.[2]

When one considers the number of adults in the United States who have an alcohol consumption problem and the resulting loss of control associated with decreased judgment, it is apparent that alcoholism is indeed a direct threat to the health of the community.

IDENTIFICATION OF THE ALCOHOLIC

The first step in successfully dealing with alcoholism is to identify those members in the community who suffer from it. The police and the criminal court system, as well as health facilities, church organizations and industrial programs, can all be extremely helpful with this task. Some states, such as New Jersey, routinely refer all persons arrested for an alcohol-related incident to community-based alcoholism treatment centers. Health facilities, progressively aware of

the signs and symptoms of this disease, are beginning to confront patients and to suggest that they seek professional counseling for drinking problems. In addition, more and more companies are becoming aware of the losses they incur as a result of this disease. Some have instituted their own alcohol treatment programs; others confront alcoholic employees and require them to seek treatment as a prerequisite for keeping their jobs.

It is unfortunate that the common notion of the alcoholic is that of the skid row derelict. In fact, only approximately five percent of alcoholics reach this stage of their illness.[3] The vast majority of

---

The common notion of the alcoholic is that of the skid row derelict. In fact, only approximately five percent of alcoholics reach this stage of their illness.

---

people with alcohol problems are able to work at least intermittently, and in the beginning stages of the illness practically all alcoholics are able to function in a job situation. It is interesting to note that the process of denial in the alcoholic is strongly supported by the common notion of the derelict alcoholic. It is not unusual for alcoholics to state that they could not possibly have a problem with alcohol because for 20 or 30 years they were able to drink a quart of alcohol a day and still maintain their jobs. It is extremely important to arrest this illness in its early stages before the physical, emotional and mental deterioration of the individual is allowed to progress to the point of dereliction. Confronting this notion of the "derelict" alcohol abuser is often the first step in treatment.

COMMUNITY-BASED TREATMENT PROGRAMS

Once the potential alcohol abuser is identified, the most effective method of treating this condition must be determined. The first step is a thorough evaluation to determine the client's particular needs. An individual treatment program based on those needs can then be designed.

There are three basic types of alcoholic clients: the reactive, the secondary and the primary. Treatment program personnel should be fully trained in the identification of these three types and should be aware of the community resources available. Differential diagnosis is the primary job of a comprehensive alcoholism treatment center, and individual treatment plans should reflect the result of this evaluation.

The Reactive Alcoholic

Some clients give a clear history of having no particular problems with their drinking until after a traumatic event in their lives. In reaction to this event, this particular group turns to alcohol for relief of feelings. The death of a spouse or parent, a major change in life, such as a job loss, physical disease or tragic accident, or the inability to deal with the feelings evoked by tragedy involving friends or loved ones can trigger this kind of alcoholic response. Alcohol becomes a method not only of decreasing feelings in general but also of temporarily forgetting the traumatic incident. Sometimes, but not always, the drinking will increase until the patient is physically addicted to the substance. If so, before it is possible to deal with the underlying problem, it will be necessary to refer this group to a detoxification center where the alcohol can be safely removed from their systems. Counseling can then address the underlying feelings which have been suppressed by the drinking. In general, if sobriety can be maintained long enough to deal effectively with the feelings that are secondary to the traumatic event, these clients have an excellent prognosis.

The Secondary Alcoholic

A significant proportion of clients use alcohol as a medication in an attempt to deal with a severe, underlying psychiatric disorder. Some schizophrenic and manic-depressive patients, as well as those with character disorders or neurotic complaints, use alcohol as a medication for their underlying problems. Drinking for this group may or may not progress to the point of physical addiction. If it does, detoxification will generally result in an increase in the symptoms characteristic of the underlying disorder. It is sometimes extremely difficult to distinguish, on a detox unit, hallucinations that are a result of the withdrawal process from those that are a result of an underlying psychotic illness. The distinction is critical if this group of patients is to receive optimum care. Once identification is made, referral to the appropriate psychiatric agency is the treatment of choice.

94 Personnel in alcohol treatment centers should be skilled in the detection of this group. Inadvertently included in a drug-free treatment program, secondary alcoholics are apt to do very poorly, because their underlying illness will not receive adequate treatment.

The Primary Alcoholic

A third group of alcohol abusing clients do not have an underlying psychiatric disorder and have not experienced a specific life event that triggered their excessive alcohol consumption. Primary alcoholics usually have a relationship with alcohol which they think was present when they discovered the effects of this substance. For these clients, the relationship with the substance, and the pathological nature of this relationship, is the primary problem. Whether or not they are physically addicted to alcohol, they will attempt to maintain this relationship at all costs. They will deny to themselves and others that their drinking is a problem, will refuse to see the connection between any physical problems they might be having and their drinking and will consistently act as if the alcohol were not a substance at all but rather a very close and dear friend. Anyone seen as a threat to this relationship will be viewed by the patient as an enemy to be resisted at all costs.

The primary alcoholic group is the most numerous of the three types of alcoholics. Although the least understood group, it has enjoyed the largest effort of current alcoholic rehabilitation programs. Primary alcoholics benefit the most from highly professional, compre-hensive rehabilitation programs and require the most consistent treatment plans. Efforts in the past to define the personality type that is representative of this group have revealed that no one particular personality type predominates. Some of the clients in this group are quite primitive and underdeveloped in their personality structure; others seem to have adequately mastered earlier stages of emotional development and are viewed in the community as strong, capable adults. The idea that all primary alcoholics are passive, dependent, oral personality types does not stand up to scrutiny.

Dynamics of the Primary Alcoholic

Even though the primary alcoholic group is composed of a variety of personality types, repeatedly when exploring their past history, similarities arise that cannot be mere coincidence. Parental problems with alcoholism, emotional disorder, physical illness, early divorce and separation, and movement of the child from one parenting figure to another are all common factors.

On closer inspection, it can be noted that in every primary alcoholic there is a history of early parental inconsistency that exceeds normal limits. Human beings are not machines, and it is clearly impossible for any parent to be completely consistent 100 percent of the time. There is, however, a range of consistency

In every primary alcoholic there is a history of early parental inconsistency that exceeds normal limits.

or inconsistency within which most parents stay. The parents, or the parenting figures, of the primary alcoholic exceed this range greatly. For example, if mother is an alcoholic herself, one day she may be a perfectly warm and loving parent, able to attend to the infant's needs and to interact with it on a reasonably normal level. The next day the same mother may be drunk and totally unable to interact normally with the child. As the child grows, he/she is unable to predict when adequate parental nurturing is to be received and when it is to be withheld. As a result, a very deeply ingrained attitude is formed: comfort and nurturing are indeed available in the world, but one cannot predict when they will be available.

Primary alcoholics incorporate this attitude into their personality structures. Approaching maturity, able to accept comfort and nurturing when they come, these persons are nevertheless unable to believe that others can be relied on for any consistent emotional support.

After this attitudinal system has been firmly established, primary alcoholics, through interaction with peer groups, experiences with cultural institutions (the neighborhood pub, etc.), or as a result of familial interactions (at weddings, parties or holiday occasions), come into contact with alcohol. For the most part this confrontation takes place during adolescence. Potential alcoholics are delighted to find that alcohol will provide both decreased unpleasant internal feelings and increased feelings of warmth, comfort and security. Most important, however, potential alcoholics discover that

alcohol can be depended upon to provide these feelings unfailingly and consistently.

This attribute of alcohol, that is, its total consistency of evoking response, becomes extremely seductive to a person with a deepset belief that people cannot be relied upon for the same thing. Alcohol, in other words, fulfills a need that, according to the patient's belief system, cannot be filled by people. Primary alcoholics subsequently develop a relationship with alcohol that is very much a love relationship. Alcohol becomes parent, friend, lover and confidant. With a great deal of willingness and joy, primary alcoholics proceed to establish a relationship with this substance until it becomes the single most important aspect of life. Anything or anybody who thereafter threatens to interfere with this relationship is resisted in whatever way is available to the client, because the threat of loss of this very important relationship is more important than life itself.

Treatment of the Primary Alcoholic

It is extremely important to understand the dynamic factors involved in primary alcoholism if one is going to design and establish treatment that is likely to be effective. Centers that are effective will incorporate methods of confronting the pathology of the relationship with alcohol while simultaneously providing the client alternative relationships which are consistently oriented toward encouraging emotional growth and development. Successful programs will be those that are viewed by the client as internally consistent. If a program fails

96 in this regard, clients will repeatedly opt for returning to the relationship with alcohol.

ESTABLISHING A COMMUNITY-BASED ALCOHOL TREATMENT CENTER

Prior to the establishment of an alcohol treatment center in the community, several decisions must be made concerning the type and scope of services that will be offered. Community resources should be evaluated to understand ongoing treatment resources and to integrate the new center with existing ones. Staff should be thoroughly aware of the other community agencies involved in the treatment of alcoholism so the best possible treatment plan can be devised.

Detoxification

Detoxification facilities must be available, because there will always be a significant number of clients who are physically addicted to alcohol. Physical addiction is defined by the presence of tolerance (more and more alcohol is needed to derive the same effect) and withdrawal symptoms (removal of the substance from the body will result in a predictable set of physical symptoms, including elevation of the blood pressure, temperature and pulse, as well as an increase in the tendency toward hallucination, agitation and seizure). Detoxification is a serious medical problem that requires staff to be skilled in dealing with medical emergencies. Untreated withdrawal can be lethal and should never be

Detoxification is a serious medical problem that requires staff to be skilled in dealing with medical emergencies. Untreated withdrawal can be lethal and should never be attempted without adequate medical supervision.

attempted without adequate medical supervision.

Evaluation and Referral

Once liaison with an appropriate detoxification facility is established, it must be decided whether or not the center will provide the service of diagnostic evaluation. If so, staff should be thoroughly trained in differential diagnosis, and staff meetings should be established to examine the findings and to provide adequate planning for disposition.

If it is decided that differential diagnosis is a service the new center is not able to provide, liaison with a community resource that can adequately provide it must be established. Of course, if this is the case, the center will be unable to deal effectively with any client who has not been thoroughly evaluated elsewhere. The danger here is that not all alcoholics are alike. Centers that attempt to treat secondary alcoholics with encouragement toward a drug-free lifestyle may inadvertently stimulate the underlying psychotic process. This can be dangerous to the client as well as to the entire program. Other clients will thereafter question the center's ability to deal with them effectively, and this will stimulate a great deal of anxiety about their own ability to live a drug-free existence. Likewise, if the secondary alcoholics so involved eventually seek effective chemotherapeutic interventions through other centers (such as psychiatric hospitals), clients who are appropriate for drug-free treatment will question whether or not they would be better off establishing a relationship with a prescription drug.

Scope of Services

Remaining problems in the establishment of an alcohol treatment center in a community include the development of a consistent program policy for the center, a decision whether residential facilities will be available and the type of counseling that will be offered. Individual, group, family and couples counseling, as well as recreational and vocational therapies, are among the available options. Depending on the size and prior experience of the staff, each center should define for itself those services they are able to provide as well as those which are beyond the scope of the program.

Availability of funding is an extremely important factor in defining the limits of any alcohol treatment program. If funds are available for only one counselor, the program will be severely limited in its ability to offer a full range of services. If, on the other hand, funds are available for a large, experienced staff, the ability for the center to provide a full range of services will be possible. Decision makers in the community who are responsible for the allocation of funds will have a great effect on the limits of the center. Optimum size of the staff is approxi-

mately 25 to 30 personnel. This includes supervisory personnel (physicians, senior counselors and other degreed professionals), as well as non-degreed counselors who have varied experience in the field. It is also necessary to provide adequate secretarial support, because it is necessary to provide statistical reports to the federal, state and local agencies which monitor the effectiveness of ongoing programs.

A HYPOTHETICAL ALCOHOL TREATMENT CENTER

For the purpose of discussion, it is assumed that funding is available to establish the most comprehensive alcohol treatment program in the community. This will provide facilities for detoxification, residential treatment, outpatient treatment and evaluation services as well as for liaison and community education. It is also assumed that an experienced, professional staff is assembled. Liaison with the police and court system, hospitals and other agencies whose role will be identification is established. Potential clients are referred for evaluation and disposition planning. The center will have the capability of providing a wide range of services to clients as needed.

Intake Evaluation

As clients begin arriving, they will be assigned to counselors for initial intake evaluation. Each center will establish its own intake procedure, including the extent and depth of the interview, what psychological tests will be used and the amount of time the counselor is expected

98 to spend for this purpose. (If the client is obviously in need of detoxification, then prompt referral should be made. Assuming that a comprehensive center will provide detoxification facilities, the patient should be admitted to these facilities directly from the intake evaluation. It is usually a good idea for the counselor who does the intake evaluation to maintain contact with the patient throughout the detoxification period. This not only provides continuity of care, but also covertly tells clients that, because they are cared about as human beings, they can expect a degree of consistency from treatment.) When all the intake data are available, the counselor should present them to either a supervisor or to a meeting of assembled staff members.

Devising Treatment Plans

A treatment plan should then be devised which corresponds to the client's particular needs. If the client is a reactive alcoholic, after sobriety is obtained counseling should focus on the difficulties the client has in dealing with the feelings evoked from the traumatic incident. This may be done on either a residential or outpatient basis. Depending on the individual client's personality structure, individual, group or any combination of other counseling experiences may be designed. The client who is a secondary alcoholic, after sobriety is obtained, should be either transferred to the appropriate psychiatric facility or dealt with in a special section of the treatment center reserved for this particular group. Often it is confusing for staff to deal simultaneously with secondary and primary alcoholics. Many cen-

ters, therefore, make the decision that they will not attempt to treat secondary alcoholics, but rather will refer them elsewhere.

If the patient is found to be a primary alcoholic, then the focus of treatment should be sobriety and the restructuring of the patient's life in order to develop support systems capable of providing consistent nurturing as needed. Alcoholics Anonymous (AA) is a community-based facility that is most helpful in this regard. Primary alcoholics who can involve themselves actively in the AA program generally have a more hopeful prognosis. However, other community-based support organizations are also useful in this respect. Churches, study groups or recreational facilities all may provide the primary alcoholic with the nurturing experience that is necessary for successful recovery. It is important to remember that primary alcoholics have a continuing need to test the consistency of all sources of nurturing and comfort. Care should be taken to establish a program for each client that will be responsive to this need.

It is often useful and effective to include treatment with Antabuse, at least in the beginning stages of therapy. Antabuse is a chemical substance that has little effect on clients unless they drink. When a client drinks alcohol, Antabuse causes the accumulation of a toxin in the body which causes the alcoholic to get extremely sick. Nausea, vomiting, headache and disturbances in blood pressure are all symptoms of an Antabuse reaction. Antabuse reactions are potentially lethal and should not be used in an attempt to adversely condition alcoholics to stop drinking. The reaction should be explained to the client in detail. The client should be informed that Antabuse is used not to stop drinking, but rather to reinforce personal commitment to stop drinking. Antabuse is a sort of insurance. Each day, when taking Antabuse, the client should be instructed to think of the act as a behavioral statement of commitment to sobriety. The client should be warned that if this commitment is changed, it takes approximately four to seven days for the Antabuse to safely leave the body. During that time drinking will remain dangerous. No one should be given Antabuse who is not seriously committed to sobriety. Alcoholics who are organically impaired, that is, who are unable to remember their commitment to sobriety, should never be given Antabuse. Antabuse reactions in these clients are likely to increase their organic damage and may ultimately kill them. If possible, medical personnel should be among the staff of the treatment center if Antabuse is used. Otherwise, access to medical facilities for evaluation in the case of an Antabuse reaction is necessary.

Ideally, each individual client should be evaluated, and an individual treatment program designed based on specific needs. Treatment modalities available will vary depending on the individual preferences and capabilities of the staff. Counselors who are skilled in individual, group, recreational and occupational therapies, as well as relaxation training, can be included in a comprehensive treatment facility. The greater the range of treatment modalities available, the more

likely it will be that individual treatment programs will be tailored accurately. For programs that are severely limited in the size of the staff and in funding, individual and/or group counseling sessions are the minimum modalities required in order for the program to function. In these cases, associations with outside organizations like AA are absolutely essential.

ESTABLISHMENT OF A COMPREHENSIVE COMMUNITY-BASED TREATMENT CENTER

Of primary importance in the establishment of a new treatment facility in a community is the firm commitment from available funding sources. The federal, state or local government, and private organizations, such as community mental health clinics, hospitals and clinics, all may be potential funding sources. It is foolish to begin establishing an alcohol treatment center without an adequate commitment to funding. Of course, once the center is established, continued funding remains a high priority. Recent cutbacks in governmental spending in this area have severely compromised many fine alcoholism programs. Where compensatory funding is not available, some programs have been forced to cut back their services and/or close.

Staffing

Assuming that adequate funding is available, the next step is assembling a competent, professional staff. Experienced supervisory personnel should be located and, as their first task, should

100   interview all prospective counselors to evaluate their level of expertise, experience in dealing with alcoholism, and ability to work in a group setting. There should be, if possible, at least one medically trained supervisor who can deal with medical problems. Care should be taken to avoid hiring staff inexperienced in the treatment of alcoholism unless the supervisory staff feels confident about their ability to train such personnel.

Ex-alcoholics often make very excellent counselors. As a rule of thumb, at least two years of sobriety should be required. Careful screening and evaluation is critical, because ex-alcoholic staff members become role models for the clients. If they should return to their drinking behavior, devastating effects on the client population may result. On the other hand, sober alcoholics are often willing to invest much more of themselves in the program, and patients can more easily identify with them. A strong, healthy, sober alcoholic can be a treatment program's most valuable asset.

Establishing Program Policy

Once the staff has been assembled, a meeting should be held to exchange views and to establish a program policy. The more consistent this policy, the more likely it is that the program will be an effective rehabilitation agent in the community. It should be stressed to staff that program consistency is extremely important and that problems of disagreement should be worked out in private staff meetings. Clients should not be included in these disputes. The exception to this rule is the client who has main-

tained sobriety within the program for an adequate time (usually six months or longer) who is viewed by staff as an unofficial cotherapist. Obviously, when a new program is established, there would be no clients who would qualify in this manner.

SUPERVISION AND MAINTENANCE OF STAFF MENTAL HEALTH

Whereas it is often understood that the role of the supervisor is to help staff develop clinical expertise, it is not always appreciated that supervisors must also monitor staff mental health. Working

---

Whereas it is often understood that the role of the supervisor is to help staff develop clinical expertise, it is not always appreciated that supervisors must also monitor staff mental health.

---

with a population of clients who repeatedly test the dedication of the counselor, who call at all hours of the night in crisis situations and who sometimes revert to old patterns of behavior (drinking and other acting out phenomena), is a tremendous emotional strain. The more dedicated the counselor, the greater the likelihood that his or her mental and emotional well-being will be affected. In severe cases the counselor may begin to act out frustrations. This may take the form of absenteeism, lateness, ineffectiveness in the provision of routine administrative duties (such as keeping statistics and filing reports) and may even lead to substance abuse and/or serious emotional deterioration, possibly leading to hospitalization. It is extremely difficult for a counselor to invest a great deal of emotional effort in a client and then watch the client fail to progress in treatment. Counselors can, as a result, get depressed, anxious and angry. More often than should be the case counselors will leave a program (the so-called "burn out syndrome") when they no longer can cope with the frustration.

It is therefore important to provide adequate mechanisms for the maintenance of staff emotional well-being. Individual supervisor sessions are helpful if the counselor and supervisor can relate in an open, warm manner. It is often helpful to provide a group experience for staff members (for this purpose groups should be kept in the area of eight to 12 members) to improve interstaff communications, to share frustrations and to seek, as a group, methods of dealing with the frustrations in a healthy manner. If possible, the staff group or groups should meet on a weekly basis. Often, problems with sex, race, rank and salary can be very effectively dealt with in this setting.

As staff will have a continuing need for education, it is often helpful to allow one or two staff members, on a rotating basis, to attend educational seminars away from the program. Not only will these staff members be able to share their education with the other staff members, but the time away from their clients will give them an opportunity to clear their heads of the tensions inherent in this work. If funding permits, each staff member should be given this opportunity at least once a year.

It is also helpful if staff can get together for shared social experiences from time to time. A barbecue, outing, fishing retreat or some such activity can help cement staff relations. In some cases staff have chosen a group retreat experience (such as spending a weekend together in a mountain cabin) and, given adequate supervisory support, have used this type of experience to improve working relations and to reduce job difficulties.

SUMMARY

The first and foremost problem in the establishment of an adequate alcoholism rehabilitation treatment program in the community is the establishment of a secure funding base. Once that is accomplished, supervisory personnel with clinical experience in the treatment of alcoholics should be assembled. The supervisors then should screen all prospective counselors and choose a staff with the broadest possible range of clinical experience and expertise. The staff then should decide, as a group, how best to deliver services to the alcoholic population. Consultation and liaison with appropriate community agencies should be established. Efforts should be made to provide round-the-clock, seven-day-a-week contact with the program, and, if this is not possible, clients should be provided with information as to where they can turn when the program is not available. Of

102 course, staff should discuss methods of evaluation of the program and constantly strive to upgrade the results of treatment. Supervisors should monitor counselors not only for the quality of services delivered, but also in respect to the maintenance of the counselors' mental and emotional stability as well. Efforts should continuously be made to evaluate and reevaluate the program so that it may grow and function with a staff that is reasonably well adjusted doing its job maximally.

REFERENCES

1. Hall, L. C. *Facts about Alcohol and Alcoholism* (Rockville, Md.: National Institute on Alcohol Abuse and Alcoholism 1976) p. 5.
2. Dorris, R. T. and Lindley, D. F. *Counseling on Alcoholism and Related Disorders* (Beverley Hills: Glencoe Press 1969) p. 37.
3. Hall. *Facts about Alcohol and Alcoholism* p. 15.

SUGGESTED READINGS

Alcoholics Anonymous World Services, Inc. *Alcoholics Anonymous* (New York: 1939).

Bales, R. F. "Cultural Differences in Rates of Alcoholism." *Quarterly Journal of Studies on Alcohol* 6 (1946) p. 480–499.

Bandura, A. and Walters, R. H. *Social Learning and Personality Development* (New York: Holt, Rinehart and Winston 1963).

Bennett, R. M., Bass, A. H. and Carpenter, J. A. "Alcohol and Human Physical Aggression." *Quarterly Journal of Studies on Alcohol* 30 (1969) p. 870–876.

Blane, H. T. *The Personality of the Alcoholic* (New York: Harper and Row 1968).

Blum, E. and Blum, R. *Alcoholism: Modern Psychological Approaches to Treatment* (San Francisco: Jassey-Bass 1969).

Cahalan, D., Cisin, I. H. and Crossley, H. M. *American Drinking Practices: A National Study of Drinking Behavior and Attitudes.* Monograph no. 6 (New Brunswick, N.J.: Rutgers Center of Alcohol Studies 1969).

Catanzaro, R. J. *Alcoholism: The Total Treatment Approach* (Springfield, Ill.: Charles C Thomas, Publisher 1968).

Cheek, F. and Mendelson, M. "Developing Behavior Modification Programs with Emphasis on Self-Control." *Hospital and Community Psychiatry* 24 (1973) p. 410–415.

Coleman, J. *Abnormal Psychology and Modern Life* (Glenview, Ill.: Scott, Foresman and Co. 1976).

Erickson, G. D. and Hogan, T. P. *Family Therapy: An Introduction to Theory and Technique* (New York: Aronson, Jason, Inc. 1976).

Forrest, G. G. *The Diagnosis and Treatment of Alcoholism* (Springfield, Ill.: Charles C Thomas, Publisher 1978).

Glasser, W. *Reality Therapy: A New Approach to Psychiatry* (New York: Harper and Row 1965).

Goslinga, J. J. "Biofeedback for Chemical-Problem Patients: A Developmental Process at the V.A. Hospital in Topeka." *Journal of Biofeedback* 2:4 (1975) p. 17–27.

Hindman, M. "Rational Emotive Therapy in Alcoholism Treatment" in *Alcohol, Health and Research World* (Spring 1976) p. 14–16.

McClelland D. C. et al. *The Drinking Man* (New York: Free Press 1972).

Shapiro, J. L. and Gust, T. "Counselor Training for Facilitative Human Relationship." *Counselor Education and Supervision* 13 (1974) p. 198–206.

Trice, H. "The Job Behavior of Problem Drinker" in Pittman, D. and Snyder, C., eds. *Society, Culture and Drinking Patterns* (New York: John Wiley & Sons 1962).

Ullman, L. and Krasner, L. *A Psychological Approach to Abnormal Behavior* (Englewood Cliffs, N.J.: Prentice–Hall 1974).

Warkov, S., Bacon, S. and Hawkins, A. "Social Correlates of Industrial Problem Drinking." *Quarterly Journal of Studies on Alcohol* 26 (1965) p. 59–71.

Wolff, K. "Hospitalized Alcoholic Patients: Motivating Alcoholic through Group Psychotherapy." *Hospital Community Psychiatry* 19 (1968) p. 706-709.

Negative and Positive Addictions

Gary G. Forrest, Ed.D., P.C.
Licensed Clinical Psychologist
Executive Director
Psychotherapy Associates, P.C. and
The Institute for Addictive Behavioral
  Change
Colorado Springs, Colorado

NEGATIVE ADDICTIONS

The past decade has witnessed a preoccupation which is culturally almost an obsession with the negative addictions. Alcohol and drug addiction have been the focus of attention. Certainly this growing awareness of the multiplicity of factors relating to the negative addictions has contributed to the development of numerous change-oriented rehabilitation and treatment modalities and other measures aimed at curtailing the drug crisis which confronts western culture.

Adjustment Orientation

Clinical experience has resulted in stressing the adjustment-oriented nature of substance abuse, especially when dealing with the treatment and rehabilitation of alcoholics and problem drinkers rather than other substance abusers and addicts. Such a position is paradoxical, because according to this paradigm the ingestion

104 of alcohol, and eventually the process labeled alcoholism, allows particular individuals the opportunity to transcend or partially overcome the powerful inner conflicts and struggles with which they are otherwise unable to cope. This becomes a most costly interpersonal and intrapersonal enterprise for most addicted individuals. In many cases the alcoholic adjustment style becomes so expensive and unpleasant that the addicted individual simply reaches a point at which the maintenance of the addiction dictates a radical change in lifestyle. This means the termination of drinking for many alcoholics.

Destructive Qualities

Learning new and more effective patterns of interpersonal behavior becomes essential to the maintenance of long-term sobriety, because negative addictions are ultimately destructive. Quite simply, at some point alcoholic behaviors are no longer adaptive for the addicted individual. The sources of gain derived via the addiction process are lessened, while the cost is increased. Thus the addicted person is forced to give up the substance dependency. This exact situation pertains to many behaviors and patterns of adjustment which we label neurotic. Cost in this sense is virtually unlimited: interpersonal relationships (including those with spouse and children), jobs, financial security, personal self-respect and esteem, ego and integrity and, not uncommonly, life itself become the price that is paid to maintain the addiction.

This model of addiction is basically negative for a number of rather obvious reasons. The cost of these addictions and substance dependencies eventually outweighs the gain and pleasure derived from this adjustment choice. On a long-term basis negative addictions represent by definition a stance and position with both self and others that is at its core destructive. The hallmark of all negative addictions is, in fact, destruction and nonbeing, as opposed to growth, integration and the meaningful experience of living life in an existentially relevant fashion. Alcoholics slowly and systematically destroy the tissues of their bodies. Identity, self-esteem and the other essentials of psychological well-being are in a similar fashion destroyed by the negative addictions.

Unfortunately, the destructive core of all negative addictions frequently first manifests itself in the interpersonal realm. Those closest to the substance

> *Unfortunately, the destructive core of all negative addictions frequently first manifests itself in the interpersonal realm.*

abuser are first to bear the brunt of interpersonally oriented destruction. Divorce, child neglect and abuse, daily living problems and vocational difficulties are but a few of the ingredients of the interpersonal destruction precipitated via negative addictions.

Culturally we have become cognizant of the direct method of destruction that negative addictions facilitate through incidences of violent automobile accidents, suicide, homicide, beatings and similar acts of violence attributable to alcohol consumption. For the addict, all of this is at the expense of the potential for learning more effective and rewarding patterns of interpersonal behavior. The potential for engaging in more adaptive behaviors is eliminated once the individual becomes actively caught in the trap of a negative addiction. This always becomes the case at some point in the addiction process.

Negative addictions are self-perpetuating and eventually become compulsive, precluding positive growth and change. The process of daily living becomes a static experience in destruction for those caught in the negative addiction process. It must be remembered that this process of destruction, inherent in the negative addiction, is facilitated and maintained by the inclusion of a basically foreign substance or chemical in the body of the negatively addicted individual. The alcoholic or drug addict perpetually injects into the body a destructive agent or chemical which is foreign to the organism.

Another primary characteristic of negative addictions has to do with the destructive distortion of reality. As alcohol and drugs function to block and distort reality input, addicted individuals progressively avoid and move away from the reality of their experiential beings and that of the external world.

Multiplicity of Pathological Factors

In brief, consideration of the multiplicity of pathological factors specific to the development and maintenance of addictive behavior is necessary. Information concerning the pathology and maladjustive nature of addictions is required by all health professionals, because addicted patients under treatment manifest a plethora of symptomatology. Focusing upon the inner conflicts, struggles and psychopathology of all people, at the expense of missing the healthy behaviors, creativity and adaptive potential of the human organism is the dilemma of the clinician and behavioral scientist. Quite unfortunately we are steeped in the tradition of viewing man as basically maladjusted or sick.

The adaptive nature of the addictions has been recognized for quite some time. Dr. William Glasser's recent book (1976) has also discussed the concept of "positive" addictions which is another matter. (See Suggested Readings.)

POSITIVE ADDICTIONS

Certain individuals obtain a positive effect or gain from engaging in a number of specific ritualistic, obsessive-compulsive behaviors which can be labeled positive addictions. While some might question the validity of considering such behaviors addictive, for particular individuals these activities represent the example par excellence of just that. To name a few, these behaviors include jogging, yoga and other forms of transcendental meditation, religious activities, sewing and needlepoint work, and reading and writing. There are essential similarities and differences between negative and positive addictions, but it should be emphasized that for certain individuals

106　the positive addictions mentioned are addictive in a very real sense.

Case Study

One striking case study of a positive addiction is that of a forty-six-year-old married male who in the last seven years has had occasion to miss his daily jogging only nine times, due to medical problems. This individual has jogged on 2,546 consecutive days out of a possible 2,555 days. Vacations, holidays, weekends and adverse climatic conditions have had no bearing whatsoever upon his daily habit. A resident of northern North Dakota, he has jogged on at least 30 or 40 days a year in which the temperature has been sub-zero. In addition to the marked consistency and frequency of this jogging behavior, it is of no lesser clinical significance that the entire routine is a highly ritualized obsessive-compulsive matter. Almost without exception, he jogs from the hours of 4:00 PM to 5:00 PM, and the jogging is never interrupted. He never takes time out to walk or engage in social discourse with others. The distance covered must always be virtually the same, and even the business of dressing for this exercise is highly predictable. The sweat-suit has always remained the same (new ones have been purchased from time to time, but the color and style have remained essentially the same); the Adidas running shoes have been essential to the jogging attire (the color and style have not changed); and the same socks, worn daily, have for all practical purposes disintegrated. The towel around the neck, always tucked into the top of the sweat-shirt, has remained an ever present part of his jogging apparel—regardless of weather conditions or other factors.

Characteristics

Perhaps this case seems a bit exaggerated, but its characteristics are common. While many individuals manifest a positive addiction syndrome which is perhaps less circumscribed in nature, nonetheless these individuals have become addicted to a specific set of behaviors. What is it that people get out of their positive addictions? All positive addictions can be viewed as essentially life generating and sustaining activities. Being able to engage in these addiction-based behaviors seems to give certain individuals an inner source of strength and enhanced ability to meet the demands of daily living.

Many addicted individuals will express only good feelings about this aspect of their being. This seems to be especially true following the completion of their daily ritual. When, for whatever reasons, they are unable to engage in their addiction, they report becoming somewhat anxious and uncomfortable and verbalize not being "up to par." Clinically it is cogent to note that positive addictions involve a very limited segment of the addicted individual's time. It is also of significance that positive addictions are totally self-oriented: they do not involve, and are not dependent upon, the incorporation of a foreign chemical or substance into the body of the addicted individual.

If such individuals do, in fact, gain an inner source of strength and enhanced coping ability as a result of their positive addictions, how and why is this accomplished? Although there are no definitive answers, there are some clinical hunches and speculation. Perhaps the most salient source of gain derived from positive addictions lies outside the interpersonal realm.

INTERPERSONAL DISENGAGEMENT

It is the ability to periodically disengage from the realm of human contact and the demands of interpersonal living that becomes a primary source of strength and gain inherent in the positive addictions. Somewhat paradoxically, effective interpersonal relations and optimal patterns of adjustment require periodic disengagement from significant others. Studies dealing with self-actualization and people who simply cope well indicate that these select individuals manifest significant autonomy needs. They require a good deal of time to themselves and seem to display a healthy ability to "get away from it all."

Preconsciously, if not consciously, the individual who becomes positively addicted learns that his or her addictive behaviors work quite well. They are both pleasurable and stress-alleviating. This means that the positive addiction becomes practiced and repeated to the extent of becoming over-learned. What is perhaps most significant about this entire process is that it is for the most part quite

---

In a real sense, the positively addicted individual can escape the taxing demands of interpersonal living and reestablish inner psychological resources.

---

healthy. In a real sense, the positively addicted individual can escape the taxing demands of interpersonal living, reestablish inner psychological resources and then once again enter the interpersonal arena of life, feeling integrated and stronger. Generally, positive addictions are not interpersonally oriented.

MENTAL DISENGAGEMENT

Another significant clinical aspect of the positive addictions has to do with figuratively "getting out of one's head," or of becoming mentally disengaged on a periodic, temporary basis. Positive addictions seem to demand almost total concentration, to the extent of blocking out environmental feedback and stimulation not related to the behavioral repertoire of the addiction per se. A number of individuals who were positively addicted revealed, when questioned, that they were unable to recall fantasies and other ideational content during their periods of involvement in the positive addiction process. When asked to try to remember what they were thinking about during the course of exercising their positive addiction, they were simply unable to remember. Moreover, when asked to speculate upon fantasies and thoughts they might experience in the process of their future positive addiction activities, there is again an almost total dearth of information. Individuals who addictively write or read can recall quite well what they have written or read, but they are virtually oblivious to their immediate surroundings, fantasies and other environmental stimuli. "When I'm jogging, that's about it, Doc. I guess I'm totally committed to

108 running and really not aware of anything else," was an explanation one jogger used to explain the situation. This response exemplifies the type of feedback received from the other positively addicted individuals. This is an experience with oneself and the phenomenal world which is a bit more removed than ordinary attempts to tune out, suppress or in other ways deny the various anxieties and stresses of interpersonal living.

The ability to remove oneself psychologically from the interpersonal world seems to be a basic ingredient in the positive addictions. While this situation is similar to the "getting away from it all" dynamic mentioned earlier, it is fundamentally different in that the positively addicted individual simultaneously is able to escape the anxieties and stresses of private intrapersonal and interpersonal experience through the medium of the positive addiction. Rehashing and reliving the difficulties of the day "in the head" while attempting to relax at some activity may be partially effective as a means of removing oneself from all the stresses and strains of the day. Just as often, however, little relief results from this type of transaction with the self. Fantasizing or reliving the experiences of the day may, in fact, make one even more uncomfortable. Realizing better alternatives and knowing that a decision has been final and cannot be reversed may only contribute to the frustration. The positively addicted individual is able to turn off the affective tapes that have been mentally recorded during the course of the day and that tend to continue to play incessantly upon the completion of the

work day. This becomes a significant source of strength. Once free from the additional emotional drain of dealing with an upsetting or disturbing self-dialogue, the positively addicted individual is able to "bounce back" and get on with the demands of living imposed in the present.

CHARACTERISTICS OF ALL ADDICTIONS

Rather obviously, Figure 1, a schematic model of the essential characteristics, similarities and differences between positive and negative addictions, is incomplete. Yet it does present a conceptual model which depicts the various parameters of both positive and negative addictions. In clinical practice the essential fundamentals of the negative addictions are understood more fully at present. The concept and implications of positive addictions have been almost totally neglected.

Pathological and Adaptive Similarities

Two significant points emerge from the schematic diagram presented in Figure 1 concerning the pathological and adaptive similarities of both types of addiction. First, positive and negative addictions appear to exist on a continuum. Rather

Rather than representing dichotomous categories of behavior, positive and negative addictions overlap in many respects.

FIGURE 1. SCHEMATIC REPRESENTATION OF POSITIVE AND NEGATIVE ADDICTIONS

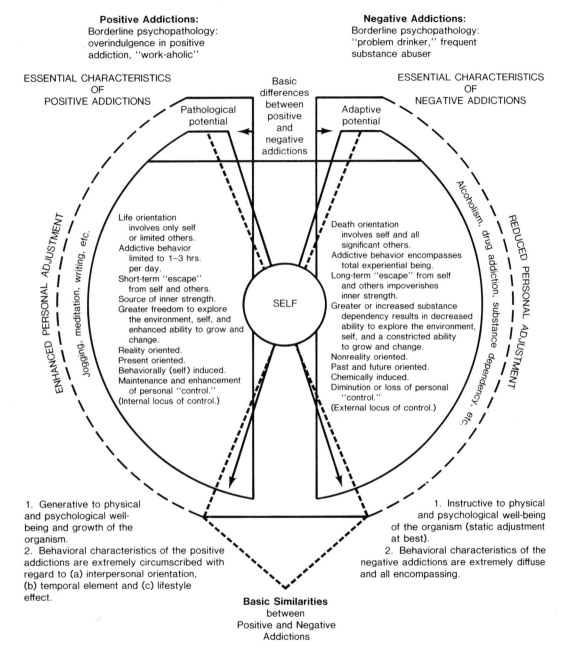

Positive Addictions:
Borderline psychopathology: overindulgence in positive addiction, "work-aholic"

Negative Addictions:
Borderline psychopathology: "problem drinker," frequent substance abuser

ESSENTIAL CHARACTERISTICS OF POSITIVE ADDICTIONS

ESSENTIAL CHARACTERISTICS OF NEGATIVE ADDICTIONS

Basic differences between positive and negative addictions

Pathological potential

Adaptive potential

ENHANCED PERSONAL ADJUSTMENT

Jogging, meditation, writing, etc.

Alcoholism, drug addiction, substance dependency, etc.

REDUCED PERSONAL ADJUSTMENT

Life orientation involves only self or limited others.
Addictive behavior limited to 1–3 hrs. per day.
Short-term "escape" from self and others.
Source of inner strength.
Greater freedom to explore the environment, self, and enhanced ability to grow and change.
Reality oriented.
Present oriented.
Behaviorally (self) induced.
Maintenance and enhancement of personal "control."
(Internal locus of control.)

SELF

Death orientation involves self and all significant others.
Addictive behavior encompasses total experiential being.
Long-term "escape" from self and others impoverishes inner strength.
Greater or increased substance dependency results in decreased ability to explore the environment, self, and a constricted ability to grow and change.
Nonreality oriented.
Past and future oriented.
Chemically induced.
Diminution or loss of personal "control."
(External locus of control.)

1. Generative to physical and psychological well-being and growth of the organism.
2. Behavioral characteristics of the positive addictions are extremely circumscribed with regard to (a) interpersonal orientation, (b) temporal element and (c) lifestyle effect.

1. Instructive to physical and psychological well-being of the organism (static adjustment at best).
2. Behavioral characteristics of the negative addictions are extremely diffuse and all encompassing.

Basic Similarities
between
Positive and Negative
Addictions

1. Interpersonal escape from reality (getting out of one's head).
2. Avoidance of interpersonal contact.
3. Relative gain offered by both addiction processes.
4. Obsessive-compulsive behavioral orientation.
5. Focus of effect is the addict.
6. Termination of addictive substance or addictive behavior precipitates anxiety or other unpleasant affective feelings.

110 than representing dichotomous categories of behavior, positive and negative addictions overlap in many respects. Practically this means that positive and negative addictions share a common grey area in which the positive addictions may become pathological to varying degrees, and in a congruous fashion the negative addictions may become adaptive to a limited extent. This becomes the case when positive addictions begin to control an inordinate proportion of the individual's experiential and interpersonal being.

Perhaps the "work-aholic" is a good example of this condition relative to the positive addictions. While this person manifests a positive addiction via the various dimensions outlined in Figure 1, at some point the role of "work-aholic" quite realistically can become a negative addiction. Similarly, negative addictions of the problem drinker and substance abuser types encompass a number of the characteristics of positive addictions. Getting drunk occasionally, smoking marijuana a number of times a week and other forms of borderline negative addictions enable certain people to transiently reap many of the sources of gain and pleasure derived from the positive addictions. At what point positive addictions become negative and vice versa becomes a most recondite issue.

Figure 1 delineates a second point. Negative and positive addictions in fact share a number of fundamental similarities. Both negative and positive addictions have to do with reality operations, interpersonal relations, the obsessive-compulsive dynamism, etc. It is a truism that a thin line exists between sanity and insanity, normal and abnormal. Identifying and defining an addiction as either negative or positive can be difficult, if not impossible. Somewhere along the continuum anagogic (adaptive, growth-oriented) trends become katagogic (pathological) trends, and by the same token katagogic trends may well become anagogic trends. The quantification and qualification of human addictive behavior is an exercise in the understanding of paradoxes.

Potential for Change

Implicit in this schematic diagram of negative and positive addictions is the potential for change. Negative addictions can be changed for the better. In fact, many of the interpersonal modalities of behavioral change found effective in the treatment of addicted patients fundamentally owe their therapeutic effect to the process of changing negative addictions into more positively oriented addictions. Therapists involved in the work of alcoholic rehabilitation live with this reality on a daily basis. Within the framework of negative and positive addictions, a primary clinical and treatment-oriented reality has been that of facilitating role reversal behaviors upon the part of the addicted or substance-abusing patient. In short, reinforcing client engagement in more positive addictions as opposed to negative addictions often becomes the

Reinforcing client engagement in more positive addictions as opposed to negative addictions often becomes the essence of successful rehabilitation or effective treatment.

essence of successful rehabilitation or effective treatment.

Treatment Implications

Evaluation of work with alcoholic patients, as well as other substance abusers and addicts, reveals an awareness of the addictive nature of the treatment modalities of Alcoholics Anonymous (AA), Al-Anon, the Synanon milieu and similar groups and communities engaged in rehabilitating addicts. It is rather unfortunate that many behavioral scientists have viewed these treatment modalities from such a negative perspective. Certainly some view the active AA member as less than successfully rehabilitated, according to what therapists have been trained to believe the ultimate product of successful psychotherapy is.

The literature on this matter abounds with clinical documentation of the pathology of terminating one's alcoholism only to become addicted to the lies of AA. A mere change in obsessive-compulsive dynamisms is the essential grist of much of this clinical orientation. Clinical therapists investing most of their professional time in the work of alcoholic rehabilitation have become more impressed with the pragmatic value and global gain offered through the medium of positive addictions. There is indeed in many respects a thin boundary separating the religious fanatic and the alcoholic or drug addict. With regard to rehabilitation and treatment modalities found to be effective with this clinical population, it is of significance to point out that AA and similar treatment models and programs based upon religious principles and doctrines have consistently been among

the most successful. This finding supports the position that the strategy of shaping negative addictions into positive addictions is a clinically worthwhile and effective endeavor. Certainly this is not the case with every individual caught in the trap of negative addiction, but it may well apply to over 70 percent of those individuals becoming engaged in the process of a negative addiction.

Although negative addictions have historically been very much a part of human behavior and social and interpersonal reality, there is only now a collective awareness of the many variables specific to this particular typology of pathological or destructive behavior. Emphasis upon negative addictions has been at the expense of acknowledging and investigating positive addictions. People have been addicted to positive behaviors and rituals for just as long as they have been addicted to destructive behaviors and rituals. What is especially germane to the schematic diagram or model of negative and positive addicts is the potential for modifying negative addictive behaviors. While addictions of the more positive type manifest this same change potential, in this case change in the direction of a more pathological adjustment, what is of particular significance for the professional change agent is that effective strategies of change presently and historically have had to do with switching addictions or compulsions. Certainly this is not a clinical revelation. It is evidence, however, that it is time to begin investing research-oriented efforts in the area of positive addictions that are equally as intense as those directed to the study of negative addictions.

112

SUGGESTED READINGS

Forrest, G. G. "Alcohol Rehabilitation: For Better or for Worse?" Paper presented at Southeastern Counselor Education and Supervision Convention, Biloxi, Miss., October 1972.

Forrest, G. G. "Problem Drinkers in the Workforce." *Personnel Management Bulletin* (Washington D.C.: Civil Service, February 5, 1973).

Forrest, G. G. "Resolution of the Alcoholic Power Fantasy." Conversation Hour, Division of Psychotherapy, American Psychological Association Convention, New Orleans, September 2, 1974.

Forrest, G. G. *The Diagnosis and Treatment of Alcoholism* rev. 2nd ed. (Springfield: Charles C Thomas Publishing Co. 1978).

Forrest, G. G. "Alcoholism, Object Relations and Narcissistic Theory." Lecture presented at Psychotherapy Associates, P.C. Fifth Annual Treatment and Rehabilitation of the Alcoholic Workshop, Colorado Springs, Colo., January 29, 1979.

Glasser, W. *Positive Addictions* (New York: Harper & Row, Publishers 1966).

Perspective from a Private Practice: The Differential Diagnosis of Alcoholism

Arthur P. Knauert, M.D.
Board Certified Psychiatrist
Private Practice
New York, New York
Medical Director of Transitional
*   Services and Alcoholism Services*
Guidance Clinic
Catholic Welfare Bureau
Trenton, New Jersey

DIFFERENTIAL DIAGNOSIS in the field of alcoholism can be the first and most important step in the treatment of the alcoholic. The word *diagnosis* has many negative connotations in our society. If someone has been diagnosed as being ill, many of us consider this a bad thing, yet accurate differentiation can reveal or guide the direction for decisions and treatment plans.

There are many definitions of alcoholism. Those used by the National Institute on Alcohol Abuse and Alcoholism and the National Council on Alcoholism have much value.[1,2] The essence of both is that when a person uses alcohol to the extent that it impairs or interferes with any area of life functioning, that person has alcoholism. The areas of life functioning are: physical health, social health (interactions with other people, including family), emotional health (ability to deal with feelings and cope adequately) and job health. If drinking interferes with one or more of these, the presence of alcoholism

114 is indicated, but more data are required to differentiate the type of alcoholism and the appropriate treatment. Clients ordered by the courts to participate in alcohol treatment programs present the professional with a differential diagnosis situation. For example, New Jersey recently mandated that everyone arrested for an alcohol-related offense such as drunk driving, public intoxication or causing a public nuisance must be sent to an alcohol rehabilitation program for evaluation and/or treatment.

Not all of these people are alcoholics. Some are social drinkers who have demonstrated poor judgment while intoxicated. They are arrested and sent to the alcoholism treatment program; evaluation reveals that no area of life functioning is impaired and the incident is an isolated instance rather than a pattern of behavior; and the decision is made to refer to an educational series on the effects of alcohol. Treatment is not indicated in this group, but education can reduce the risk of repetition. If it is determined that a person does have an alcohol problem, the professional must then decide the direction of treatment.

If there were only one type of alcohol problem, the task would be easy, because the professional could apply the same treatment to everyone. Since there are several types of alcohol problem, however, professionals cannot treat everyone with the same method. Skilled differential diagnosis will help in the construction of a relevant treatment plan. In the past, alcoholics have been classified as alpha, beta and gamma alcoholics;[3] early-, middle- and late-stage alcoholics;[4] and episodic, habitual and addicted alcoholics.[5]

Alcoholism counselors are usually familiar with these classifications. However, except for the fact that addiction indicates referral to a detoxification unit, these classifications are not much help in creating a plan that is relevant and workable and has a reasonable chance for success. (Here *addiction* is defined as the presence of tolerance to the effects of alcohol and the presence of withdrawal symptoms as a result of alcohol's removal from the body.)

Why does a person become an alcoholic? What categories are most useful in decision making? How do professionals treat alcoholics appropriately? Based on experience with several thousand alcoholics, the author has developed a three-part diagnostic system that answers these questions.

CLASSIFICATION OF ALCOHOLICS

Reactive Alcoholics

Reactive alcoholics are persons who become preoccupied with alcohol only after being overwhelmed by some external stress.[6] Most of them have functioned well as social drinkers and have never had a problem with alcohol until the traumatic event. Then they begin drinking as an attempt to deal with the feelings evoked by the trauma. In time reactive alcoholics may become physically addicted. Common events that may induce reactive alcoholism are the loss of a loved one, extreme public humiliation, bankruptcy, amputation of a limb and job termination.

Reactive alcoholics know that (1) alcohol is available; (2) alcohol changes feelings and can blot out pain; and (3) when there are no feelings of pain it is unnecessary to think about the traumatic event or to deal with its consequences. Each time the feelings or thoughts threaten to become conscious, it is a simple matter to walk into a liquor store or bar and drink them away.

People who have limited coping resources and are insufficiently advised against using alcohol in this manner may fit into any of the categories in the literature. They may drink episodically or habitually, or they may be tissue addicted. The drinking pattern is not as important as the reason behind the pattern.

If reactive alcoholics are seen shortly after the traumatic event, they may be considered in the early stages of the disease, two or three years after the event in the middle stage, or five to 20 years after in the late stage. No matter what category they fall into, such persons are reactive alcoholics. Reactive alcoholics are a minority of the people who will be seen in treatment. Treatment of alcoholics in this group differs markedly from that of secondary and primary alcoholics.

Secondary Alcoholics

Secondary alcoholism occurs only in the presence of major psychiatric illness. Like reactive alcoholics, secondary alcoholics drink for a specific purpose. They use alcohol as a kind of medication to control something that is going on inside their heads.

For example, people may use alcohol in an attempt to control schizophrenia, a disease which causes them to lose control over the ability to think logically. Their minds do not work correctly, and they may have delusions or hallucinations. Schizophrenia can be extremely frightening. Secondary alcoholics have learned that intoxication not only masks the fear, but it also temporarily suppresses the symptoms of the disease. They drink in an attempt to correct an internal process that is not functioning correctly.

Another disease that can induce secondary alcoholism is manic-depressive psychosis. This disease results in loss of control of emotional response. Clients with manic-depressive psychosis feel overly happy, overly sad, overly fearful or overly angry. Like losing control of thought, losing control of feelings is a frightening experience. Drinking to control feelings which are out of control leads to secondary alcoholism.

Psychotic depression, a disease where the ability to feel good about oneself is lost, may also lead to secondary alcoholism. Clients with psychotic depression may try to obliterate their pain with alcohol and may use alcohol to satisfy suicidal impulses generated by the depression. Mixing alcohol with tranquilizers or sleeping pills and/or driving while intoxicated certainly results in loss of life.

Failure to identify secondary alcoholism can lead to a treatment plan that is exactly opposite of what is desired. A secondary alcoholic who goes to a drug-

116 free treatment program may stop drinking only to find that the symptoms of the underlying disease increase in intensity. Often, the client returns to drinking and is identified as a habitual, recurring or chronic alcoholic; the underlying problem remains undiagnosed and untreated.

When secondary alcoholics are correctly diagnosed and have their underlying psychiatric disease properly treated, they no longer have a need to drink excessively. Medications are available that have been shown to significantly control the symptoms of psychiatric disorders without interfering with areas of life functioning; therefore, secondary alcoholics can be viewed as using the inappropriate medication. A drug-free treatment program deprives secondary alcoholics of appropriate medications and the intensity of interactions (especially if treatment groups are used) may stimulate the underlying disorder resulting in failure to maintain sobriety.

Primary Alcoholics

The third and largest category of alcoholism is primary alcoholism. Primary alcoholics find, at the time of their first drink or shortly thereafter, that drinking is an extremely positive, highly desirable experience. They choose to involve themselves with alcohol and to capture the feelings evoked from this special *relationship* time and time again and disregard any negative consequences of their drinking.

ALCOHOL AS NURTURER

Successful treatment outcomes with alcoholics can be obtained without inquiring into their early childhood history, but questioning primary alcoholics about their childhood provides the counselors with valuable information regarding the genesis of primary alcoholism. Careful exploration invariably reveals a history of excessive inconsistency in the nurturing experience. Parents of primary alcoholics have supplied their children with love and caring some of the time, but never in a consistent, dependable manner.

A significant percentage of primary alcoholics have one or more parents who are themselves alcoholics. Sometimes the parent will be able to fulfill the nurturing need and other times will not be available. Violence may be present at times in the home, and a child may be unable to understand its source or predict its occurrence. The child's viewpoint is, "I cannot tell whether Mom and Dad hate me or love me. Sometimes they are okay, but sometimes they act like they are going to kill each other. Then I won't have anybody." Some primary alcoholics have parents with histories of psychosis or physical illness which results in intermittent hospitalization. Others have parents who were separated or divorced early. Still others have had multiple parental figures (such as a series of foster homes) which convey to the child mixed messages about the nature of love and caring. Children who are inconsistently nurtured learn that it is possible to be loved, but impossible to predict when love will come.

Early psychoanalytic theorists generally considered alcoholics as people fixated at an oral level of development.[7,8] They viewed the bottle as a symbol of the breast and believed deprivation of nurturance to be the reason why personality development stopped at such a primitive level. These theorists failed to account for the fact that many primary alcoholics demonstrate a greater ability to function than does an orally fixated person, and that any active alcohol program has primary alcoholic clients whose personality structures encompass the entire range of personality types, including primary alcoholics who are obsessive-compulsive, hysterical, passive-aggressive and passive-dependent. Clinical experience shows that primary alcoholics can exhibit any personality style at all, but that most believe it is impossible to receive nurturance in a dependable manner.

The common denominator then is not a fixation of character style, but rather the incorporation of a character trait, i.e., a belief system which shapes the primary alcoholic's view of the world. This belief system does not result in a cessation of personality development, but influences perceptions of others, the ability to accept love comfortably and perceptions of the self. It appears that this character trait is usually formed by three years of age. It is definitely present by age six. It becomes part of the personality core of potential primary alcoholics, but may be indiscernible until circumstance introduces the primary alcoholic to the substance of alcohol.

THE LOVE RELATIONSHIP

Primary alcoholics often look back on their initial experience with alcohol as a very positive thing. They remember it as a wonderful experience. Usually during adolescence, they attend a party where alcoholic beverages are served. They take a drink and feel warm inside. Their problems seem to fade away. They take their second drink *and the same thing happens*. They have found something they can count on, something that is consistent, and at that moment they fall in love with alcohol. It is as if they had found a person who can give them warmth, caring, understanding and nurturance and who is always there. For this reason, primary alcoholics choose to form a "relationship" with alcohol for as long as they can to the exclusion of other areas of life functioning.

It is not until later, when primary alcoholics find out that they cannot really count on alcohol, that they even consider giving it up. Alcoholics Anonymous (AA) talks about "raising the bottom"—alcoholics have to hit bottom before they will be able to give up alcohol. The counselor should understand what raising the bottom really means: showing alcoholics that they cannot count on alcohol. Even when a person develops the physical signs of deterioration from alcoholism the love relationship is so powerful that the person will deny the symptoms and reject the idea of being alcoholic. Skilled counselors who are able to break through this denial become adept at demonstrating to alcoholics that alcohol is hurting them and not providing nurturance as the client perceives.

Because counselors are telling primary alcoholics to abandon the most meaningful thing in their lives, they often become angry and reject the counselor's help. To encourage abstinence, the counselor must

118　help to introduce a substitute into the alcoholic's life that can provide consistent nurturing.

THE ROLE OF AA

Providing an extremely consistent nurturing experience for alcoholics is the essence of AA. Meetings in New York, Honolulu, Arizona, Florida, Chicago or Wisconsin use the same words and convey the same concepts. A critical component is that members nurture one another. There are certainly some AA groups that do not succeed because they lack consistent nurturing, but the ones that have this quality are usually very effective. In an effective AA program, a person can receive consistent nurturance all the time, 24 hours a day, seven days a week.

Counselors should inform clients of the AA hot-line for those times when they need someone to talk to and the counselors themselves cannot be available. They should inform clients that the hot-line provides someone to talk to, someone who will listen and try to understand at all times.

A CASE STUDY

Counselors able to differentiate among the types of alcoholism will be able to design effective treatment plans. It is important to remember the primary alcoholic character trait and the reason for it, since successful treatment of primary alcoholics depends upon the establishment of consistent nurturance. When this factor is neglected it is unlikely that the client will be able to maintain sobriety comfortably.

Recently, the author discovered a case where an exception seemed to exist. The client had been drinking alcoholically for 30 years and did not appear, on evaluation, to be either a reactive or secondary alcoholic. He had been drinking to the extent that it interfered with his physical, social and vocational well-being. Although the counselor who evaluated this client understood the concepts of the primary alcoholic character trait and its evolution, the client denied any history of parental inconsistency. Even though the counselor asked specific questions designed to uncover this history if it existed, the client maintained that neither parent was an alcoholic, neither suffered from any significant physical or emotional problem that would render him or her incapable of consistent nurturance and, as far as the client comprehended, there was no inconsistency in his parents' ability to nurture.

The patient was referred to the author for evaluation and disposition planning. At first the interview reproduced the findings of the counselor. The client gave no history of alcoholism in the family and no history of significant problems. He maintained that his childhood had been perfect and that it could not be related to his drinking problem. However, as the session progressed, the following history emerged.

The author asked, "Are your parents still alive?"

The client responded, "No, my mother died when she was 55."

"From what did she die?"

"Cirrhosis of the liver." (The counselor had asked if either parent was alcoholic or had significant physical illness, but the client had not thought the cirrhosis was present when he was a child.)

"Was she a drinker?"

"Never in front of us (the children)."

"Did she have any emotional problems?"

"None that were important."

"What do you mean, 'none that were important'? What did she have?"

He reluctantly answered, "Well, every once in a while, *for no apparent reason* she would run through the house screaming and yelling and throwing her arms around. My father and older brother would have to carry her into the bedroom and hold her down while the doctor came and gave her a shot to put her out."

The author said, "But she had no important emotional problems and was not an alcoholic?"

"Right." (The client viewed this history as normal.)

"Well, what did you do when this occurred?"

The client, who was second from the youngest in a family of ten, said, "Well, the youngest ones had to sit in the living room when this happened and we were not allowed to say anything about it. We just sat there."

"Do you remember those times?"

"Yes, I remember them very well."

"What goes through your mind when you remember?"

"I didn't know if I was going to have a Mommy the next day or not."

This case illustrates the elements of inconsistency and unpredictability in the nurturing experience in primary alcoholics. Here was a mother who provided inconsistent nurturance, but the client believed this was normal and concluded that all parents must be this way. He was unaware that his view of the world had been distorted and did not understand that his love of drinking was in any way related to his early history. Only with persistent exploration did the history emerge.

TREATMENT METHODS

Treatment of Reactive Alcoholics

Diagnosing reactive alcoholics requires skill and careful evaluation, since both primary and reactive alcoholics have experienced emotional traumas in their lives. The counselor must be able to identify which clients are truly reactive and which ones are primary alcoholics representing themselves as reactives.

Clients may state that they did not drink excessive amounts of alcohol prior to some event. This should not be taken at face value, but should be explored further.

An iron-clad history which reveals no excessive drinking prior to a traumatic incident is required to diagnose reactive alcoholism. Consider the case of a 35-year-old male Army sergeant who had broken his ankle. He presented himself as a reactive alcoholic who drank to deal with his pain. He denied the fact that he had broken his ankle after drinking 15 cans of beer while on duty and was divorced because his ex-wife thought he drank too much.

Once the diagnosis of reactive alcoholism is established, it follows that the most appropriate treatment is sobriety followed by psychotherapy (either individual or group) aimed at helping the client understand the emotional response to the traumatic event and resolve it in the most

120 appropriate manner. Successful treatment will eliminate the client's need to drink in order to cope with the past event and should prepare the client to cope with future traumas in alternative ways.

Resuming Drinking

Some psychologists have reeducated alcoholics to become social drinkers with a moderate degree of success.[9,10] One person who was successfully reeducated was a 55-year-old executive who was respected in the community. He was a social drinker until his company went bankrupt and he lost his job. He found it difficult to find another job, and he began drinking. Several years later he was tissue addicted.

Subsequently, the client went through a detoxification program and had withdrawal symptoms. His psychologist initiated a reeducation program for social drinking, while at the same time retraining him vocationally and helping him find employment. When the client resumed work he went back to social drinking.

Only reactive or secondary alcoholics can be retrained to be social drinkers. If a primary alcoholic attempts social drinking, he or she will reestablish the pathological relationship with alcohol, and treatment failure may result. Resuming drinking is a risky business for the primary alcoholic. It is also risky for reactive alcoholics (they may drink to cope with stress, thus avoiding the problem) and for secondary alcoholics (they may stop taking needed medications since drinking often hides underlying symptoms). To be safe counselors should advise all alcoholics, regardless of category, to abstain from alcohol.

THE TECHNIQUE OF CONFRONTATION

Abstinence from drinking is a cornerstone for the treatment of a reactive alcoholic. After evaluation, the first priority of the counselor is the expert interference with the client's drinking. If the counselor waits for somebody else to interfere with the drinking behavior or for the client to stop drinking on his own, it may never happen.

One client had been drinking alcoholically for 30 years. He had been in a number of alcohol-related programs without success and had been in treatment with a psychiatrist for two years, but had not stopped drinking. When his therapist moved to another city he was referred to the author for treatment. The client's first statement was, "One thing I want to get straight right off the bat. We're not going to talk about my drinking." The author replied, "Okay, tell me about yourself. I want to know more about you." For the next two weeks all the client talked about was his drinking and its consequences in his life.

Interfering with the drinking of this client, who was a primary alcoholic, required the implementation of a confrontation technique. The author said to the client, "You said we were not going to talk about your drinking. I did not say anything about that, but all we have been talking about is your drinking. How do you understand that discrepancy?"

Confrontation does not mean getting angry at a person. It does not mean yelling and screaming. It is the juxtaposing of two different views of reality and making the person look at them. This client's view of reality was, "we will not be talking about my drinking"; the second view was "all we talk about is your drinking and its consequences." The author, in a caring and nurturing manner, simply put them together and asked the client to clarify the confusion.

The client then said, "Are you telling me that drinking is a problem for me?"

The author replied, "No, that is what you're telling me."

The client agreed and was then ready to work with the author. He made several attempts to control his drinking as an outpatient but failed. Finally he requested admission to a hospital where he was detoxified. Since then he has maintained sobriety and is doing well.

Confrontation helped this client break through his denial of his problem. This technique can be used with both reactive and primary alcoholics. The professional needs to be actively concerned about the person, show warmth and caring, be as consistent as possible and be able to identify the distorted views of the client in order to use confrontation effectively. Sobriety is step one for treatment and is required before treatment can progress to step two. With a reactive alcoholic, step two is clear cut. Once the alcohol is removed, the feelings that have been suppressed will be available. The counselor is then able to help the client understand the feelings and deal with them. If the client has suffered a significant loss, the counselor can help with the grieving process. If indicated, vocational rehabilitation may be helpful. Whatever the need, with the removal of the alcohol the client and the counselor should work together to help the patient reestablish a reasonable life.

Reactive alcoholics benefit from parti- cipating in AA because, once sober, they gain support from group interaction and learn to resolve problems. Once their problems are truly resolved, the question of whether reactive alcoholics can drink again arises. The answer is yes, with qualifications. If the person is truly a reactive alcoholic, drinking will not be that important to him or her. If the person is really insistent about continuing to drink at some level, perhaps he or she is not a reactive alcoholic. The practitioner must be very careful. Primary alcoholics often try to convince professionals that they are reactive alcoholics.

Treatment of Primary Alcoholics

The treatment appropriate for primary alcoholics is more complicated than that for reactive alcoholics. Sobriety is, of course, the first step, but once achieving this step, primary alcoholics often do not have anything specific to discuss. They may not have experienced a trauma that they have suppressed. They may be willing to talk about any number of problems in their life, but resolution of the problems is not enough. Primary alcoholics require consistent nurturing. For many, joining AA is the most convenient way of meeting this need. Alcoholics Anonymous is in every city and is always available. There are, however, some people who will not attend AA. Regardless of their reasons, to treat these primary alcoholics properly, the professional must help the client establish some alternative consistent nurturing. The alcohol treatment program itself can fill this need. One such program used clients in the residential component of the program as a 24-hour hot-line service. The number was avail-

122 able to nonresidential clients in the program for use whenever a crisis occurred and they needed to talk to someone.

Groups tend to be more consistent than individuals. Group therapy works better with primary alcoholics than individual therapy, unless the individual counselor is constantly aware of the consistent nurturance factor. The worst error a counselor can make with primary alcoholics is to tell them one thing one week and the opposite the next week. Professionals who are late for appointments, give conflicting advice, are dishonest or make false predictions are failing to be consistent and may encourage the client to continue drinking. Consistent nurturing can be obtained from church groups, friends or other anonymous groups such as Gamblers Anonymous, Overeaters Anonymous or Neurotics Anonymous. Whatever is available in the community should be evaluated by the counselor and used appropriately.

Treatment of Secondary Alcoholics

Treating secondary alcoholics is difficult. First, the client must abstain from alcohol. This may not be easy if the alcohol is keeping the client from experiencing delusions or hallucinations. The longer the secondary alcoholic remains sober the more intense their underlying illness becomes. Treatment of the underlying illness then becomes the focus of therapy; medications are usually required. Some programs choose to refer all secondary alcoholics to appropriate psychiatric facilities.

Primary alcoholics who convince counselors that they are secondary alcoholics are difficult to treat. Some primary alcoholics have met psychiatric patients through previous treatment programs and know how to convince physicians to give them prescriptions for psychoactive medications. They may be trying to substitute prescription medications for alcohol and are actually continuing their problem.

Counselors should generally avoid treatment of secondary alcoholics unless their programs are specifically designed to handle them. A thorough knowledge of psychiatric disorders or the availability of close supervision by a psychiatrist is necessary in order to work successfully with this group.

If secondary alcoholics are addicted, detoxification is required. Detoxification itself may induce hallucinations, but with time these withdrawal symptoms lessen. Secondary alcoholics' hallucinations will increase with time, and the staff of the detoxification unit will need to be sensitive to this difference if the patient is to receive optimum care. Detoxification units are excellent places for the identification of secondary alcoholics, since the reactions to detoxification are usually marked. Alcoholics who react more strongly than usual as detoxification progresses should be recognized as potential secondary alcoholics and should be carefully evaluated for the presence of psychiatric disorders. Once properly diagnosed, appropriate medication and referral can be initiated.

Unfortunately, the withdrawal process is often complicated by polyaddictions— addictions to barbiturates, tranquilizers and other chemical substances. Withdrawal from multiple substances can present a complicated and confusing clinical picture. The patient may initially improve as one withdrawal is accomplished only to get worse as the second substance's withdrawal makes its presence known. The professional might misperceive the client as a secondary alcoholic when this occurs. The key issue is time. The longer a secondary alcoholic is sober, the worse the symptoms become, and the underlying process consequently becomes clearer and easier to diagnose. However, the possibility of multiple withdrawals must always be remembered and ruled out before it is concluded that the client is a true secondary alcoholic.

Secondary alcoholics may not relate well to AA. Their illness may result in severe discomfort in a group setting. If they are being successfully treated with medications, they may feel pressure from AA members to stop their medications, and if they do they will become ill again.

Occasionally some AA groups work successfully with secondary alcoholics, but this is the exception. There are usually more appropriate centers for this group than AA.

GENERAL CONSIDERATIONS

In order to provide alcoholic clients with the highest level of care, the professional must be able to distinguish between groups of alcoholics and respond appropriately. Individual treatment plans, based on the type of alcoholism and the needs of each client, should be constructed on an individual basis. Counselors who are knowledgeable about psychiatric disorders, are understanding of the nature of primary alcoholism and are skilled in psychotherapy techniques will have more successful outcomes than their colleagues who are not.

REFERENCES

1. National Institute on Alcohol Abuse and Alcoholism. *Alcoholism Treatment and Rehabilitation* (Rockville, Md.: NIAAA 1975).
2. National Council on Alcoholism, Criteria Committee. "Criteria for the Diagnosis of Alcoholism." *American Journal of Psychiatry* 129 (1972) p. 127–135.
3. Jellinek, E. M. *Phases of Alcohol Addiction, Society, Culture and Drinking Patterns* (Pittman and Snyder, 1962).
4. Alcoholics Anonymous World Services Corporation. *Alcoholics Anonymous* (New York: AA 1939).
5. American Psychiatric Association. *Diagnostic and Statistical Manual of Mental Disorders* ed. 2 (Washington, D.C.: APA 1968).
6. Friedman, A. M., Kaplan, H. I. and Sadock, B. J. *Comprehensive Textbook of Psychiatry* ed. 2 (Baltimore: Williams & Wilkins Co. 1975).
7. Knight, R. P. "Psychodynamics of Chronic Alcoholism." *Journal of Nervous and Mental Disease* 86 (1937) p. 538.
8. Adler, A. "Individual Psychiatry of Alcoholism Patients." *Journal of Criminal Psychopathology* 3 (1941) p. 74.
9. Sobell, M. and Sobell, L. "Individual Behavior Therapy for Alcoholics." *California Mental Health Research Monograph* 13 (1972).
10. Sobell, M. and Sobell, L. "Training Responsible Drinking with State Hospital Alcoholics." Paper presented at the American Psychological Association meeting, Chicago 1975.

SUGGESTED READINGS

Forrest, G. *The Diagnosis and Treatment of Alcoholism* (Springfield, Ill.: Charles C Thomas, Publisher 1978).

Knauert, A. P. "The Treatment of Alcoholism in a Community Setting." *Family and Community Health* 2:1 (May 1979) p. 91–102.

Masterson, J. F. *Treatment of the Borderline Adolescent: A Developmental Approach* (New York: John Wiley, Publisher 1972).

Liver Disease in Alcohol-Addicted Patients

W. Jeff Wooddell, M.D.
Gastroenterologist
Cooper Clinic, PA
Fort Smith, Arkansas

THE ALCOHOL-ADDICTED patient's general health is of concern to the health care professional trying to utilize the most appropriate methods of treatment. Chronic heavy drinking affects the body's physiological mechanisms, produces pathological changes in the liver and creates problems that are difficult to manage when alcohol is withdrawn. An understanding of the complexity of alcoholic liver disease and cirrhosis is imperative for all professionals involved in treating alcohol-addicted patients.

Of the approximately ten million alcoholics in the United States, an estimated 5 to 15 percent will develop cirrhosis of the liver.[1] In many urban areas, cirrhosis is the fourth leading cause of death in persons from 25 to 60 years old, exceeded only by heart disease, lung disease and cancer.[2] This does not take into consideration the other diseases to which the alcohol-addicted patient has an increased predisposition.

Cirrhosis is the end result of the

126 complicated metabolic pathways for alcohol in the liver. Of all the body's systems and organs, the liver is the most vulnerable to the potentially dangerous effects of chronic alcohol intake.

Alcoholic liver disease, particularly cirrhosis and its complications, can be like a malignancy; often it is worse. A patient with a terminal malignancy has the empathy and sympathy of others; a chronic alcoholic or patient dying from alcoholic liver disease rarely receives sympathy, and the very nature of chronic alcoholism usually has adverse effects on the entire family and not just the alcohol-addicted individual.

METABOLISM OF ALCOHOL

The end products of the metabolism of alcohol in the liver are relatively simple, with 90 percent of them being either carbon dioxide or water. The liver metabolizes alcohol primarily by two pathways. The first pathway utilizes the enzyme alcohol dehydrogenase and is responsible for approximately 80 percent of the metabolism of alcohol in the liver in *normal* individuals.[3,4] An alcohol dehydrogenase subsystem catalyzes or oxidizes alcohol, resulting in acetaldehyde which in turn gives off excess hydrogen ions. This subsystem catalyzes another reaction in which pyruvate breaks down into a lactate.

The above reactions may cause side effects, such as decreased gluconeogenesis, which may result in hypoglycemia (low blood sugar); decreased urate production, which may present clinically as an attack of gout; and increased lipid or fat formation, which may result in a deposition of fat in the liver or hyperlipidemia (excess fat in the blood).

The second main pathway of alcohol metabolism is of lesser significance for normal individuals but plays a prominent part in the metabolism of alcohol in the alcohol-addicted patient: the microsomal ethanol oxidation system (MEOS). The complete significance of this pathway is not yet fully known, and is of considerably more significance in individuals with chronic heavy alcohol ingestion than in individuals who consume only small amounts of alcohol or who drink excessively only on occasion. The MEOS is partially responsible for the development of alcohol tolerance. It lacks specificity and alters the metabolism of other drugs as well as alcohol. It may interfere with the metabolism of sedatives, anticoagulants and hypoglycemics as well as acetaminophen. Administering medications such as these when the patient has consumed a large amount of alcohol for a long period of time may prolong the drug effect and necessitate smaller doses of the medication. However, when the body has completely metabolized the alcohol, the MEOS reverts to "normal" and the drug effect is no longer prolonged; therefore, more medication will be required to obtain the same desired effects as when the patient was consuming large amounts of alcohol.

A normal individual weighing 70 kg. may metabolize from 100 to 250 mg. of alcohol per kilogram per hour. The *maximum* amount of alcohol that could be metabolized in a 24-hour period is about 430 g. One pint of 86-proof liquor contains approximately 160 g. ethyl alcohol. This amount of alcohol is equivalent to the amount in 2.2 bottles of wine or three six packs of beer consumed in a 24-hour period. Four hundred and thirty grams of alcohol in 24 hours is the *maximum* amount that can be metabolized when the MEOS is functioning properly. The metabolic rate of alcohol is considerably lower when the MEOS has not yet attained its maximum efficacy.

Some drugs, such as opiates and other narcotics, have specific receptor sites and can be treated with specific medications. Naloxone, for example, blocks the effects of opiates. Alcohol, however, acts on the lipid bulk phase of membranes (the fatty layer of the cell) and does not have a specific receptor site. Thus there is no medication that will counteract the effects of alcohol.

Alcohol may adversely affect the metabolism of other potentially toxic drugs taken concomitantly. It increases the toxicity of isoniazid (INH), a common medication used for the treatment of tuberculosis. It also increases the potential toxicity of acetaminophen and carbon tetrachloride.

The metabolism of testosterone, the primary male sex hormone, may be significantly affected in alcohol-addicted patients. Alcohol decreases the production of testosterone and converts some of the metabolites of testosterone into estrogenic substances (female hormones). Clinically the male patient with impaired testosterone production may exhibit decreased body hair, enlargement of the breasts and decreased testicular size. Mentioning these possible side effects

127

Alcohol decreases the production of testosterone and converts some of the metabolites of testosterone into estrogenic substances.

may deter male alcoholics from excess consumption of alcohol and may be part of a comprehensive treatment plan.

TOXICITY OF ALCOHOL TO THE LIVER

For many years it has been thought that alcohol has no direct toxic effect on the liver and that many of the changes attributed to liver disease associated with alcoholism were secondary to malnutrition. A leading medical reference of 30 years ago reveals that alcohol itself is probably not a hepatotoxin.[5] In the past decade or so many have thought that indeed alcohol was directly toxic to the liver. Rubin and Lieber recently studied the effects of chronic alcohol consumption in baboons. During their study baboons received 50 percent of their total calories from ethanol and the remaining 50 percent from a nutritious balanced diet. In spite of their adequate diet the baboons developed different stages of alcoholic liver disease and finally cirrhosis just as has been seen in humans. Rubin and Lieber concluded that "chronic alcohol consumption in baboons in the absence of nutritional deficiencies is hepatotoxic and produces all the stages of liver disease clinically associated with chronic alcoholism in man."[6]

128 STAGES OF ALCOHOLIC
LIVER DISEASE

Most gastroenterologists feel that there
are three main stages of alcoholic liver
disease: (1) the presence of a fatty liver or
steatosis; (2) the development of alcoholic
hepatitis; and (3) the progression into
alcoholic cirrhosis (Laennec's).

Presence of Fatty Liver

The presence of excess fat in the liver
of alcohol-addicted patients has been
known for some time. Rubin and Lieber's
work was significant inasmuch as it
showed conclusive proof that the deposition of fat was related to alcohol
consumption and not to malnutrition.

Alcohol interferes with some of the
body's normal physiological metabolic
pathways. It increases the synthesis of
fatty acids in the liver; it decreases the
metabolism of fatty acids which in turn
interferes with the Krebs cycle; and it
enhances the incorporation of dietary fat
into hepatic fat. All 23 of the baboons
studied by Rubin and Lieber did develop
a fatty liver as was evident in liver biopsies. It is felt that all alcoholics at some
time will have excess fat in the liver
secondary to excess ethanol. It has been
shown in humans that a fatty liver can
result from drinking from 120 to 270 cc.
of alcohol a day for approximately two
days (a pint has 500 cc.). Most patients
with a fatty liver will only have an
enlarged liver and may or may not have
some associated right upper-quadrant
pain. They are often asymptomatic in this
stage of alcoholic liver disease. If all

alcohol is stopped and the patient has a
nutritionally adequate diet, the fatty liver
can return to its normal state in approximately two weeks. Since there are no
specific laboratory tests for the diagnosis
of a fatty liver, unless a liver biopsy has
been obtained, the diagnosis is usually
based on clinical suspicion and the
patient's history. If the patient continues
to drink, the fatty liver may progress to
the second stage of alcoholic liver disease,
alcoholic hepatitis.

Development of Alcoholic Hepatitis

It is extremely important for clinicians
to be able to differentiate between alcoholic hepatitis and hepatitis resulting
from other etiologies. This is often difficult, especially since alcohol-addicted
patients often deny the consumption of
alcohol as well as have poor recollection
of other medications they may be taking.
It is important to rule out other causes of
hepatitis such as viruses, transfusions,
prescription medications, over-the-coun-
ter medications and toxins. Obtaining a
history from the patient, family members
and/or friends which reveals alcohol
consumption of at least a half pint of
alcohol a day over an extended time is
helpful in determining whether the
patient has alcoholic hepatitis; however,
the only way to prove the diagnosis is to
perform a liver biopsy.

The liver biopsy usually shows changes
characteristic of alcoholic liver disease
and permits it to be differentiated from
other causes of hepatitis. Although some
patients with alcoholic hepatitis are
asymptomatic, most are somewhat jaun-
diced and show other signs and symptoms

of liver disease, including loss of appetite, occasional nausea, vomiting, fever (usually not greater than 103°F) and abdominal pain. About 75 percent of patients with alcoholic hepatitis have liver enlargement and jaundice. Almost half the patients with alcoholic hepatitis have ascites (accumulation of fluid in the abdomen) and over one-third develop hepatic encephalopathy (coma) due to liver disease. Patients with alcoholic hepatitis may become comatose and die when this stage of alcoholic liver disease is reached.[7-10]

There are no specific laboratory tests for diagnosing alcoholic hepatitis; however, the white cell count may be increased, liver tests may be abnormal inasmuch as the serum glutamic-oxalotransaminase (SGOT) is elevated usually to levels less than 300, and bilirubin and serum alkaline phosphatase levels are frequently increased. These abnormal levels, however, may be present in other forms of hepatitis and do not indicate alcoholic hepatitis conclusively.

Many gastroenterologists believe that between 24 and 50 percent of alcoholics eventually develop alcoholic hepatitis, and some believe it may be present as early as three months after the beginning of excessive alcohol consumption.[11,12] Alcoholic hepatitis may remain stable even in the presence of continued alcohol intake, or it may progress to the third stage of alcoholic liver disease, alcoholic cirrhosis.

The estimated mortality associated with alcoholic hepatitis varies from 10 to 40 percent, depending on what studies of patients one includes.[13-16]

The suggested treatment for alcoholic hepatitis is the cessation of all alcohol ingestion, adequate rest (absolute bed rest is not necessary) and a nutritious diet supplemented with multivitamins. No specific drugs are available for the treatment of alcoholic hepatitis. Several researchers have studied steroids in the treatment, but thus far no consistent beneficial effect has been demonstrated.[17,18]

Education is one of the most important means of treating alcoholic hepatitis. By educating alcohol-addicted patients, professionals can encourage the cessation of alcohol consumption, thereby avoiding

By educating alcohol-addicted patients, professionals can encourage the cessation of alcohol consumption, thereby avoiding the potentially serious effects of alcoholic hepatitis and the development of cirrhosis.

the potentially serious effects of alcoholic hepatitis and the development of cirrhosis.

Progression into Cirrhosis of the Liver

Cirrhosis of the liver is best defined as scar formation (fibrosis) within the liver with loss of normal architectural pattern. It is usually accompanied by some regeneration of the liver and the formation of regenerative nodules. Unfortunately, the regenerative process is not sufficient to

130 functionally compensate for the already-damaged liver.

The liver biopsy of a patient with suspected cirrhosis may also show some of the same changes seen in the liver biopsy of a patient who has fatty liver as well as a patient with alcoholic hepatitis. These changes can be seen in addition to the abnormalities observed in cirrhosis.

Recent studies have shown that some of the fibrosis or scarring resulting from cirrhosis may be reversible (the fibrosis is apparently reabsorbed) as long as there is no further damage to the liver by prolonged alcohol consumption.[19,20] This has stimulated research on drugs to help reverse fibrosis; however, as yet attempts to discover a nontoxic drug that will do this have been unsuccessful. It must be remembered that the development of alcoholic cirrhosis is not inevitable and only a small percentage (10 to 15 percent) of alcoholic patients develop cirrhosis. In the above-mentioned baboon study, only 6 of 23 baboons developed cirrhosis (26 percent).[21]

SIGNS, SYMPTOMS AND COMPLICATIONS
OF CIRRHOSIS

Patients with alcoholic cirrhosis may be asymptomatic just as may patients with excess fat in the liver or alcoholic hepatitis. Physicians rarely see these patients since they usually do not seek treatment. But patients with cirrhosis frequently have a noticeable protuberance of the abdomen, peripheral wasting of the extremities which is most apparent in the lower arms and legs, prominent parotid glands, pedal edema, breast enlargement and tenderness, and skin lesions or spider angiomata. Once they develop these signs, most patients with cirrhosis seek help.

Development of the protuberant abdomen in patients with cirrhosis is usually due to ascites. Many patients initially attribute it to the accumulation of fat, or obesity. Ascites is a result of fluid seeping from veins that are under increased hydrostatic pressure and from the liver itself. The fluid accumulates for two reasons: (1) the liver's ability to synthesize albumin, a substance which normally retains fluid within the vascular compartment, is decreased; and (2) the formation of aldosterone, a hormone which causes increased sodium and water retention, is increased.

As a result of the scarring from cirrhosis, the normal blood flow in and to the liver is altered. With advanced cirrhosis, the portal vein which normally brings venous blood to the liver becomes partially obstructed because of the scarring and disease in the liver. The blood flow tends to "back up" and cause dilatation of the weaker veins. The resultant increased pressure in these blood vessels is termed *portal hypertension*. Portal hypertension is responsible for the dilatation of veins (varices) in the wall of the stomach as well as in the esophagus. Varices often rupture, resulting in profound gastrointestinal bleeding and death.

Spider angiomata appear as small superficial dilated blood vessels on the skin, often in the configuration of a spider. These small arterioles are thought to be the result of abnormal metabolism of estrogen and testosterone by the alcoholic liver.

Internal gastrointestinal bleeding in an alcohol-addicted individual is usually secondary to causes other than varices. It is often a result of esophagitis, gastritis or peptic ulcer disease. Bleeding may be more profuse because of the decreased coagulability of blood frequently seen with alcoholic liver disease. Tears in the lining of the lower esophagus or upper stomach, often caused by vomiting or the "dry heaves," may result in profuse bleeding because the area of the tear may involve blood vessels. The origin of upper gastrointestinal bleeding in a patient with cirrhosis is almost impossible to determine by the patient's history, and its diagnosis requires the care of a skilled physician; often gastroscopy as well as barium x-rays of the esophagus and stomach are necessary.

Hepatic encephalopathy (hepatic coma) is seen in the more advanced stages of cirrhosis. It is thought by many to be related to the abnormal metabolism of ammonia derived from protein digestion; however, many still feel that the true etiologic agent or agents responsible for hepatic encephalopathy have yet to be found.

Patients with cirrhosis have an increased incidence of primary cancer of the liver (hepatoma). There is also an increased incidence of cancer of the pharynx and esophagus seen in alcoholic patients. Conclusive cause-and-effect relationships regarding the above have not been established, but it is thought that the chronic ingestion of alcohol irritates the mucosal linings and that this increases the susceptibility to cancer.

DIAGNOSIS

The liver biopsy is the most definitive method of establishing or proving the diagnosis of cirrhosis.[22,23] In addition to the clinical signs and symptoms discussed above, there are laboratory tests which may assist in the diagnosis of cirrhosis though thus far there are none specific for alcoholic liver disease or cirrhosis. Tests for serum albumin levels; the albumin–globulin ratio; and serum bilirubin, SGOT and serum alkaline phosphatase levels may help diagnose cirrhosis, but may also fall within the normal range.

In the past few years there has been interest in the measurement of the level of the enzyme glutamate dehydrogenase (GDH) in the diagnosis of cirrhosis.[24] This enzyme, found in the mitochondria in the liver, seems to be elevated in the presence only of alcoholic liver disease and not other forms of liver disease. A positive correlation seems to exist between GDH level and alcoholic liver damage, but GDH elevation does not require the presence of cirrhosis. The GDH is thought to be significant when two times greater than the normal level. As yet this enzyme assay is not available in most hospital laboratories.

Another enzyme that has stimulated increased interest recently is gamma glutamyl transpetidase (GGTP). This enzyme, in contrast to SGOT, seems to be

132

elevated only in liver disease but is not specific for alcoholic liver disease.[25]

A test measuring the prothrombin time—one of the tests used to measure the clotting ability of blood—may also help in diagnosing cirrhosis. Prothrombin time is often abnormally prolonged in cirrhosis and alcoholic liver disease; however, it may also be abnormal in other forms of liver disease.

LABORATORY TESTS ACT AS DETERRENTS

For some alcohol-addicted patients, laboratory tests and/or liver biopsies may serve as deterrents to continued alcohol consumption. For example, the liver biopsy usually reveals some pathological

---

For some alcohol-addicted patients, laboratory tests and/or liver biopsies may serve as deterrents to continued alcohol consumption.

---

abnormality in alcohol-addicted patients. Since the biopsy may be abnormal while the patient is as yet asymptomatic, it offers concrete evidence that drinking affects the liver and acts as a deterrent.

TREATMENT

The initial evaluation, diagnosis and treatment of patients suspected of having alcoholic liver disease are best done in a hospital. Liver biopsies to establish this diagnosis are rarely conducted on outpatients. The initial evaluation of patients suspected of having alcoholic liver disease should include rather intense medical, psychiatric, psychological and social evaluation. The patient should be observed very carefully for complications of the alcoholic withdrawal syndrome. Baseline liver function studies and a liver biopsy are most essential.

Rehabilitation and education of the patient are probably the two most important parameters of treatment. Each patient should be treated as an individual and should feel that the professional has a genuine interest in his or her welfare.

Approximately 90 percent of patients with alcoholic cirrhosis who do not have portal hypertension and *who stop* drinking alcohol will live for an average of at least five years after they have developed cirrhosis.[26] Only an estimated two-thirds of those patients who do not have portal hypertension *but who continue* to drink survive for more than five years beyond the development of cirrhosis.[27] Of the patients who continue to drink and have portal hypertension, only 10 to 20 percent have a five-year survival rate.[28]

RECENT DEVELOPMENTS

A new laboratory test that does not rely on blood alcohol levels is being studied which can detect whether a patient has been drinking excessive amounts of alcohol. It is not currently available, but may subsequently be helpful in treating patients who deny alcohol ingestion yet who are suspected of having alcoholic liver disease. It measures the level of the enzyme alpha amino n-butyric acid (AANB). Although an elevated level does not require the presence of liver disease, it reflects a history of prolonged drinking. Elevated levels of AANB usually return to normal within one week following the cessation of alcohol intake. As yet the test is not conclusive, and interference of measurements may occur from a protein deficiency or a decreased level of serum protein in the blood.

Recent developments in the area of alcoholic liver disease have been stimulating and will be more rewarding in the near future. Since only 5 to 15 percent of alcoholics develop cirrhosis, it would be of great value to be able to predict which patients will develop cirrhosis. Lieber is currently using liver biopsies to predict who will develop cirrhosis. He is searching for specific changes in the liver which he terms pericentral or perivenular necro-

sis. So far most of Lieber's work has been done on laboratory animals with alcoholic liver disease; however, very early studies in alcohol-addicted patients look promising. Since it is known that all alcoholics develop fatty livers, obtaining a biopsy at the stage of this development and determining which individuals are predisposed to cirrhosis would be a tremendous asset in the treatment of alcohol-addicted patients.

Evaluating and diagnosing alcohol-addicted patients is the first step in their treatment. By knowing the signs and symptoms of alcoholic liver disease and cirrhosis, health care workers can do their share in treating those patients who are addicted to alcohol and can recognize alcoholic liver disease prior to the development of cirrhosis.

REFERENCES

1. Lieber, C. S. "Pathogenesis and Early Diagnosis of Alcoholic Liver Injury." *New England Journal of Medicine* 298:16 (1978) p. 888–893.

2. Ibid.

3. Ibid.

4. Fleming, C. R. and Higgins, J. A. "Alcohol: Nutrient and Poison." *Annals of Internal Medicine* 87:4 (1977) p. 492–493.

5. Lieber. "Pathogenesis and Early Diagnosis of Alcoholic Liver Injury."

6. Rubin, E. and Lieber, C. S. "Fatty Liver, Alcoholic Hepatitis and Cirrhosis Produced by Ethanol in Primates." *New England Journal of Medicine* 290 (1974) p. 128–135.

7. Alexander, T. F., Lichner, M. W. and Galambos, J. T. "The Natural History of Alcoholic Hepatitis: II—Long Term Prognosis." *American Journal of Gastroenterology* 56 (1971) p. 515–525.

8. Fallon, H. J. "The Management of Alcoholic Hepatitis." *Hospital Practice* (February 1974) p. 115–121.

9. Fallon, H. J. "Alcoholic Liver Disease." *Practical Gastroenterology* 2:6 (1978) p. 10–17.

10. Gregory, D. H. and Levi, D. F. "The Clinical-Pathologic Spectrum of Alcoholic Hepatitis." *American Journal of Digestive Diseases* 17:6 (1972) p. 479–488.

11. Alexander, Lichner and Galambos. "The Natural History of Alcoholic Hepatitis."

12. Fallon. "Alcoholic Liver Disease."

13. Alexander, Lichner and Galambos. "The Natural History of Alcoholic Hepatitis."

14. Campra, J. L. et al. "Prednisone Therapy of Acute Alcoholic Hepatitis." *Annals of Internal Medicine* 79 (1973) p. 626–631.

15. Gregory and Levi. "The Clinical-Pathologic Spectrum of Alcoholic Hepatitis."

16. Hardison, W. G. and Lee, F. I. "Prognosis in Acute Liver Disease of the Alcoholic Patient." *New England Journal of Medicine* 275:2 (1966) p. 61–66.

17. Campra et al. "Prednisone Therapy of Acute Alcoholic Hepatitis."

18. Fallon. "The Management of Alcoholic Hepatitis."

19. Fallon. "Alcoholic Liver Disease."

134

20. Lieber. "Pathogenesis and Early Diagnosis of Alcoholic Liver Injury."
21. Rubin and Lieber. "Fatty Liver, Alcoholic Hepatitis and Cirrhosis."
22. Fallon. "The Management of Alcoholic Hepatitis."
23. Gregory and Levi. "The Clinical-Pathologic Spectrum of Alcoholic Hepatitis."
24. Lieber. "Pathogenesis and Early Diagnosis of Alcoholic Liver Injury."
25. Shaw, S., Lue, S. and Lieber, C. S. "Biochemical Tests for Detection of Alcoholism: Comparison of Plasma, Alpha-Amino-n-Butyric Acid with Other Available Tests." *Alcoholism: Clinical and Experimental Research* 2:1 (1978) p. 3–7.
26. Conn, H. O. "Cirrhosis" in Schiff, L., ed. *Disease of the Liver* 4th ed. (Philadelphia: J. B. Lippincott Co. 1975).
27. Ibid.
28. Ibid.

The Alcohol Withdrawal Syndrome

W. Jeff Wooddell, M.D.
Gastroenterologist
Cooper Clinic, PA
Fort Smith, Arkansas

ALCOHOL-ADDICTED patients who cease or significantly decrease their alcohol consumption frequently develop the symptoms associated with the alcohol withdrawal syndrome. To safely and effectively treat alcohol-addicted patients, the medical and psychological health care team must be well educated in alcohol addiction, the various ways patients manifest withdrawal symptoms and currently accepted methods of treating those symptoms.

Before one can successfully treat the withdrawal syndrome, it is necessary to understand the meanings of tolerance and dependence.

Tolerance is present when, over a period of time, increasing doses of a drug are needed in order to achieve the same effect as the initial dose. Tolerance is often difficult to detect clinically. As an individual increases the amount of alcohol consumed, his or her rate of alcohol metabolism also increases; therefore the individual requires more alcohol to attain

136 the same effect as the initial consumption level. An individual who consumes a fifth or more of whiskey or its equivalent per day is usually considered to have developed a tolerance to alcohol.

Dependence is present when an individual experiences adverse symptoms or behavior following the withdrawal of a drug or other chemical from the body. When alcohol-addicted individuals decrease their alcohol intake, withdrawal symptoms often occur. In one study, subjects received from one-half to one pint of 95-percent (190-proof) alcohol every 24 hours in addition to a balanced, vitamin-supplemented diet. Some continued to drink this amount for several months before ceasing alcohol intake. Observation of these individuals revealed a wide clinical spectrum of the withdrawal syndrome, ranging from an asymptomatic state to death. Subjects revealed different stages of withdrawal, including nervousness, seizures and delirium tremens (DTs).[1]

The consumption of large quantities of liquor, beer, wine or other alcoholic beverages over a long period of time results in compensatory neurophysiological changes in the body. The body senses a "depressant effect" and attempts to compensate by altering its nervous pathways. This compensation functions well until the ingestion of alcohol is stopped or significantly decreased. Then the compensatory changes become maladaptive and inappropriate. In effect, one becomes "overcompensated," and a rebound effect develops. A hyperacuity of all sensory modalities develops. Visual and auditory acuity as well as touch become oversensitive and inappropriate.

The severity of the withdrawal syndrome is usually, but not always, proportional to the duration of a drinking period and the amount of alcohol consumed. One night of excessive imbibition rarely results in significant withdrawal symptoms. Heavy drinkers do not need to completely stop drinking to experience withdrawal symptoms.

STAGES OF WITHDRAWAL SYMPTOMS

Withdrawal symptoms are not always predictable, but their development can be categorized into general time periods or stages during which they are most likely to occur.

Stage I

Approximately eight hours after alcohol ingestion has been significantly decreased or stopped the patient may develop tremors, become jittery and nervous or experience headache or nausea. An observer at this time might note that the patient's hands seem unsteady, or that the patient has difficulty holding a drink or a cigarette. There may be evidence that the patient has had some difficulty shaving as manifested by cuts or nicks.

In the hospital setting, the physician is often not the first to identify the early withdrawal symptoms. Nurses have more of an opportunity to observe patients and are often the initial ones to suspect that a patient is experiencing withdrawal.

Stage II

Between 8 and 24 hours after the decrease in alcohol intake the patient

In the hospital setting, nurses have more of an opportunity to observe patients than physicians and are often the initial ones to suspect that a patient is experiencing withdrawal.

may become still more jittery and nervous. He or she is often irritable and easily startled. Tremors may worsen and hyperactivity develops. The patient may become more restless, have difficulty sitting in one place for long and complain of not sleeping well. Nightmares may occur at this time; and visual, auditory or tactile hallucinations usually develop. The hallucinations may occur when the patient is well oriented to time, place and person. Although asking such questions as "what is your name," "where are you" and "what is the date" may yield appropriate answers, the patient may still be hallucinating. For example, the patient may perceive that "there are goldfish in the hanging intravenous solution bottle."

Tactile hallucinations may include a sensation of the "creepy crawlies," or a feeling that insects are crawling on the skin. A combination of hallucinations can result in a misinterpretation of objects in the environment. For example, the patient may interpret a blowing curtain as a wave of water, or female nurses as waitresses. When the patient verbally expresses such misinterpretations nurses invariably inform the physician of the patient's inappropriate behavior.

Seizures often occur 8 to 24 hours after drinking ceases. If an electroencephalogram (EEG) is obtained during the seizures, it usually demonstrates erratic spikes, a result of the now overcompensatory mechanisms which have persisted. The brain is in a hyperexcitable state.

Seizures in alcohol-addicted patients may also result from conditions other than alcohol withdrawal, such as epilepsy, brain trauma, systemic infections, brain abscess, subdural hematoma, or serum potassium or serum calcium deficiencies. Seizures also may result from the withdrawal of drugs other than alcohol. Therefore, when seizures occur, a differential diagnosis is necessary to determine whether a patient is experiencing withdrawal.

Stage III

Delirium tremens may occur from three days to two weeks after a significant decrease in alcohol intake. Delirium tremens is a pathological state of consciousness resulting from interference with brain metabolism, causing confusion and disorientation. Either confusion or disorientation may be present at times in patients undergoing withdrawal but when occurring separately are not associated with delirium. When both are present simultaneously the patient is usually delirious. The DTs have been defined as "the acute alcohol abstinence syndrome"; however, for DTs to occur, total abstinence is not required, as has been discussed above.

On some occasions patients with DTs are ambulatory, making it difficult for professionals providing care. For example, patients with DTs may walk into the wrong room or a closet, or they may urinate in inappropriate places.

The temperature of patients with DTs

138 is often elevated and may be as high as 104°F. However, alcoholics are highly susceptible to infections, and it is important to rule out other etiologies of the febrile state before concluding that fever is associated with DTs.

Along with the DTs and fever, hyperventilation, nausea, vomiting and seizures often occur. The state resulting from their combination with hyperexcitability, overactivity and sweating is often termed the "autonomic storm."[2]

The percent of mortality at this stage of alcoholic withdrawal varies from 4 to 20 percent depending on what case studies one selects.[3-6] The cause of death is usually secondary to a complication of the DTs rather than DTs themselves. For example, the withdrawal symptom, hyperactivity, increases the frequency of myocardial infarctions. Other conditions associated with withdrawal which may lead to death are metabolic imbalances, abnormal serum electrolyte levels, hypoglycemia and head injury.

Two relatively infrequent complications seen in chronic alcoholic patients, but not necessarily associated with withdrawal are the Wernicke syndrome and the Korsakoff syndrome. Symptoms of the Wernicke syndrome include rapid lateral eye movement, nystagmus, ataxia and muscular incoordination. These symptoms occur when the patient is not inebriated. Symptoms of the Korsakoff syndrome are disorientation, poor memory recall and confabulation. Patients with the Korsakoff syndrome often talk in sentences composed of short bursts of words that have no logical connection. These two syndromes may occur simulta-

neously in a patient. This is known as the Wernicke-Korsakoff syndrome. Nystagmus, ataxia and muscular incoordination may be reversed by the administration of thiamine, a B vitamin. The Korsakoff syndrome is usually not reversible. Patients may continue to live for many years with the Wernicke-Korsakoff syndrome.

TREATMENT

The ultimate goal in treating withdrawal is to prevent the occurrence of the symptoms. When the symptoms do occur the goal is to make the patients more comfortable and to avoid complications that often accompany withdrawal. If medications are required—and they frequently are—the establishment of a new drug dependence as well as any associated toxicity must be avoided. Rehabilitation of the alcohol-addicted patient should be initiated.

Hospitalization

The physician must determine whether hospitalization is necessary. Some alcohol-addicted patients experience mild withdrawal symptoms and do not require hospitalization. In such cases patients can be treated effectively at home *if* there is a good physician–patient relationship and *if* the patient follows the prescribed medications. Requiring the patient to pick up medications at the physician's office or clinic allows health care professionals to observe the patient to determine if hospitalization or a change in medication is indicated.

For patients who live alone withdrawal may be more difficult. Patients require competent supervision, observation and companionship. An attentive family or close friend is often more valuable than any medication administered. If the patient is in an environment where he or she receives little or no attention, hospitalization may be necessary for adequate treatment.

A thorough medical evaluation is indicated in the treatment of the patient experiencing withdrawal. In addition to the stress associated with the physiological withdrawal, alcoholics are highly susceptible to head injury and diseases such as tuberculosis, pneumonia, diabetes, liver disease, disease of the cardiovascular system and neurological disease.

Hospitalized patients should be placed in well-lighted rooms which can be observed by nurses. A light left on in the patient's room at night may assist in the patient's orientation. A nutritious high-caloric diet with increased amounts of protein and a large volume of oral fluids should be provided. Intravenous fluids may be required to achieve adequate hydration, which is extremely important. The patient may require up to six liters of intravenous fluid in a 24-hour period. Potassium, magnesium and folate levels are often decreased in alcohol-addicted patients. Supplements can be provided in the intravenous fluids. The magnesium level is routinely decreased and the patient may require up to 8 g. in 24 hours. The serum potassium level is easily checked and can be corrected orally or through intravenous fluids. One hundred milligrams of thiamine given intramuscularly at the time of admission usually prevents the development of the Wernicke-Korsakoff syndrome.

Occasionally hospitalized patients experiencing withdrawal require transfer to the intensive care unit. When feasible they should be placed in an isolated room in the unit so that their often disruptive behavior will not disturb other seriously ill patients. If restraints are necessary the patient should be placed face down or on the side to prevent or decrease any possible aspiration of vomitus. If the patient's condition permits, restraining him or her in a sitting position in a chair is even more desirable.

Medication

Most hospitals, alcoholic centers and clinics use some form of drug therapy in treating withdrawal. Many different opinions exist as to the drug or group of drugs that are the most efficacious, least toxic and least likely to become the source of a new drug dependence.

Paraldehyde, a liquid with a pungent odor, has been used for some time and is still used by many physicians. It may be administered orally, intramuscularly or rectally as an enema. Paraldehyde seems to be most effective when used in combination with chloral hydrate which is only given orally. Problems with the administration of paraldehyde include the following. Paraldehyde, like ethanol, is metabolized in the liver, and some physicians believe this causes liver damage. Abscesses may develop at the sites of intramuscular injection. Local irritation of the rectum (proctitis) can be secondary to

140

rectal enemas of paraldehyde. Gastritis may be secondary to prolonged oral administration. Most of these complications resolve with time and simple symptomatic treatment; however, it has been reported that some patients develop periods of apnea after the administration of paraldehyde, and there have been some unexplained deaths associated with its administration.[7-10]

Chlorpromazine (Thorazine®) has been used for many years. A relative disadvantage of its administration is that it does not prevent seizure activity and in fact seems to increase the frequency of seizures.[11] It is also associated with some postural hypotension. Chlorpromazine can impair the thermoregulatory centers and cause side effects such as facial tics and uncontrolled muscular movements. It is a member of a group of drugs, the phenothiazines, and acts similarly to Sparine® and Stelazine® which are also phenothiazines.

Phenobarbital is not used as frequently as it was a decade ago. It can be administered intravenously or intramuscularly as well as orally. Some patients exhibit a cross tolerance to phenobarbital and therefore may require rather large amounts of the drug for it to be effective. Since the drug appears to have a cumulative effect, close observation is necessary for the safe administration of large doses. In the presence of liver disease the metabolism of phenobarbital is often altered, which results in excess accumulation of phenobarbital in the body. It may be given in a dosage as high as 200 mg. every six to eight hours as long as the patient is being closely monitored. It is effective in

decreasing the seizure activity. Non-life-threatening side reactions such as nystagmus can be seen when the serum phenobarbital level becomes elevated.

The hydroxyzine hydrochlorides (Vistaril®, Atarax®) are in wide use today. These drugs appear to be relatively safe and have a great variability in the therapeutic dose ranges. They may be given orally or intramuscularly. When given in combination with some of the other withdrawal treatment drugs, the hydroxyzines may decrease the other drugs' potency, necessitating an increased dosage administration of the latter. The hydroxyzines seem to lower the seizure threshold making patients more susceptible to seizures.[12]

Alcohol itself, administered either intravenously or orally, is still used by some physicians for treating withdrawal. Alcohol is more toxic than most of the above-mentioned drugs, and prolonged administration may exacerbate complications of alcoholism such as metabolic abnormalities, gastritis and its associated upper gastrointestinal bleeding, and liver disease.[13,14]

Alcohol consumption at home by the patient may be an acceptable temporary stop-gap measure for treating withdrawal until appropriate evaluation and treatment can be obtained.[15]

If the patient has a history of seizures, phenytoin sodium (Dilantin®) may well be the drug of choice and should be used if the patient has been previously successfully treated for seizures with this medication. The drug seems to have little beneficial effect on symptoms of withdrawal other than seizures. Phenytoin sodium is poorly absorbed intramuscularly and should be administered orally or intravenously.

A newer medication, haloperidol (Haldol®) has been available for use for several years and seems to act similarly to chlorpromazine. In its limited use thus far it seems to be beneficial in treating hallucinations. However, it is ineffective for preventing seizures and has been observed to increase their frequency.

The benzodiazepines (Librium®, Valium®, Serax®, Tranxene®, Atavin®) have gained great favor in the treatment of withdrawal. They tend to accumulate in the blood with time, however fatalities directly attributed to their therapeutic use are extremely rare. This group of drugs does decrease the frequency of seizures. The intramuscular absorption of the members of this group which can be given intramuscularly is very erratic, so it is best not to administer them in this manner. The proper dose of the benzodiazepines depends not only on the individual drug used but on the patient. Each patient requires a different dose. A patient who smokes or who is already using a similar medication often requires a larger dose of the benzodiazepines.

Chlordiazepoxide (Librium®) is often given in 100 to 400 mg. doses orally or intramuscularly. The patient must be observed closely if the intramuscular method is used because of the erratic absorption. This should be titrated according to the patient's response.

Diazepam (Valium®) should be given intravenously, should not be given intramuscularly and should not be mixed with other solutions. The effect of diazepam is quite rapid, and repeat doses can usually be safely administered intravenously 10 to 15 minutes after the initial dose. If the desired effects are still not observed additional medication can be given intravenously with continued observation. The frequency of the administration of diazepam can be increased to obtain the relative state desired. This should be given slowly intravenously, and caution should be exercised especially in patients with chronic obstructive lung disease since diazepam can depress respiratory activity.

Diazepam is not the ideal drug. However, it and chlordiazepoxide are the drugs most frequently chosen for treating withdrawal. The side effects of these drugs include drowsiness, lethargy, ataxia, respiratory depression and slurred speech. The benzodiazepines are better anticonvulsants than the phenothiazines and are less toxic than most of the other drugs mentioned above.[16-19] However, dependency on the benzodiazepines is to be avoided, and they are best discontinued prior to the patient's discharge from the hospital.

It is most important for professionals treating alcohol-addicted patients to recall that it is not so much which drug is

---

It is not so much which drug is chosen for treating alcohol-addicted patients, but which method of administration is used and how each drug is titrated to individual patient needs.

142 chosen but which method of administration is used and how each drug is titrated to individual patient needs.

The number of alcoholics in the United States is ever increasing. A knowledge of withdrawal symptoms and the stages of their development will provide health care professionals with a better understanding of alcohol addiction and will enable them to better treat patients who are undergoing detoxification. In gaining knowledge about alcohol withdrawal, health care professionals will better be able to do their share in reducing the magnitude of the problems associated with alcoholism, as well as reducing its cost to society.

REFERENCES

1. Isbell, H. et al. "An Experimental Study of the Etiology of 'Rum Fits' and Delirium Tremens." *Quarterly Journal of Studies on Alcohol* 16 (1955) p. 1–33.
2. Koch-Weser, J., Sellers, E. M. and Kalant, H. "Alcohol Intoxication and Withdrawal." *New England Journal of Medicine* 294 (1976) p. 757–762.
3. Behnke, R. H. "Recognition and Management of Alcoholic Withdrawal Syndrome." *Hospital Practice* (November 1976) p. 79–84.
4. Thompson, W. L. "Management of Alcohol Withdrawal Syndrome." *Archives of Internal Medicine* 138 (1978) p. 278–283.
5. Thompson, W. L. et al. "Diazepam and Paraldehyde for Treatment of Severe Delirium Tremens." *Annals of Internal Medicine* 82 (1975) p. 175–180.
6. Victor, M. "The Alcohol Withdrawal Syndrome: Theory and Practice." *Post-Graduate Medicine* 47 (1970) p. 68–72.
7. Greenblatt, D. J. and Greenblatt, M. "Which Drug for Alcohol Withdrawal?" *Journal of Clinical Pharmacology* (1972) p. 11–12, 429–431.
8. Knott, D. H., Beard, J. D. and Fink, R. D. "Acute Withdrawal from Alcohol." *Emergency Medicine* (February 1974) p. 87–93.
9. Koch-Weser, Sellers and Kalant. "Alcohol Intoxication and Withdrawal."
10. Thompson et al. "Diazepam and Paraldehyde for Treatment of Severe Delirium Tremens."
11. Thompson. "Management of Alcohol Withdrawal Syndrome."
12. Dilts, S. L. et al. "Hydroxyzine in the Treatment of Alcoholic Withdrawal." *American Journal of Psychiatry* 134:1 (1977) p. 92–93.
13. Koch-Weser, Sellers and Kalant. "Alcohol Intoxication and Withdrawal."
14. Tavel, M. E. "A New Look at an Old Syndrome, Delirium Tremens." Editorial, *Archives of Internal Medicine* 10 (1962) p. 57–62.
15. Rappolt, R. T. "D.T.'s and Alcohol." *Clinical Toxicology* 12:1 (1978) p. 97–99.
16. Greenblatt and Greenblatt. "Which Drug for Alcohol Withdrawal?"
17. Koch-Weser, Sellers and Kalant. "Alcohol Intoxication and Withdrawal."
18. Thompson. "Management of Alcohol Withdrawal Syndrome."
19. Thompson et al. "Diazepam and Paraldehyde for Treatment of Severe Delirium Tremens."

The Psychotherapist as a Twelfth Step Worker in the Treatment of Alcoholism

Thomas Edward Bratter, Ed.D.
*Trustee, Forest Institute of Professional
   Psychology
Des Plaines, Illinois
Independent Practice
Scarsdale, New York*

When the author began treating narcotic addicts in 1964 he was influenced greatly by the nondirective approach of Rogers who believed the therapist should have a "warm regard for him [the client] as a person of unconditional self-worth—of value no matter what his condition, his behavior, or his feelings."[1] The author subsequently studied the psychodynamic analytical approach to treating addicts and adopted the therapeutic stance of being "professional," "uninvolved," "analytical" and "neutral."

An incident occurred in 1964 which altered the author's therapeutic orientation and approach. While working in the Bedford-Stuyvesant area of Brooklyn, New York, he encountered an addict-pusher who financed his narcotic habit by selling narcotics to junior high school students. As the addict related the details of his trade to the author, he conjured up images of "dope fiends" who viciously prey on the weak and innocent,

144

who entice youths into dark hallways and force them to become drug addicts. The author became angry and lost his detachment. He insulted and rejected the client. When the session ended, the author doubted he would see the client again. However, the addict returned the next week and told the author, "You are right, I am a monster. I hate myself . . . . And you know what? I haven't sold any drugs all week!"

What happened? The author had lost his objectivity and violated the sacred beliefs regarding the role of the therapist. But these actions had prompted the addict to change his behavior, to cease selling drugs.

This case illustrates the effectiveness of Reality Therapy, an approach developed by William Glasser and practiced by the author.[2,3] This approach can help alcohol-addicted individuals to become abstinent and responsible.

PROBLEMS IN WORKING WITH ALCOHOLICS

Goals of Treatment

PROBLEMS in working with alcoholics relate both to treatment goals and to conceptualizing and understanding the nature of alcoholism.

The primary goal of treatment for persons addicted to alcohol is abstinence. Until the psychotherapist, the alcoholic individual and significant others can agree that abstinence is a realistic and attainable goal, there can be no basis for a therapeutic alliance. The conclusion

drawn by certain researchers that some alcoholics will be able to resume their "social drinking"[4-8] is unsubstantiated and will prove harmful to the achievement and maintenance of sobriety among problem drinkers. Those psychotherapists who hold out the hope that an alcoholic can drink moderately indicate their lack of understanding that someone who has become alcohol addicted is by definition unable to control his or her alcohol consumption. Tragically, these researchers and psychotherapists inadvertently sabotage the long-term prognosis for alcohol-addicted persons; treatment oriented toward reduction rather than elimination of drinking almost always ends in relapse.

Defining Alcoholism

Prevailing definitions of alcoholism compound the difficulties of treating it. The Cooperative Commission on the Study of Alcoholism has defined alcoholism "as a condition in which an individual has lost control over his alcohol intake in the sense that he is consistently unable to refrain from drinking or to stop drinking before getting intoxicated."[9] According to the Uniform Alcoholism and Intoxication Treatment Act (1971), alcoholism is "the inability to abstain from drinking for any significant time period." This relatively narrow definition has been the basis for court decisions holding alcoholics not criminally responsible for their intoxication.[10] The American Medical Association describes alcoholism as an illness "characterized by a preoccupation with alcohol and loss of control over its consumption such as to lead usually to intoxication, if drinking is begun, by chronicity; by progression; and by tendency toward relapse. It is typically associated with physical disability and impaired emotional, occupational, and/or social adjustment as a direct consequence of persistent and excessive use of alcohol."[11]

These definitions explicitly assume that alcohol-addicted individuals are powerless to control their consumption of liquor. Their implicit, and more insidious, message is that such individuals should not be held accountable for their drinking behavior by psychotherapists. Conventional psychoanalytic stereotypes regard inappropriate behavior or emotional disorders as the acting out of unconscious interpersonal conflicts associated with concepts such as the Oedipus complex, infantile sexuality, the death wish and others. These elaborate constructs reinforce the contention that the individual has indeed suffered a loss of internal control.

Fox, in contrast, has developed a more operational description of alcoholism as "a behavioral disturbance in which the excessive drinking of alcohol interferes with the physical or mental health of the individual. It is usually accompanied by a disturbance in the interpersonal relationships within the family, in the work life, and in the social environment. It is also an addiction, which means that there is both an emotional and a physiological dependence on the drug alcohol."[12]

Glasser rejects the sacred dogma of etiology, of alcoholism rooted in unconscious conflicts, and holds the alcoholic responsible for his or her behavior. An alcoholic drinks "because he wants peace and contentment from the anxiety which plagues him when he is sober."[13]

The Disease Concept of Alcoholism

The increasingly accepted disease concept of alcoholism may appear, at first glance, to fall unequivocally in the category of loss-of-control concepts of alcoholism, and to be irreconcilable with notions of personal responsibility and accountability such as those proposed by Glasser. The disease concept states that alcoholic individuals are those who, after taking the first drink, are *unable* to regulate the amount of their alcohol consumption thereafter, which results in their becoming inebriated.[14]

What is often not understood is that the disease concept actually suggests not two but three states of being in relation to alcohol. Powerlessness is preceded by a state in which the individual is capable of not taking the first drink, i.e., is capable of self-control. It is this primary state of control, of potential responsibility for self that most psychotherapists neglect to consider in using the disease concept as a paradigm for treatment; consequently, a very powerful motivating force is lost.

The unmodified disease concept obscures, as does psychoanalysis, the real issues of alcoholism; further protracts myths that have survived too long without question; and provides few viable treatment options for helping alcohol-addicted individuals experience a positive response from the world. Psychoanalytic and physiological research, thus far, has not produced anything decisive beyond the

146 "discovery" that alcoholism is due to a psychopathogenic fixation at the oral stage and/or the disturbances of early object relations.

The Myth of the Unmotivated Alcoholic

The psychoanalytic model of human behavior is unproven; it is also counter-therapeutic.[15,16] Paradoxically, in traditional psychiatric settings and parlance, the unmotivated client/patient does not exist. Any person who appears resistant to change is labeled "not amenable for treatment" and therefore excluded from psychotherapy. There are only four places for unmotivated individuals: skid row, the back ward of the hospital, prison and the cemetery. Yet all alcohol-addicted individuals who enter treatment enter unmotivated and unconvinced.

Because they want to continue to escape the pain and stress of everyday life by drinking, alcoholics view psychotherapy as a threat and the therapist as the enemy.[17] Therapists become discouraged when they realize that the alcoholic does not "want to quit playing his alcoholic game and play my game instead."[18]

TOWARD A MORE HUMANISTIC VIEW OF BEHAVIOR

Today a more operational and humanistic view of human behavior is evolving, one which allows room for positive, productive therapy for alcoholics. This view holds that it is useless to evaluate individuals by their thoughts and feelings because these cannot be controlled. Behavior thus becomes the most significant criterion of the individual's identity—i.e., goodness or badness. This position assumes explicitly that individuals can control their behavior in that they retain the elements of choice as well as the capacity to grow and develop. While it may not be possible to control the external environment that challenges them, individuals can control their responses to it. In this model, self-destruction is a matter of choice.

Alcoholics and the Failure Identity

Alcohol-addicted persons do not have a chemical problem; instead they have a people problem to which they are seeking

---

Alcohol-addicted persons do not have a chemical problem; instead they have a people problem to which they are seeking a chemical solution.

---

a chemical solution. They enter treatment desperately trying to maintain an impenetrable, arrogant, hostile facade, but inadvertently revealing they are frightened, fragile people who feel no intrinsic self-worth and value. All indicate they have felt betrayed, abandoned and abused by others. They are people who, in Glasser's term, suffer from a "failure identity"[19]—people who have convinced everyone (including themselves) that they are unreliable, unworthy, unwanted, unlovable and untreatable. They trap themselves in their own expectations that their fate is to fail and experience a lifetime of failure: behaviorally, psychologically, educationally and socially. They have branded themselves as helpless and hopeless. They have no sense of identity other than that of being failures. Many, in an effort to escape from such a painful, pathetic and pessimistic reality, have discovered that self-medication via alcohol can provide immediate, if ephemeral, relief.

The Alcoholic's Needs in Therapy

The therapeutic imperative is to break the failure cycle, the self-perpetuating sense of helplessness, by holding these seemingly helpless individuals accountable for their own behavior and destinies. It is useless for the alcohol addicted to rationalize their dysfunctional behavior in terms of family or societal disadvantage, suffering or abuse; what they need is to accept responsibility for their own inappropriate choices. Only by doing so can they activate their capacity to make better choices.

Glasser prescribes that people who have adopted failure identities need responsible helpers who will not accept excuses when they fail but instead will insist that they will recommit themselves to achieving success. In so doing, Glasser contends that people will "gain respect, love, and a successful identity."[20]

Sterne and Pittman have pointed out that alcoholics are labeled "unmotivated" by workers who do not wish to examine their own failure to motivate these people.[21] But alcoholics *can* be motivated; they do have the capacity to transcend their previous mistakes. What they need are people who will become involved with them, who will expect and demand the best they can contribute. They need people who will struggle with them. They need people who care enough to continue trying to convince them of their intrinsic

Alcoholics can be motivated; they do have the capacity to transcend their previous mistakes. What they need is people who will become involved with them, who will expect and demand their best, who will struggle with them and who will never give up.

worth, their ability to perform meaningful acts and justify their own existences. They need people who will never give up.

The Meaning of Responsibility

Let us look more closely at the meaning of responsibility. It is necessary first to understand the term *addiction*. Van Kaam discusses it as an "emphasis on surrender, on giving up . . . it seems to be related more to the passive than to the active dimension of man's life."[22] Surrender is antithetical to responsibility. Responsibility becomes the crucial concept. The English word *response* appears to be less active than the French term *repondre* or the German *antworten,* which mean to reply or answer. The German term *verantwortung* appears more comprehensive in that it means to answer for a person's actions. *Ability* connotes being able to accomplish a task which coincides with the therapeutic community's overall definition of *responsibility.* Emphasis is placed on the person's ability to respond to external challenges with reasonable judgment. Patterson contends that while no one can control the environmental conditions which confront and challenge them, they can control their reactions. People thus

148 can be held accountable for their behavior, their choices and their actions.[23]

Carkhuff and Berenson write that "the essential task of all therapy is to enable man to act and to accept the awesome freedom and responsibility for his action."[24] Freud defined therapy as an attempt "to give the patient's ego freedom to choose one way or the other."[25] Maslow labeled it a "third force in psychology" which endows the individual with freedom and responsibility.[26] Choice and responsibility are profoundly linked to one another.

Psychologically, individuals can adjust their defenses so that there is a capacity for new experiences; this implies liberation. Learning presupposes some unlearning. No development can occur unless the current level of integration (homeostasis) is disturbed so that a transitory disequilibrium can produce a new differentiation. The primary goal for the addicted individual, as Bratter and Hammerschlag suggest, "is to assist him to be aware of the impact of his behavior, to understand the consequences of his acts, and to become more responsible to himself, others and to society."[27] Horney has defined the goal of psychotherapy to help the individual actively assume responsibility for him- or herself by making decisions and accepting the consequences. "With this goes an acceptance of responsibility toward others, a readiness to recognize obligations in those values he holds whether they relate to his children, parents, friends, employees, colleagues, community, or country."[28] Individual responsibility and accountability are at the center of Reality Therapy. It is this primary state of control that most psychotherapists neglect to consider in using the disease concept as the basis for treatment.

ANTECEDENTS AND DEVELOPMENT OF REALITY THERAPY

Reality Therapy is one of the newer, more humanistic psychotherapeutic approaches. It has developed over the past two decades under the leadership of William Glasser. Glasser conceptualizes Reality Therapy as "a system of ideas designed to help those who identify with failure learn to gain a successful identity and to help those already successful to maintain their competence and help others become successful."[29]

Reality Therapy has antecedents in the psychotherapeutic literature. Koenig contends that "Glasser's originality is marginal"[30] and Glasser and Zunin have discussed some of the psychotherapeutic predecessors of Reality Therapy.[31] Reality Therapy is a partial answer to Eysenck's assertion that traditional psychotherapy has proven ineffective.[32] Modifying his position, Eysenck concludes that whatever psychotherapeutic outcomes and gains have been documented have had learning theory as their basis.[33] Learning theory is central to Reality Therapy; in its most simplistic form, Reality Therapy can be considered an educational problem-solving process which helps people maximize their chances of success while minimizing failure. Learning presupposes some unlearning. Wolpe assumes "since neurotic behavior . . . originates in learning, it is only expected that its elimination will be a matter of unlearning."[34]

Ford and Urban, after comparing ten psychotherapeutic approaches, "believe that psychotherapy must be developed around the concept of behavioral change."[35] Reality Therapy stresses the cognitive and behavioral components of human development while de-emphasizing the emotional. Glasser is explicit: "in Reality Therapy we are much more concerned with behavior than with attitudes."[36]

Contemporary society is confronted by the problem of the "ME decade,"[37] or what Malcolm has called the "generation of narcissus." "One of the most inescapable characteristics of large numbers of young people today is the degree to which infantile narcissism—or, as the psychoanalysts call it, 'primary narcissism'—dominates their lives."[38] Not surprisingly some of the newer psychotherapeutic orientations espouse self-indulgence. Perls, for example, distorts the concept of responsibility along narcissistic lines:

> You are responsible only for yourself. I am responsible only for myself . . . I am not in this world to live up to other people's expectations, nor do I feel the world must live up to mine.[39]

The "three R's" of Reality Therapy are: responsibility, reality and respect. Glasser is adamant that the reality therapist will "never agree that [the patient's] irresponsibility is justified no matter how much they have suffered at the hands of others."[40] Reality Therapy encourages individuals to take responsibility for their behavior; it also stresses that no person has the right to deprive others of fulfilling their needs "through loving and being loved, and by doing something one believes is worthwhile."[41]

Finally, Reality Therapy differs importantly from traditional psychotherapies in that reality therapists do not stand back detached, analytical and uninvolved; instead they become involved with clients and take an active-directive approach to help them help themselves. The role of the psychotherapist is to teach alcoholics more self-fulfilling ways to achieve happiness.

> We spend much time painstakingly examining the patient's daily activity and suggesting better ways for him to behave. We answer many questions that patients ask and suggest ways to solve problems and approach people.[42]

MAJOR ELEMENTS OF REALITY THERAPY

The Therapeutic Alliance: Responsible Therapeutic Eros

The primary ingredient in a love relationship is the sharing of the most precious gift—the self. Fromm suggests that the individual gives of himself "the most precious gift he has, he gives of his life . . . He gives him of that which is alive in him; he gives him of his joy, of his interest, of his understanding, of his knowledge, of his humor, of his sadness. . . ."[43] Glasser radically challenged the traditional psychotherapeutic literature when he urged the helper to become *involved* with the person who needed help. According to him, the psychotherapist "must have the strength to become

150 involved, to have his values tested by the patient, and to withstand intense criticism by the person he is trying to help. . . . To some extent he must be affected by the patient and his problems and even suffer with him."[44]

While this humanistic approach may appear to be common sense, it is clearly revolutionary when compared to the existing medical model. Szasz accurately represented the benign detachment of the conventional psychoanalytic posture. "You need not show that you are human, that you care for him [the patient]. . . . Your sole responsibility to the patient is to analyze him." The analyst needs to refrain from making therapeutic decisions about hospitalizing patients or preventing them from committing suicide. The analyst, Szasz contends, "cannot make vague promises to the patient, such as 'I will take care of you,' 'I will protect you.' "[45] Szasz extends his thinking when he argues "I don't see how anyone can take seriously the idea of personal self-determination and responsibility and not insist on his [the patient's] right to poison and kill himself."[46] Such a position is extremely alienating and dehumanized:

> Can we be therapeutically immobilized to the democratic ideal of freedom of choice when we believe the client/patient may commit suicide? If viewed from this perspective, the benign neglect by the psychotherapist appears to be the ultimate irresponsible and no-caring [sic] act. When clients/patients are encouraged explicitly by a lack of crisis intervention by the psychotherapist to indulge their feelings when they feel like killing themselves must be more than a misguided act; it is accessory to murder.[47]

Angry, alienated, self-annihilative alcoholics equate the psychotherapist's degree of caring with the loudness of the therapeutic protest and intensity of thera-

---

Angry, alienated, self-annihilative alcoholics equate the psychotherapist's degree of caring with the loudness of the therapeutic protest and intensity of therapeutic anger expressed.

---

peutic anger expressed. People, as Samorajczyk concludes, "want to know where the limits are—and that someone 'gives a damn' enough to guide [them] in [their] search of what's expected of [them]."[48] They both need and want some tangible assurance that the psychotherapist cares sufficiently to become involved and, if necessary, act to stop them from their self-destructive behavior. Unless the psychotherapist is prepared to become involved, it is doubtful that he or she will be able to maintain any therapeutic alliance in such instances. Ex-addict mental health specialists, themselves the most extreme chemical casualties, describe the ultimate act of caring in terms of "responsible concern."

RESPONSIBLE CONCERN

Responsible concern implies sufficient concern to be willing to become involved with other persons to the extent of intervening directly if need be to prevent them from harming or destroying themselves. These responsibly concerned ex-addicts are prepared to aggressively restrain substance abusers from purchasing illicit drugs. They view themselves as their "brother's keeper." Alcoholics Anonymous (AA), in comparison, has adopted a less active-directive approach.[49,50] Reality Therapy is compatible with AA.[51] Twelfth Step workers (who are recovered alcoholics) will respond to a plea for help 24 hours a day, seven days a week but will not attempt to impose themselves in the lives of drinkers and force them to abstain.

The primary criticism ex-addict and Twelfth Step workers make of the analytic approach is against the reluctance of its practitioners to abandon their noninvolvement, their "objectivity." Bernstein contends that treatment failures occur because psychoanalysts are reluctant to show any compassionate behavior. He says, "Unfortunately, a misreading of the counter-transference prohibition makes analysts . . . afraid of having any feelings. . . .Thus, instead of feeling compassion in the face of a patient's demand to "help me" they feel coldness, objectivity, and withdrawal.[52] These concerns are valid. For too long psychotherapists have feared they might have a positive transference to clients. For too long they have believed it is taboo—i.e., "unprofessional"—to become involved with clients in a responsible way.

As Glasser says, "Unless the requisite involvement exists between the responsible psychotherapist and the irresponsible client, there can be no therapy." He goes on to define the therapist's responsibility in operational terms.

> Discipline must always have within it the element of love. "I care enough about you to force you to act in a better way. . . ." Similarly, love must always have an element of discipline. "I love you because you are a worthwhile person."[53]

THERAPEUTIC PROTEST AND ANGER

When the alcoholic individual tells the psychotherapist of plans to abuse drugs, he or she is testing the degree of responsible therapeutic eros. If the psychotherapist remains silent, the problem drinker can conclude either that this means indifference, or worse, tacit approval. When the psychotherapist communicates displeasure, however, the person feels reassured. It can be therapeutically effective to exaggerate the concerned response to the extent of offering to detain the individual, to notify a friend or a member of the family and, in extreme cases, to contact the police.

A final testing of the established limits can occur when the alcohol-addicted person challenges the sincerity of the psychotherapist by remarks such as "All you care about is your fee" or "What do you know, you never used drugs." Rather than inquiring as to why the adolescent is acting out and attacking or interpreting the underlying feelings—as the psychoanalyst would do automatically—the therapist can respond effectively with much therapeutic concern and aggression. For example, "See how crazy you are! You don't even understand what a friend is. Your definition of a friend is someone who will supply you with enough drugs to kill you. I care enough about you to recognize that your potential never will be achieved if you continue to abuse alcohol. I am trying to prevent you from killing yourself." This type of therapeutic exchange may be required before any meaningful helping relationship can be

152 formed. As long as substance abusers feel the psychotherapist does not care and remains impotent to effect positive behavior change, they will continue their self-destructive lifestyles. In working with self-destructive individuals, the initial impetus for change is stimulated by the psychotherapist, who not only becomes involved but also sets and enforces behavior limits.

Working with individuals who persistently engage in awesomely self-annihilative behavior forces the psychotherapist continually to reevaluate his or her own orientation and to devise innovative crisis intervention techniques. Often the psychotherapist must decide whether he or she can modify his or her own philosophical or political beliefs for the sake of their commitment to a distressed client. The concern for the ultimate survival and welfare of the alcoholic can enable the therapist to take, at least temporarily, an ordinarily uncomfortable or uncongenial approach. The most controversial aspect of the treatment relationship, and rightfully so, is when the psychotherapist elects to impose him- or herself as the central figure in the patient's situation and determines therapeutic limits to behavior. When this is done judiciously as part of the rational treatment plan, it tends to produce a corrective learning experience which speeds the formation of a therapeutic alliance.

BECOMING INVOLVED

If the psychotherapist will become effective to help alcoholics reclaim their lives, he or she must abandon their detached, analytical, objective stance in

For too long psychotherapists have believed it is taboo—i.e., "unprofessional"—to become involved with clients in a responsible way ... if they will become effective to help alcoholics, however, they must abandon their detached, analytical, objective stance.

favor of a concerned, involved helping relationship of the type advocated by Glasser. Significantly, Glasser has added a more human element to this involvement by comparing the psychotherapeutic relationship to friendship.[54] Unfortunately, the education of credentialed mental health professionals stresses the ability to diagnose the "illness" and treat its symptoms, while ignoring the crucial elements of warmth and involvement so effective in AA. Clearly, the psychotherapist needs to adopt more of the Fromm and Glasser models to establish an intimate relationship where there can be a mutual sharing. The difference between parent–child and psychotherapist–client relationships is the lack of possessiveness in the latter. In therapy, when individuals succeed it is because they elected to expend the energy, make a commitment and discipline themselves to do so. The psychotherapist can make suggestions, but, in the final analysis, it is the client's life and it is the client who must assume the responsibility and the consequences of his or her behavior. These individuals are accountable to themselves primarily, to others secondarily and thirdly to the psychotherapist. The therapist must know when it is appropriate for the individual to fail and learn from the failure. Rogers, describing the helping relationship, asks: "Am I secure enough within myself to permit the client his separateness? Can I permit him to be what he is—honest or deceitful, infantile or adult, despairing or overconfident? Can I give him the freedom to be? Or do I feel that he should follow my advice, or remain somewhat dependent on me, or mold himself after me?"[55]

It is equally important that the psychotherapist identify those instances where intervention is indicated to prevent self-destructive individuals from doing permanent damage to themselves.[56]

The Psychotherapist as Advocate

Advocacy is a relationship wherein the psychotherapist commits him- or herself not only to protect the interest of clients but also to actively seek preferential consideration for them. Briar has described the caseworker-advocate as assuming the roles of supporter, advisor, champion and representative with social agencies and courts on behalf of individuals in psychotherapy.[57] Stone and Coward and Elman suggest that the advocate in a mental health setting must be prepared to intervene on behalf of individuals to secure services which have been obscured or denied to them.[58,59] Grosser characterizes the advocate as "a partisan . . . whose expertise is available to serve client interests."[60] The psychotherapist-advocate should be assertive and competitive. The advocate must be able to respond to momentary defeats with a more creative and vigorous plan of action.[61] Advocates

must be strongly committed to clients who may lack the knowledge, qualifications or convictions to further their own cause. The dynamics of psychotherapeutic advocacy parallel those of the relationship in which an attorney zealously guards and argues for the interests of the client even when he or she believes that client may be guilty.

THE IMPORTANCE OF TIMING

The psychotherapist working with an alcoholic should not extend the treatment relationship to include advocacy until he or she has been convinced clinically that the individual not only has stopped drinking but also has become more responsible and productive. If the therapist assumes the advocate role before the person in psychotherapy is ready, it can adversely affect the client's sobriety. If recovering alcoholics are not sufficiently motivated and prepared to deal with the situations in which advocacy may place them—e.g., renewed opportunities to work or continue their education—they may fail. To place individuals who have experienced many failures in a situation where they are likely to fail again is an irresponsible, sadistic and countertherapeutic act of professional malpractice.

Aside from the harm done to those whom the psychotherapist is committed to helping, the therapist's own professional reputation and credibility with community resources can be jeopardized. Referral resources such as employers, vocational training institutions, colleges and agencies are most likely to accept additional referrals if the first ones are successful. The timing of advocacy is

154 crucial to ultimate recovery. If undertaken too soon, it can undermine all progress. If too late, the individual may be so discouraged and demoralized that he or she may choose to return to chemical relief from a reality judged too painful to endure.

DISCUSSING ADVOCACY WITH
THE CLIENT

The psychotherapist's potential advocacy commitment to the alcoholic should be discussed early in the formation of the therapeutic alliance, for three reasons:

1. All individuals who have acquired a failure identity have become resigned to the fact that their poor performance denies them access to opportunities to achieve self-respect. Once they understand that the psychotherapist is prepared to help them get access to such opportunities, they may be motivated to adopt more responsible and productive behavior. When the psychotherapist decides to become an advocate, it is tangible and irrefutable proof that someone important cares, is willing to become involved and has faith that the recovering alcoholic can make a significant contribution. This can have a profound positive impact toward restoring the alcoholic's morale. The act of advocacy, timed correctly, cements a positive therapeutic alliance which permits the psychotherapist to maintain high expectations for improved performance.

2. By offering to serve as an advocate, the psychotherapist has begun to negotiate intermediate to longer term goals of treatment. The psychotherapist will enhance his or her credibility by explaining objectively what changes the individual will need to make before trying to get a job or an educational placement. Negotiated agreement on these changes can become the basis for therapy. (Generally, it helps the process to request that the client write down in specific terms all the changes he or she agrees to make so there will be a permanent record.)

3. The recognition by the candidate for psychotherapy that the therapist will perform the special, vital service of advocacy subtly neutralizes the "you–me" dichotomy, and the humanistic "we" partnership is begun. This partnership is critical in working with resistant and unconvinced problem drinkers.

The Need for Authoritarian Structure

The literature on treatment of alcohol-addicted individuals is characterized by divergent, often contradictory, views on the need for authoritarian structure. Triana and Hinkle contend that the alcohol-addicted individual's hypersensitivity "coupled with his craving for acceptance and affection, requires the therapist either to avoid confrontations and interpretations which the alcoholic may construe as criticism or rejection or to prepare for their application by intensive supportive and sustaining techniques."[62] It has been argued that the more determined the psychotherapist appears to be about controlling the drinking behavior, the less effective he or she may be in actuality.

Thimann, in contrast, maintains that a relatively passive psychotherapist's role may be beneficial with certain subpopulations, but is less than effective with alcoholics.[63] Shea has stated that "alcoholism must be attacked directly; it cannot be expected to perish by attrition when the fundamental neurotic roots are crushed. . . . The easiest way to tackle the alcoholism directly is to make nonalcoholism an obsessive issue with the patient.[64] Tiebout elaborates on the harmfulness of permissive attitudes and emphasizes the necessity for intervening actively and forcing the alcoholic to view reality; according to Tiebout, it is therapeutically imperative to break through defenses and precipitate a crisis which forces the alcoholic to pay attention.[65] Canter offers the following picture of the active-directive role of the psychotherapist:

> The reality of the patient's life situation is constantly stressed and he is repeatedly confronted with the ways in which his drinking injures him. . . . The therapist must provide structure, direction, strengthening of defenses, and alternative channels for release of tension, and help the patient "survive the rigors of abstinence."[66]

Cleckley may have been the first to recognize that the *sine qua non* of treatment with immature individuals who exhibit psychopathic tendencies is constant confrontation and attempted therapeutic control of their behavior.[67,68] This therapeutic control and authority become critical because they prevent continued self-destructive behavior and stimulate intimate interpersonal relationships. Authoritative therapeutic confrontation can shatter the barriers the alcoholic has erected to insulate him- or herself from

being either hurt or helped. It can be "painful . . . it is also a nurturing, supportive and caring act."[69] Until the lines of authority are established, no meaningful therapeutic alliance can exist.

MAJOR PHASES OF REALITY THERAPY

Beginning Treatment

There literally is only one goal of treatment for the first session with an alcoholic: to convince him or her to return

---

There is only one goal of treatment for the first session with an alcoholic: to convince him or her to return for the second session.

---

for the second one. Alcoholics have no wish to terminate their drinking because it affords them the only relief and pleasure they experience. No matter how sincere they appear to be, they do not want to stop. They have sought "assistance" because they have been pressured by significant others or by circumstances.

THE THERAPIST AS ROLE MODEL, THE THERAPIST AS HUMAN

Rather than starting the session by inquiring "why" individuals decide to come, it is helpful to invite them to question the psychotherapist about his or her beliefs. In so doing, the therapist attempts to minimize suspicion while trying to model acceptable "therapeutic behavior." If therapists respond honestly to their clients' questions, they can more

156 reasonably expect clients to be comparatively open and honest with them. This unorthodox and humanistic approach generally fascinates those who have had previous psychotherapy experience.

The therapist can become a responsible role model and living poof that it is possible to be happy, responsible, spontaneous and creative without using or abusing chemicals. A sense of sharing and of openness can also result from locating the psychotherapist's office in his or her house so that potential clients have an opportunity to see where and how the therapist lives. Occasionally clients may meet family members or hear raised voices when children argue. Bringing clients into the home is done deliberately to attempt to reduce the mysteries of the "doctor–patient" relationship. The "patient" label has inherent countertherapeutic connotations. "Patients" are not in control of their behavior or claim they are not. They are expected to be "sick" and, by extension, less responsible. Alcohol-addicted individuals have sufficient excuses to perpetuate their self-destructive and sadistic behavior; they do not need the opportunity to justify themselves.

In working with alienated, bruised, battered, abandoned people, the therapist may find it makes more sense to emphasize his or her credibility as a human being and not as a professional. Perhaps one of the most destructive aspects of traditional psychotherapy has been the distance between the therapist who is presumably sane and healthy and the "patient" who is sick and dysfunctional. This dichotomy impedes the growth and development of the individual in psychotherapy. A person-to-person dialogue is more likely to result in improved behavior changes than a physician-to-patient exchange.

SETTING FEES

Another early problem is establishing a fee. The more traditional approach is for the psychotherapist to "set" the fee. Assuming the client cannot afford to pay, it becomes the client's responsibility to renegotiate. Rather than risk jeopardizing the therapeutic alliance, the therapist can permit the client to pay what he or she considers reasonable. Even though alcoholics have a well-deserved reputation for being dishonest, in the author's experience they have rarely abused this policy. Fees in the author's practice range from zero (for a client who is on welfare) to $100.00 for affluent families.[70] The negotiation of the fees is directly related to how much the professional cares.

A few minutes before the first session is to end, the therapist can tell candidates that they have the right to determine whether or not they wish to return and whether they believe the therapist can help them to help themselves. Having the therapist tell them that he or she will respect their choice is often startling to clients. If they decide not to continue, the therapist can offer to provide other possibilities. The psychotherapist can volunteer to talk with persons who may be pressuring candidates to enter into psychotherapy and explain why they could see someone else.

There will be sufficient time during the next few sessions to discuss candidly respective goals of psychotherapy, expectations and therapeutic limits. At no time do individuals in psychotherapy need to confess that they have a problem. While negotiating the conditions of psychotherapy, the therapeutic alliance begins to form.

DIAGNOSIS

Before establishing a treatment plan, the psychotherapist must decide whether the individual in question is actually an alcoholic or is suffering from a psychological dependency which, if unchecked therapeutically, could result in alcoholism. Use of a substance does not, in and of itself, imply compulsive abuse or psychopathology. Wise suggests learning the frequency of drug abuse and then asking whether this behavior is "based on healthy self-assertiveness and self-realization in certain spheres, or is it pathologically pervasive in all relationships? ... Can attempts at self-realization and self-identity be discerned in the esoteric interests of youth, as well as in their sometimes provocative strivings for ideals?"[71]

With individuals who are suspected of being alcoholics, diagnosis is complicated by their massive avoidance-denial reaction. Paredes offers a helpful operational definition of this behavior. Problem drinkers reject the notion that they cannot control the amount of consumption of alcohol. They resent any attempts to regulate their drinking behavior and defend it as a matter of principle. The alcoholic "drinks only to enjoy the company of others; to celebrate family occasions or a business success; or because it is required by the type of work done . . . ; to escape the unpleasantness of a dispute with a wife, a friend, or a sweetheart; to ease rancor against the boss; to

obtain some comfort if money or a job is lost; to warm up after the inclement weather"; etc.[72]

Alcohol-addicted individuals are often devious. Mann has described some of their prevarications. They use elaborate rationalizations to justify their drinking. They minimize the amount of liquor consumed. They employ numerous explanations to conceal their alcohol-dependent behavior.[73] Accurate diagnosis of alcoholics obviously is complicated by these various dishonesties. Burnett suggests that the psychotherapist recognize that alcoholics may agree they have a drinking problem but will deny they are addicted. The psychotherapist can ask for a definition of an alcoholic, but many alcoholics will attempt to provide a description that excludes themselves, such as:

> alcoholics drink hard stuff—I drink only beer; alcoholics drink in the morning—I drink only after 5 o'clock; alcoholics get drunk—I can hold my liquor; alcoholics can't hold a job—I've never missed a day of work; alcoholics have to drink—if I really wanted to I could give up drinking; alcoholics drink everything—I have Scotch.[74]

CONCURRENT REFERRAL TO
ALCOHOLICS ANONYMOUS

An effective supplement to the one-to-one therapeutic alliance is a referral, at the earliest opportunity, to AA. If possible, the therapist should accompany the alcoholic to the first few AA meetings or arrange for a member from AA to transport the new member.

Alcoholics Anonymous helps individuals stop drinking. An integral purpose of AA self-help groups is to assist alcoholics to abstain. Alcoholics Anonymous philos-

158 ophy emphasizes self-discipline and self-control. Alcoholics Anonymous views alcoholism as an illness in which individuals are powerless to control their consumption of alcohol; however, its operating premise is that alcoholics can surmount their problem by means of self-appraisal, disclosure and responsible behavioral change. An anonymous AA member writes that "we are allergic to alcohol and that is simply common sense to stay away from the source of our allergy." The alcoholic must become abstinent if he or she wishes to be a responsible and productive human being. Alcoholics Anonymous works through Twelve Steps. Crucial to its success is the idea that alcoholics can help themselves by attempting to help others who have had similar life experiences.

An anonymous person who combined psychotherapy and AA participation dramatically reported, "every gain I made in AA was reflected in my therapy, and every progress I made in therapy helped deepen and strengthen my understanding and appreciation of AA." Curlee contends that significant positive lessons are learned when individuals begin to rely on others for support instead of resorting to liquid oblivion. "(The alcoholic's) work with his therapist may help him utilize his AA socialization more fully, especially by focusing upon harmful attitudes and behavior that may be interfering with his relationship with other AA members."[75]

Hurvitz, discussing peer self-help groups, believes that more people have been helped by this form of intervention than by all types of professionally trained psychotherapists combined. The basis for his enthusiasm is that peers are active with each other by focusing on the presenting problems, identifying with each other and attempting to find a solution. Peers provide the necessary conditions for positive growth and development by being nurturing and confronting.[76]

Alcoholics Anonymous fellowship encourages interpersonal dependency and camaraderie, whereas:

A problem of the formal patient–therapist relationship is to establish this warmth and friendship with someone who needs involvement desperately, as most patients do, yet limit the involvement to what is possible in the situation.[77]

Glasser conceptualizes Reality Therapy as having seven primary components[78] (while Rachin lists fourteen[79]). These components are:
1. becoming involved and making friends;
2. examining current behavior;
3. evaluating behavior;
4. planning responsible behavior;
5. making and keeping a commitment;
6. accepting no excuses; and
7. giving no punishment.

Becoming Involved and Making Friends

The most significant contribution the psychotherapist makes to therapeutic success is his or her commitment to and involvement with clients. Before clients will begin to examine their behavior candidly, they must be convinced the therapist genuinely cares for them.

Rarely do alcoholics entering therapy have any friends. They are alienated from themselves and others; they feel rejected and misunderstood. They enter therapy anticipating yet another failure, yet another painful human encounter. Initially they are likely to seem remote, resigned and resistant; therapist involvement is essential to breaking through this facade.

Involvement between client and professional must begin right away. The psychotherapist cannot predict whether the establishment of a therapeutic friendship will take five minutes or five sessions—but until it occurs, until the client is convinced of the therapist's concern, the therapeutic process will not begin.

What does it mean to become involved, what does it mean to make friends? The outcome of therapy depends on the helping relationship. How can the therapeutic friendship be established? By inviting the client to ask some questions about the therapist. (Most persons in psychotherapy do not really want to know too much about the therapist other than how to manipulate so they can continue to drink.) Next the therapist can ask clients something about themselves, such as their hobbies, their likes and dislikes. The therapist should make an explicit declaration of responsible concern, of his or her intention of getting involved in the client's situation. Unless there is a crisis, the focus of the first few sessions can be on developing a give-and-take relationship and establishing ground rules.

CONFIDENTIALITY AND INTERVENTION

Once a relationship is established with the alcoholic, progress can begin, but may be complicated by the issue of confiden-

On the one hand, the therapist is committed to maintaining trust; on the other hand, he or she is also obliged to share certain kinds of information.

tiality. The extent to which clients' confidences are honored remains problematic. On the one hand, the therapist is committed to maintaining trust; on the other hand, as a responsible professional, he or she remains obliged to share certain kinds of information. For example, if a client seriously proposes going out and harming someone, the therapist must intervene personally or must take steps to see that an authority does. The therapist needs to be explicit regarding the parameters of confidentiality. The issue of confidentiality must be understood before any crisis is experienced.

The psychotherapist's position of active concern and involvement is one that can incur intense anger and resentment from clients. The therapist should reiterate that any interventions come from concern for the client, a concern so sincere that the therapist would be willing to risk the client's anger. When confronting this anger the therapist must recognize that the rage may be directed against the environment and not him or her personally. The anger generally camouflages a fear of being fragile, of not being able to survive without the alcohol. Many alcoholics do not believe they are capable of achieving abstinence. The professional must respond rationally to the client's anger. If the psychotherapist becomes

160 angry and emotional, he or she will be discredited.

If the psychotherapist wishes to become a responsible and reasonable limit-setting factor in the alcoholic's life, he or she must struggle not to be intimidated by the problem drinker. There are times when the psychotherapist may need to consider waging a "therapeutic war."

THE THERAPIST–CLIENT WAR

The therapeutic war, in fact, is the essence of the first phase of therapy with an alcoholic or other addict.[80] It is an intense conflict between the alcoholic's powerful self-destructiveness and the therapist's concern and skill. Alcoholics feel tremendous rage and anger. And, like all substance abusers, they want to manipulate, to "get one over" on the therapist. Of course when they "win" in this way, they are actually losing. And when they "lose," they win. The manipulative, angry—sometimes to the point of violence—alcoholic is looking for the therapist's weak spots. The therapist should attempt to present an impenetrable facade of strength and confidence. When threatened by a hostile client with "you're afraid of me," the therapist must communicate "I'm not afraid of you or anybody else," and prove his or her assertion by many nonviolent techniques.

During the war, the therapist's task is to make the alcoholic's life so miserable—which is difficult when alcoholics can medicate themselves—that the alcoholic will be forced to consider a new lifestyle, i.e., abstain from alcohol use. When the war has been won, the therapist can become more human, can permit him- or herself a certain amount of self-disclosure. While the war is on, however, vulnerability on the part of the therapist is countertherapeutic.

Examining Current Behavior

After the therapeutic alliance, predicated on involvement, has been established, alcoholics in treatment begin to examine their current behavior rather than their attitudes or emotions.[81] Although Reality Therapy does not deny that feelings are important, effective practitioners have learned that unless they focus on behavior they will not help the client. Glasser believes "people often avoid facing their present behavior by emphasizing how they feel rather than what they are doing."[82]

The questions "what have you done today," "what are you doing now" may seem simplistic, but in fact are powerful therapeutic tools. These questions encourage the alcoholic to examine and evaluate what he or she is doing. It is expedient for the therapist to ask such questions as: What time did you wake up? What did you do? To whom did you speak? Did you drink? What? With whom? This therapeutic inquisition forces the individual to relate to his or her behavior for the day. The confrontation with the reality of the alcohol-addicted existence is absolutely required before the individual will be motivated to change.

Alcoholics, regardless of socioeconomic class, are consumed by seething anger. Alcoholics generally are so frightened by their anger that they can release it only when they are inebriated. When they are sober, most alcoholics are passive and pleasant, but after a few drinks they become transformed into angry, aggressive, abrasive and abusive people.

Evaluating Behavior

CONFRONTATION

During this phase of therapy clients understand the implications of their self-defeating and irresponsible acts. Confrontation remains the most effective technique for enabling clients to penetrate their own defenses quickly and view themselves realistically.[83-85] Carkhuff and Berenson have defined confrontation as an act which "brings the client into more direct contact with himself, his strength and resources, as well as his self-destructive behavior. The purpose of confrontation is ... a challenge to the client to become integrated.... It is directed at discrepancies within the client.... It implies a constructive attack upon the unhealthy...."[86]

NOT ASKING WHY

Reality Therapy differs significantly from psychoanalysis in that it is not concerned with ascertaining *why* individuals behave as they do, but with making positive changes in their behavior. Reality therapists do not ask "why?" Asking why permits the alcohol-addicted individual the opportunity to make excuses. In listening to and trying to understand these "reasons," it is easy for the therapist to become a conspirator with persons in psychotherapy to avoid accepting responsibility for their own behavior, to suggest they cannot control themselves. The central task of therapy is concerned with positive growth and change, not to analyze or explain behavior antecedents.

THE NECESSITY OF SELF-EVALUATION

Addicted individuals will not change their behavior until they decide for themselves that they experience so much discomfort that it makes sense to enter-

---

Addicted individuals will not change their behavior until they experience so much discomfort that it makes sense to entertain the idea of change.

---

tain the idea of change. Helping alcoholics to conclude "I don't like what I'm doing, I don't like myself" is a prerequisite for progress. For example, the professional can ask "what did you do yesterday?" or "what are you planning to do today?"

If the problem drinker replies, "I stayed up until three A.M. getting drunk, and then I woke up about three P.M.—showered, shaved, did my hair, watched television, then went out and got high." The professional can inquire, "do you like doing that," or, "is it helping you?" Only when the alcoholic concedes a dissatisfaction with the current behavior or the daily routine will there be any incentive to contemplate change.

If alcoholics continue to maintain that they are satisfied with their lifestyle, the therapist, after exhausting this approach, needs to consider terminating the relationship.

162   *Planning Responsible Behavior*

During this phase of treatment, alcoholics are helped to identify how they believe they would like to act. Garner describes this process as based on "a problem-solving rather than a permissive or coercive approach"[87] which focuses attention on how individuals evaluate their behavior and what they wish to do to improve themselves. Erikson suggests that "psychotherapy is sought not primarily for enlightenment about the unchangeable past but because of the dissatisfaction with the present and a desire to better the future."[88]

When alcoholics acknowledge they are satisfied with their current behavior, the therapeutic war ceases. The therapist assumes a consultative role. The therapist may instruct the client specifically how to behave to ensure maximum probability of success and minimize failure. A plan for responsible behavior is developed by the two of them. The psychotherapist should encourage the problem drinker to conceptualize his or her ideas in the form of a written contract which specifies goals and rates.

A written plan for change serves as a reference point for judging improvement. This can be useful for purposes of external evaluation. Parlour, Cole and Van Vorst have discovered that progress is quicker when problems are defined on paper, and methods for solving them are written out.[89] Thomas and Ezell suggest that a written contract can be divided into sections and progress can be reviewed after each has been completed.[90] This enables the alcohol-addicted individual to experience frequent progress and success.

Goals are defined in behavioral terms and are deliberately limited in scope. For example, the alcoholic may be encouraged to take one less drink a day rather than become abstinent immediately. Alcoholics Anonymous apparently understand the reinforcing value of limited goals when the idea of attempting to abstain from drinking for 24 hours at a time, rather than forever, was introduced more than 40 years ago. Glasser suggests that goals should be attained easily. Persons who have failed frequently need to experience success. As they succeed, goals can be made progressively more ambitious and demanding.

Making and Keeping a Commitment

Once a plan has been determined jointly, the therapist exacts a commitment from the client to abide by it.

WHAT IT MEANS TO THE CLIENT

During the commitment phase persons in psychotherapy no longer have as many self-destructive impulses. They are learning to anticipate potential consequences and payoffs of their behavior. They are learning they can become responsible—that through self-discipline they can make thinking decisions even when they do not feel like it. They see that they can control their behavior, which implies a capacity to transcend what they have done previously, and can discard their failure identities. They can understand that while external events and conditions cannot be controlled, any person can control his or her responses to them. They become aware that they possess elements of freedom of choice as well as the capacity to grow and develop.

THE THERAPIST AS RESPONSIBLE PARENT

This type of relearning involves a most profound restructuring of outlook for alcoholics in treatment. It is not surprising that during this process much support is needed and demanded from the therapist, who in effect assumes the role of responsible parent. For example, there

---

It is perfectly appropriate for the therapist to go to great lengths to reverse mistrust, even to the extent of allowing the recovering alcoholic to form a temporary symbiotic attachment to the therapist.

---

may be a need for frequent, even daily, telephone contact between treatment sessions in order to prevent relapses. Alcoholism is not a chemical problem but a people problem. Alcoholics are people who have lost the ability to trust and depend on others. It is perfectly appropriate for the therapist to go to great lengths to reverse this mistrust, even to the extent of allowing the recovering alcoholic to form a *temporary* symbiotic attachment to the therapist.

FAMILY SABOTAGE

The therapist can regulate his or her involvement and serve as both a significant other and a responsible role model. What is more difficult to control is the

behavior of the alcoholic's family. When the alcoholic is drinking destructively the family is most supportive of the therapist. However, when the individual becomes abstinent, responsible, and autonomous the family begins to sabotage this progress.[91-93]

The anger of the spouse or parents of the substance abuser remains submerged while the person is in his or her lunatic phase. Only *after* the self-destructive behavior has been terminated, after the alcoholic gets a job and/or begins to do well in school, does family anger surface. In the case of adolescent alcoholics, the family may forget to remind the alcoholic of appointments with the therapist or may deliberately set up conflicting commitments. The therapist may need to schedule an appointment at an inconvenient time—even if it means holding sessions at midnight—until the family understands that they will not be able to destroy the treatment alliance. The psychotherapist refuses to enter into a conspiracy to sabotage growth and development.

Accepting No Excuses

The concern of the psychotherapist can be demonstrated by refusing to accept any excuses when goals are not attained and by maintaining high expectations for improved behavioral performance. Dynamically, the high expectations of the therapist differ from parental pressure because there is neither a possessive demand nor any reflection on the therapist personally if goals are not completed.

164   By not accepting excuses, the therapist reinforces the reality of his or her commitment to and belief that the individual can succeed. Not accepting excuses is an extremely important way of communicating. "I think enough of you to believe you can do well and to expect you to do so." The alcoholic may scream "You expect too much, you expect too much." The response of the committed therapist is "No, you can do it, I believe you can do it. When are you going to start believing in yourself?!!" The therapist who accepts excuses unwittingly reinforces a powerful means of perpetuating the failure identity. They can tell themselves that they were right after all, they cannot succeed. That not even their therapist thinks enough of them to demand that they measure up—so why should they?

Having the therapist expect and demand the best of them is an incentive to persons in psychotherapy to do their best. Frank, who has studied the psychotherapeutic process, notes that the therapist's positive expectations can be a catalyst which stimulates action on the part of the client.[94] Glasser believes that adolescents grow and develop when they have teachers and therapists who will continue to insist that commitments be made and fulfilled.[95]

When clients succeed and fulfill commitments and goals, praise by the therapist stimulates and reinforces their continued progress and growth. The therapist needs to consider the impact of accepting and acknowledging gratitude and therefore responsibility, for the client's progress. For if the psychotherapist allows him- or herself to be responsi-

Therapists must be wary of the extent to which they accept thanks, and therefore responsibility, for the client's progress. For if they allow themselves to be responsible for client successes, they must also be responsible for client failures.

ble for client successes, he or she must also be responsible for client failures. The reformed alcoholic in all probability will seethe inwardly with resentment. Clearly, it is more therapeutic to disavow much influence and stress the fact that the individual deserves the credit because he or she made the investment and succeeded. The psychotherapist does the recovering individual a disservice by competing against him or her for the "glory." The psychotherapist can acknowledge a sense of gratification when the recovering individual succeeds but should avoid feeling "proud of." The difference between rejoicing with and having a personal investment in is precisely the distinction between parent–child and therapist–individual.

Giving No Punishment

If a commitment is not consummated, additional discussion and planning are necessary. Perhaps the contract will need to be renegotiated. Punishment, however, serves to reinforce the notion of failure and is countertherapeutic. Fox, Graham and Gill, who utilize a psychiatric model to treat outpatient alcoholics, describe their patient population as having rigid and punitive superegos. Alcoholics suffer from a sense of guilt and shame, and of a need to place themselves in self-defeating positions so they can be punished.

> Exhortations, threats, and predictions of dire consequences are seldom effective and often prove counterproductive in the formation of a therapeutic alliance. At some level, every alcoholic realizes that alcohol is running his life; he need not be told this but rather helped to acknowledge it.[96]

The concept of no punishment is important for alcoholics. But it can be difficult to implement, because alcoholics infuriate and frustrate—the therapist may be tempted frequently to point the finger at a client and say "Get out of here, you no longer are a candidate for psychotherapy or whatever we're doing together."

WHAT IS PUNISHMENT?

The definition and conceptualization of punishment, indeed, is difficult because conditions and circumstances vary. Perhaps the most important cue is to examine the motives which govern the action. If, for example, the psychotherapist feels angry or frustrated with the individual whom he or she is trying to help and is motivated by these feelings generally the outcome is a form of punishment. Punishment is noxious. The psychotherapist needs to examine his or her reaction to the outcome. Obviously when the psychotherapist feels "good, they deserve what they got," then it is punishment.

NO PUNISHMENT VERSUS NO INTERVENTIONS

Glasser supports a no-punishment position and suggests that the therapist should not interfere with the consequences of clients' behavior.[97] This strategy is not appropriate with substance abusers, whose impulsive and unregulated behavior can culminate with overdose, incarceration, suicide or homicide. The therapist working with such persons wants to be in a position to affect outcomes to avoid irrevocable disaster, to break the bottle, take away the gun—whatever is necessary. Alcoholics Anonymous disapproves of such interventions. Admittedly, breaking the bottle may be insignificant because the alcoholic may have hidden several more in other locations.

The symbolic act of breaking the bottle dramatically demonstrates the psychotherapist's concern and antidrinking bias. While the alcoholic is locating another bottle, he or she may have the opportunity to think about taking one more drink and about the future consequences of such action. One of the critical tasks of therapy with alcoholics is to help them understand the correlation between actions and consequences, to teach them to make the connection. This kind of understanding is important to living successfully and happily, which are the ultimate goals of psychotherapy.

TREATING ALCOHOLICS: IS IT WORTH IT TO THE THERAPIST?

The Difficulties

Working with alcohol-addicted individuals presents many problems for the psychotherapist who seeks to help them to help themselves. A survey by Glasscote et al. showed that more than 90 percent of the responding psychiatrists considered alcoholics "harder to treat" than other

166 patients.[98] Robinson and Podnos found 45 out of 46 psychiatrists and psychiatric residents reporting negative reactions to working with alcoholics.[99] Schulberg, who surveyed the attitudes of psychiatrists in private practice in Massachusetts, found that almost 25 percent of them would reject an alcoholic for treatment.[100]

Most psychotherapists have received little or no training for working with alcohol-addicted individuals and do not understand the disease of alcoholism. Alcoholics do not respond to conventional treatment. They are manipulative and dishonest, often refusing to acknowledge they have a drinking problem. Psychotherapists are trained to work through resistance and psychological defenses in their clients, but not to challenge overt deceit. Most therapists do not recognize that distrust rather than trust is the basic adjustment reaction for alcoholics.

The therapist who works with alcoholics needs to recognize that they frequently miss appointments, call at inopportune times, make unreasonable demands, refuse to pay bills, sometimes do not learn from their mistakes and sometimes do not profit from advice. The problem drinker continually experiences crises to which the therapist must respond, often at great personal inconvenience.

The occupational hazards of working with alcoholics and other substance abusers exceed the degree of inconvenience and frustration with more traditional people who seek psychotherapy. The therapist can feel overwhelmed at times by the trust, the faith, the dependency and the desperation of substance abusers whom he or she tries to help. Addicted persons are relentlessly ingenious in devising ways to hurt and destroy themselves. The therapist will not always be able to intervene. Some clients will punish themselves again and again and inflict incredible suffering on those who love them. Some will have to be institutionalized. Some will die. When these are the outcomes of their struggle to help, the therapist suffers intense grief and anger. There are times when, confronted with a severe treatment failure, the psychotherapist may question his or her own sanity, wisdom and competence.

Taking Personal Inventory

The most crucial step to recovery for members of AA is the fourth—i.e., to take their "personal inventory"; it is a process that can be equally beneficial to therapists, but it is one they undertake all too rarely. Many feel they have concluded their own treatment and analysis.

Clearly not every psychotherapist should or can work with alcohol-addicted persons. To do so takes an indestructible commitment, concern, caring, faith and resilience. Alcohol counselors need to ask themselves to what extent they are prepared to become involved, to intervene, to risk being hurt and to be inconvenienced—what constitutes their professional and personal limits. They need to be wary of becoming too preoccupied with the awesome responsibilities of their work. They need to be sure they are not indulging in feeling superior to the people they are trying to help. They need to know when to refuel and regenerate, or else they will burn themselves out and become useless to themselves, their families and those they are trying to help.

The Rewards

If the demands and risks of treating alcoholics are high, the rewards are equally so. The confrontations, the constant ups and downs can be a source not only of frustration but of exhilarating challenge and stimulus. The confrontations also force therapists to face up to their own hypocrisies and weaknesses and to grow along with their clients.

Most importantly, by virtue of training, energy and concern, committed professionals working with alcoholics can contribute clearly to the difference between success and failure, between life and death. They can experience the unique satisfaction of knowing they have helped at least some clients reclaim their lives from the liquid chemical oblivion and self-destruction of alcoholism. There can be no finer, no more meaningful reward than helping others actualize their potential and justify their existences to themselves.

REFERENCES

1. Rogers, C. R. "A Therapist's View of the Good Life: The Fully Functioning Person" in Rogers, C. R., ed. *On Becoming a Person: A Therapist's View of Psychotherapy* (Boston: Houghton Mifflin Co. 1961) p. 185.
2. Bratter, T. E. "Treating Alienated, Unmotivated Drug Abusing Adolescents: A Reality Therapy and Confrontation Approach." *American Journal of Psychotherapy* XXVII:4 (October 1973) p. 585–598.
3. Bratter, T. E. "Group Therapy with Affluent, Alienated Adolescent Drug Abusers: A Reality Therapy and Confrontation Approach." *Psychotherapy: Theory, Research and Practice* 9:4 (Winter 1972) p. 308–313.
4. Armor, D. J., Polich, M. J. and Stambul, H. B. *Alcoholism and Treatment* (Washington: Rand Corporation 1973).
5. Bigelow, G. and Cohen, M. "Abstinence or Moderation? Choice by Alcoholics." *Journal of Behavior Research and Therapy* 10:2 (1972) p. 286–289.
6. Schaefer, H. H. "Twelve Month Follow-Up of Behaviorally Trained Ex-Alcoholic Social Drinkers." *Journal of Behavior Therapy* 3:2 (1972) p. 286–289.
7. Pattison, E. M. et al. "Abstinence and Normal Drinking, an Assessment of Changes in Drinking Patterns in Alcoholics after Treatment." *Quarterly Journal of Studies on Alcohol* 28A:3 (1968) p. 610–622.
8. Davies, D. L. "Normal Drinking in Recovered Alcohol Addicts" *Quarterly Journal of Studies on Alcohol* 23 (1962) p. 94.
9. Cooperative Commission on the Study of Alcoholism. *Alcohol Problems: A Report to the Nation* (London, England: Oxford University Press 1967). 1967).
10. Uniform Alcoholism and Intoxication Treatment Act, in *First Special Report to the U.S. Congress on Alcohol and Health* (Washington, D.C.: Government Printing Office 1971).
11. Shearer, R. J., ed. *Manual on Alcoholism* (Chicago: American Medical Association 1968).
12. Fox, R. "A Multidisciplinary Approach to the Treatment of Alcoholism." *Journal of Drug Issues* 2:2 (1972) p. 20.
13. Glasser, W. *Mental Health or Mental Illness?* (New York: Harper & Row, Publishers 1960).
14. Jellinek, E. *The Disease Concept of Alcoholism* (New Haven: Hillhouse Press 1960).
15. Jurjevich, R. M. *The Hoax of Freudism: A Study of Brainwashing the American Professionals and Laymen* (Philadelphia: Dorrance & Co. 1974) p. 468.
16. Salter, A. *The Case Against Psychoanalysis* (New York: Holt 1952).
17. Hartocollis, P. "Some Phenomenological Aspects of the Alcoholic Condition." *Psychiatry* 27:2 (Summer 1964) p. 345.
18. Berne, E. *Games People Play* (New York: Grove Press 1964).

168

19. Glasser, W. *The Identity Society* (New York: Harper & Row Publishers 1972).

20. Glasser, W. *Schools without Failure* (New York: Harper & Row Publishers 1969).

21. Sterne, M. and Pittman, D. "The Concept of Motivation: A Source of Institutional and Professional Blockage in the Treatment of Alcoholism." *Quarterly Journal of Studies on Alcohol* 26 (1965) p. 41.

22. Van Kaam, A. "Addiction and Existence." *Review of Existential Psychology and Psychiatry* 7:1 (1968) p. 54–64.

23. Patterson, C. H. *Theories of Counseling and Psychotherapy* (New York: Harper & Row Publishers 1966) p. 466.

24. Carkhuff, R. B. and Berenson, B. G. *Beyond Counseling and Therapy* (New York: Holt, Rinehart and Winston 1967) p. 77.

25. Freud, S. *The Ego and the Id* (London: Hogarth Press 1947).

26. Maslow, A. H. *Toward a Psychology of Being* (Princeton: Van Nostrand 1962) p. 178.

27. Bratter, T. E. and Hammerschlag, C. A. "Advocate, Activist, Agitator: The Drug Abuse Program Administrator as a Social Revolutionary-Reformer" in Rachin, R. L. and Czajkoski, E., eds. *Drug Abuse Control: Administration and Politics* (Lexington, Mass.: D. C. Heath & Co. 1975) p. 121–145.

28. Horney, K. *Our Inner Conflicts: A Constructive Theory of Neurosis* (New York: W. W. Norton & Co. 1945) p. 241.

29. Glasser. *The Identity Society* p. 103.

30. Koenig, P. "Glasser: The Logician." *Psychology Today* 7:9 (1974) p. 66–67.

31. Glasser, W. and Zunin, L. M. "Reality Therapy" in Corsini, R., ed. Current Psychotherapies (New York: A. I. Peacock 1972) p. 287–315.

32. Eysenck, H. J. "The Effects of Psychotherapy: An Evaluation." *Journal of Consulting Psychology* 16 (1952), p. 319–324.

33. Eysenck, H. J. "Learning Theory and Behavior Therapy" in Eysenck, H. J., ed. *Behaviour Therapy and Neuroses* (New York: Pergamon Press 1960) p. 62.

34. Wolpe, J. *Psychotherapy by Reciprocal Inhibition* (Stanford, Calif.: Stanford University Press 1958).

35. Ford, D. H. and Urban, H. B. *Systems of Psychotherapy: A Comparative Study* (New York: John Wiley and Sons 1963) p. 3.

36. Glasser, W. *Reality Therapy: A New Approach to Psychiatry* (New York: Harper & Row Publishers 1965).

37. Wolfe, T. "The 'ME' Decade and the Third Great Awakening." *New York Magazine* 9:34 (1976) p. 26–40.

38. Malcolm, H. *Generation of Narcissus* (Boston: Little, Brown and Co. 1971) p. 142.

39. Perls, F. "Four Lecturers" in Fagan, J. and Shepherd, I., eds. *Gestalt Therapy Now* (Palo Alto, Calif.: Science and Behavior Books 1970) p. 30.

40. Glasser. *Reality Therapy* p. 32.

41. Glasser, W. *Positive Addictions* (New York: Harper & Row Publishers 1976) p. 3.

42. Glasser. *Reality Therapy* p. 60.

43. Fromm, E. *The Art of Loving* (New York: Harper & Brothers Publishers 1956) p. 24–25.

44. Glasser. *Reality Therapy* p. 21–23.

45. Szasz, T. S. "Medicine and the State; The First Amendment Violated." *The Humanist* 33:2 (1973) p. 7.

46. Ibid.

47. Bratter, T. E. "Responsible Therapeutic Eros: The Psychotherapist Who Cares Enough to Define and Enforce Behavior Limits with Potentially Suicidal Adolescents." *The Counseling Psychologist* 5:4 (1975a) p. 97–104.

48. Samorajczyk, J. "The Psychotherapist as a Meaningful Parent Figure with Alienated Adolescents." *American Journal of Psychotherapy* XXXV:1 (January 1971) p. 115.

49. Alcoholics Anonymous. *Twelve Steps and Twelve Traditions* (New York: Alcoholics Anonymous World Services 1952).

50. Alcoholics Anonymous. *Alcoholics Anonymous* (New York: Alcoholics Anonymous World Services 1939).

51. McElroen, L. J., Falhco, G. J., "Reality Therapy and Alcoholics Anonymous: A Comparison of Two Approaches to Behavior Change." *Corrective and Social Psychiatry* 23:3 (October 1977) p. 79–82.

52. Bernstein, A. "The Fear of Compassion" in Wolman, B., ed. *Success and Failure in Psychoanalysis and Psychotherapy* (New York: MacMillan 1972).

53. Glasser. *Reality Therapy.*

54. Glasser. *The Identity Society* p. 109.

55. Rogers, C. R. "Characteristics of a Helping Relationship." *Personnel and Guidance* 37:1 (1958) p. 13.

56. Bratter, T. E. "Responsible Therapeutic Eros: Setting Limits with Self-Destructive Adolescents Who Abuse Drugs." *The Addiction Therapist* 1:4 (1976) p. 69–78.

57. Briar, S. "The Current Crisis in Social Casework" in *Social Work Practice* (New York: Columbia University Press 1967) p. 28.

58. Stone, B. J. "The Rehabilitation Counselor as a Client Advocate." *Journal of Applied Rehabilitation Counseling* 2:1 (1971) p. 46–54.

59. Coward, R. A. and Elman, R. M. "Advocacy in the Ghetto." *Transaction* 4 (1966) p. 27–35.

60. Grosser, C. V. "Community Development Programs for Serving the Urban Poor." *Social Work* 10:3 (1965) p. 17.

61. Bratter, T. E. "The Psychotherapist as Advocate: Extending the Therapeutic Alliance with Adolescents." *Journal of Contemporary Psychotherapy* 8:2 (1977) p. 119–126.

62. Triana, R. R. and Hinkle, L. M. "Psychoanalytically Oriented Therapy for Alcoholic Patients." *Social Casework* (May 1964) p. 285–291.

63. Thimann, J. *The Addictive Drinker* (New York: Philosophical Library 1966) p. 42.

64. Shea, J. "Psychoanalytic Therapy in Alcoholism." *Quarterly Journal of Studies on Alcohol* 15:3 (Summer 1954), p. 595.

65. Tiebout, H. "Intervention in Psychotherapy." *The American Journal of Psychoanalysis* 22:1 (1962) p. 5.

66. Canter, F. M. "The Future of Psychotherapy with Alcoholics" in Frederick, C. J., ed. *The Future of Psychotherapy* (Boston: Little, Brown and Co. 1969) p. 280.

67. Cleckley, H. "Psychopathic States" in Arieti, S., ed. *American Handbook of Psychiatry* (New York: Basic Books 1959) p. 567–588.

68. Cleckley, H. *Mask of Sanity* (St. Louis: The C. V. Mosby Co. 1941).

69. Raubolt, R. R. and Bratter, T. E. "Games Addicts Play: Implications for Group Treatment." *Corrective and Social Psychiatry* 20:4 (1974) p. 7.

70. Bratter, T. E. "Group Therapy With Affluent, Alienated Adolescent Drug Abusers: A Reality Therapy and Confrontation Approach." *Psychotherapy: Theory, Research and Practice* 9:4 (1972) p. 308–313.

71. Wise, L. "Alienation of Present-Day Adolescents." *Journal of the American Academy of Child Psychiatry* 9:2 (1970) p. 265.

72. Paredes, A. "Denial, Deceptive Maneuvers, and Consistency in the Behavior of Alcoholics" in Sexias, F., ed. *The Person with Alcoholism* (New York: Harper & Row Publishers 1966) p. 466.

73. Mann, M. *New Primer on Alcoholism* (New York: Rinehart & Co. 1959).

74. Burnett, M. M. "Toward a Model for Counseling Alcoholics." *Journal of Contemporary Psychotherapy* 8:2 (1977) p. 129.

75. Curlee, J. "Attitudes that Facilitate or Hinder the Treatment of Alcoholism." *Psychotherapy: Theory, Research and Practice* 8:1 (1971) p. 69.

76. Hurvitz, N. "Peer Self-Help Psychotherapy Groups and Their Implications for Psychotherapy." *Psychotherapy: Theory, Research and Practice* 7:2 (1970) p. 44.

77. Glasser. *The Identity Society* p. 109.

78. Glasser. *The Identity Society* p. 107–132.

79. Rachin, R. L. "Helping People to Help Themselves" in Bassin, A., Bratter, T. E. and Rachin, R. L., eds. *The Reality Therapy Reader* (New York: Harper & Row Publishers 1976) p. 313–325.

80. Bratter, T. E. "Helping Those Who Do Not Want to Help Themselves: A Reality Therapy and Confrontation Orientation." *Corrective and Social Psychiatry* 20:4 (October 1974) p. 1–8.

81. Bratter, T. E., "Reality Therapy: A Group Psychotherapeutic Approach with Adolescent Alcoholics." *Annals of the New York Academy of Sciences* 233 (April 15, 1974) p. 104–114.

82. Glasser, *The Identity Society* p. 108.

83. Bratter, T. E. "Confrontation Groups: The Therapeutic Community's Gift to Psychotherapy" in Vamos, P. and Devlin, J., eds. *Proceedings of the First World Conference on Therapeutic Communities* (Montreal: Portage Press 1976) p. 164–174.

84. Bratter, T. E. "Confrontation: A Group Psychotherapeutic Orientation with Heroin Addicts" in Uchtenhagen, A., Battegay, R. and Friedemann, A., eds. *Group Therapy and Social Environment* (Switzerland: Hans Huber 1975) p. 360–367.

85. Bratter. "Treating Alienated, Unmotivated Drug Abusing Adolescents."

86. Carkhuff and Berenson. *Beyond Counseling and Therapy* p. 176.

87. Garner, H. G. *Psychotherapy: Confrontation Problem-Solving Technique* (St. Louis: Warren H. Green, Inc. 1970) p. 4.

88. Erikson, M. H. "Foreword" in Watzlawick, P., Weakland, J. H. and Fisch, R. *Change: Principles of Problem Formation and Problem Resolution* (New York: W. W. Norton & Co. 1974) p. ix.

89. Parlour, R. R., Cole, P. Z., Van Vorst, R. "Treatment Teams and Written Contracts as Tools for Behavior Rehabilitation," *The Discoverer* 4:1 (1967) p. 7.

90. Thomas, P. and Ezell, B. "The Contract as a Counseling Technique." *Personnel and Guidance* 51:1 (1972).

91. Bratter, T. E. "The Methadone Addict and His Disintegrating Family: A Psychotherapeutic Failure." *The Counseling Psychologist* 5:3 (Summer 1975) p. 110–125.

92. Bratter, T. E. "Wealthy Families and Their Drug

170

Abusing Adolescents." *Journal of Family Counseling* 3:1 (Spring 1975) p. 62–76.

93. Bratter, T. E. "Helping Affluent Families Help Their Acting-Out, Alienated, Drug Abusing Adolescent." *Journal of Family Counseling* 2:1 (Spring 1974) p. 22–31.

94. Frank, J. D. "The Role of Hope in Psychotherapy," *International Journal of Psychiatry* 5:5 (1968) p. 383.

95. Glasser. *Schools without Failure* p. 24.

96. Fox, R. P., Graham, M. B. and Gill, M. J. "A Therapeutic Revolving Door," *Archives of General Psychiatry* 26:2 (1972) p. 181.

97. Glasser. *The Identity Society* p. 129.

98. Glasscote, R. M. et al. "The Treatment of Alcoholism" (Joint Information Service of the American Psychiatric Association of National Association for Mental Health 1967) p. 67.

99. Robinson, L. and Podnos, B. "Resistance of Psychiatrists in Treatment of Alcoholism." *Journal of Nervous and Mental Disease* 143 (1966) p. 220–225.

100. Schulberg, H. C. "Private Practice and Community Mental Health." *Hospital and Community Psychiatry* 17 (1966) p. 363–366.

Setting Alcoholic Patients up for Therapeutic Failure

Gary G. Forrest, Ed.D., P.C.
Licensed Clinical Psychologist and
Executive Director
Psychotherapy Associates, P.C., and the
Institute for Addictive Behavioral
Change
Colorado Springs, Colorado

M OST ALCOHOLIC patients entering treatment have assumed the
interpersonal position of victim or scapegoat prior to engagement in therapy.[1]
Counselors who initiate therapeutic relationships with these patients often assume
the rescuer role, consequently establishing a psychonoxious atmosphere and
"setting up" the patient for therapeutic
failure. The psychonoxious atmosphere
may well become an intolerable reality
resulting in suicide for some alcoholic
patients; at best it reinforces continued
intoxication.

Research, as well as clinical evidence,
indicates that alcoholics or problem
drinkers are significantly depressed and
anxious when they begin therapeutic
treatment.[2] This is particularly true with
individuals seen in the public setting—in
community mental health settings, Veterans Administration facilities, state hospital facilities and/or other agencies. For
the most part, patients treated in public
agencies manifest symptomatology of a

172   more diffuse type and to a greater degree than patients seen in private practice. In addition to showing symptomatic drinking behavior, the alcoholic patient seen in public agencies often has marked vocational difficulties, legal involvements, educational handicaps, significant family problems and other potent debilitating factors. This may contribute significantly to their increased depression and anxiety.

[Note: The observations relative to psychonoxious counselor and agency behaviors presented in this article were derived explicitly from direct therapeutic contact and supervision with alcoholics and problem drinkers treated in a military alcoholic rehabilitation facility. The observations may only partially apply to counselors in the private practice setting. Counselors should exercise care in attempting to relate these impressions to other clinical settings.]

COUNSELOR AS RESCUER

How do counselors typically respond to the depressed, frequently overwhelmed individual initially seen in a social agency providing rehabilitation and psychotherapy services for alcoholism or problem drinking? Most counselors respond with humanism and support. They assume the role of "rescuing" the patient.

The inordinate dependency needs of the alcoholic, the tremendous need for attention ("strokes") and the multiplicity of other interpersonal deprivation-oriented needs, which account for the internal and social transactions of the alcoholic patient, help "set up" the counselor for assuming the rescuer role.

Another element which encourages the counselor to assume the rescuer role is the victim role of the patient. The alcoholic patient often enters therapy because he or she is "forced" to do so. Various legal, family or spouse-oriented pressures, pressures often external to the patient, account for perhaps 70 percent of the patients seen in many agencies.[3] In these cases the patient has usually assumed the role of victim or scapegoat. This dynamic directly reinforces counselor rescue behaviors, since the counselor attempts to "save" the patient from the ramifications and behavioral consequences of engagement in the victim role.

Aside from the various patient dynamics, counselor dynamics—a need for omnipotence, narcissistic conflicts,[4] depressive personality characteristics and unresolved feelings of inadequacy—also encourage the counselor to accept the rescuer role.

Dangerous Role

Counselor engagement in the rescuer role may be the first, and fatal, step in the process of setting up alcoholic patients for therapeutic failure. Although the counselor-as-rescuer role often proves comfortable for both counselor and patient initially, the counselor–patient relationship constructed around this dynamic ultimately fails. Alcoholics have an unconscious need to defeat or destroy others, and they often exhibit obsessive-compulsive behavior. The rescuer role proves most exhausting, since alcoholics have an unending need to be rescued. Counselors engaging in the role soon find themselves to be physically tired, "burned out" and generally depressed.[5] This leads to an eventual collapse of the rescue-oriented relationship.

Counselor Rejection

Eventually most counselors become angry with the rescuer role and reject the patient, which in essence fulfills the patient's unconscious need to defeat the counselor. This in turn reinforces the victim role of the patient. The patient's response is typically, "I told you nobody can help me . . . What's the use?"

Patient Regression

What happens at this juncture in the therapeutic relationship? If the patient has thus far been able to remain sober and in other ways show therapeutic gain, he or she may at this point undergo a massive regression, or "go sour," typically including the reengagement of drinking behavior. If the patient has engaged in intermittent drinking episodes and in other ways shown only moderate or minimal gain, the rupture in the therapeutic alliance may in all probability be much less acute, less regressive and traumatic in scope. In any case, rupture validates the patient's feelings of inadequacy and his or her preconscious belief that "nobody cares," that others really do wish him or her to remain in the dysfunctional state or that he or she is not really capable of changing. In short, the patient responds to the rupture as if it were a rationale for remaining intoxicated or emotionally "sick." For the alcoholic patient with marked depression, the rupture often exacerbates the feeling of being overwhelmed and helpless and precipitates a total "giving up," which in turn results in overt suicidal acting-out.

To the chagrin of the treatment staff, depressive psychiatric patients sometimes end their lives upon release from the hospital, when things appear to be on the upswing. Similarly, some alcoholic patients "give up" once they have dried out and are eating and sleeping regularly again. Roughly one-half of patients completing rehabilitation programs return to intoxication and old behaviors and roles shortly after treatment.[6,7] It appears that actual suicide potential is greatest when patients are in the process of emerging from a depressive episode.[8]

Counselors assuming the primary rescuer role, particularly if they are involved in taxing individual and group therapy with more than one alcoholic patient, often respond to the role with anger and "give up" on the patient. In other conscious and preconscious ways they reinforce patient depression and despair. These ineffective and psychonoxious counselor behaviors may then result in counselor burnout and counselor turnover in various alcoholic rehabilitation settings.[9,10]

COUNSELOR AS PERSECUTOR

A role reversal takes place when the patient begins to regress, principally when the patient resumes drinking. It is at this time that counselors may begin to reject the assumed rescuer role and begin to assume the persecutor role.

Patients who "go sour" or act out continually while in an alcoholic rehabilitation program at times cause feelings of resentment on the part of the counselor. The counselor expresses rage and assumes the persecutor role. This process is

174 contingent upon counselor ego strength, training and other variables related directly to therapist behavior and interpersonal skills. Assuming the persecutor role further reinforces the patient's role as victim. Professionals who fall into the persecutor role become the most potent representatives of the alcoholic's interpersonal past which has historically contributed to the addiction process. The counselor persecutor role reinforces patient paranoia, continued intoxication and suicidal ideation and acting out, thus setting the patient up for therapeutic failure.

AGENCY AS RESCUER-PERSECUTOR

Alcoholic rehabilitation agencies may also assume the basic rescuer-persecutor role. As patients become involved in the rehabilitation process, they become well known to the general agency staff. They have significant interactions with personnel and establish an ego-involvement with the facility. This relationship is reciprocal in nature.

Once in the agency, successful patients—those who are able to maintain sobriety and show personality and behavioral growth—receive "strokes" and are otherwise rewarded for their "good behavior" by the agency. The agency assumes the rescuer role. In effect, the "rescue" frequently appears to have worked during the early stages of the therapeutic or rehabilitation process: drinking behavior, violent acting out and other primary symptoms of alcoholism become more controlled if not nonexistent.

However, this relationship deteriorates during the long-term therapeutic management of the vast majority of alcoholic patients. As the ego-involvement and collective identity of the treatment agency become increasingly fused with and dependent upon patient evidence of behavioral gain, the probability of the agency's engagement in the persecutor role correspondingly increases. And, if a particular patient "goes sour," he or she often becomes a threat to the identity of the agency.[5]

A number of patients regressing at the same time can be interpreted as evidence of an agency's inability to successfully treat alcoholic patients. This interpretation may even be extended to mean that the agency is not capable of providing other adequate or worthwhile services. Similar to the counselor's reaction, the agency may respond to such a threat by rejecting or abandoning the alcoholic patient. When this happens, the agency has in essence moved into a persecutor role, and the patient's victim role is validated. The assumption of the persecutor role by both agency and counselor can lead to the failure to rehabilitate or the death of some alcoholic patients.

NEED FOR "HEALTHY" RESCUING

Counselors of alcoholic patients often deny their role in the development and maintenance of a psychonoxious atmosphere and its influence on therapeutic failures. They often rationalize by saying, "the patient resisted," "the patient was not ready," "the patient had not hit bottom yet" or "there really was no reason for the patient to sober up." Because of frustration, which is often the result of not knowing what to do next, and because of other more psychodynamically oriented reasons, the staff may at this point recommend hospitalization or incarceration of the patient. While such decisions may be practically based and possibly represent the option of choice, the decisions are frequently accompanied by counselor guilt, feelings of therapeutic impotence and similar negative-affective behavior components.

Paradoxically, some form of rescuing is indicated for a significant proportion of patients during the initial stage of treatment in an alcoholic rehabilitation agency. Counselor agency concern, support, warmth and similar "helping behaviors" are both appropriate for and facilitative to alcoholic patients. They are essential to helping extinguish the marked depression and anxiety with which the patient is struggling. Detoxification is one form of medically oriented intervention that represents appropriate rescuing. Two other appropriate behaviors are interpersonal detachment and extended therapeutic contact.

Interpersonal Detachment

Healthy rescue-oriented intervention includes a significant degree of interpersonal detachment on the part of the counselor/agency. It is imperative that the counselor/agency continually reinforce patient decision making, responsibility and independence—behaviors which in effect act to extinguish the inordinate dependency needs of the alco-

holic patient. The verbal messages, "you must sober up for your own benefit" and "you are responsible for your own behaviors," are essential. The counselor/agency must also consistently reinforce concrete patient behaviors that reflect the patient's acceptance of responsibility for his or her own actions, and confront the patient with those behaviors that do not reflect this acceptance of responsibility, i.e., drinking while in treatment. Patient behaviors that are related to legal involvements while in treatment or other negative cause-and-effect situations relative to drinking behavior should be talked about and openly discussed immediately within the therapeutic context. Emphasizing to the patient that legal consequences, marital separations and job reprimands are often the direct result of intoxication can be central to healthy rescue-oriented intervention.

Extended Therapeutic Contact

Another crucial element is extended therapeutic contact. Detoxification, short-term counseling or psychotherapy and Antabuse maintenance programs are ineffective over the long haul for the vast majority of alcohol-addicted patients. Therapy, preferably group therapy, must encompass at least six to eight months of weekly contact with the patient to establish a basis for continued sobriety, significant behavioral change and growth of a more generalized nature. Counselors engaging in pathological rescue behaviors simply are not capable of maintaining this type of extended therapeutic relationship.

176   AVOIDING THE PITFALL

Counselors and agencies that respond to alcoholic patients with "overdoses" of rescue-oriented behavior set the stage for eventual therapeutic failure. By being aware of the potential dangers, counselors and agencies can more effectively avoid these dangers and lead the alcoholic patient toward successful rehabilitation.

REFERENCES

1. Forrest, G. G. "Alcoholism, Object Relations and Narcissistic Theory." Lecture presented at Psychotherapy Associates, P. C. Fifth Annual Treatment and Rehabilitation of the Alcoholic Workshop, Colorado Springs, Colorado, January 29, 1979.
2. Forrest, G. G. *The Diagnosis and Treatment of Alcoholism* (Springfield, Illinois: Charles C Thomas 1978).
3. Ibid.
4. Forrest. "Alcoholism, Object Relations and Narcissistic Theory."
5. Knauert, A. P. "Methods for Maintaining the Sanity of Addiction Counselors and Therapists." Lecture presented at Psychotherapy Associates, P.C. Fifth Annual Treatment and Rehabilitation of the Alcoholic Workshop, Colorado Springs, Colorado, January 31, 1979.
6. Forrest. *The Diagnosis and Treatment of Alcoholism.*
7. Forrest, G. G. "Psychotherapy with the Alcoholic Patient." Workshop, Denver, Colorado, June 2, 1979.
8. Forrest. *The Diagnosis and Treatment of Alcoholism.*
9. Ibid.
10. Knauert. "Methods for Maintaining the Sanity of Addiction Counselors and Therapists."

Maintaining the Sanity
of Alcoholism Counselors

Arthur P. Knauert, M.D.
Board Certified Psychiatrist
Private Practice
New York, New York
Medical Director of Transitional
  Services and Alcoholism Services
Guidance Clinic
Catholic Welfare Bureau
Trenton, New Jersey

Sharon V. Davidson, R.N., M.Ed.
President
Continuing Professional Education and
  Nursing Review Programs, Inc.
Ob-Gyn Unit Coordinator
Memorial Hospital
Colorado Springs, Colorado

MAINTAINING the sanity of the alcoholism counselor is a serious concern. It is important to understand what an immense task it is to deal with alcoholism. The latest estimates indicate that in the United States alone there are at least nine million alcoholics, and many of these are still drinking. With so many clients, counselors often feel like they are standing knee deep in the ocean with a bucket, dipping it in the ocean and throwing water out to sea only to be inundated by the next breaker.

Overcoming alcoholism is a very difficult task. It is also a very complex one, for alcoholics are of almost all ages, occupations and personality types and certainly of all known psychiatric diseases as well.[2] Consequently, people who come into the alcoholism professionals' offices are members of the largest, most diverse and complicated group treated by professionals in the field of mental health.

178

THE DEMAND OF THE PROFESSIONAL

Certain criteria are necessary to successfully treat alcoholics. Professionals must be creative and intelligent, possess tremendous internal energy and be very caring. Professionals who are not caring, but who have become counselors to "punish" alcoholics or to retaliate for previous personal traumas (such as being raised by alcoholic parents) will experience serious difficulty in treating alcoholics and should seek other employment.

With such an overwhelming population of clients who have such complex problems, the professional can be quickly and easily drained of emotional resources. Alcoholics can be extremely demanding of caring and constantly test the counselor. They may try to prove that the counselor does not care and is not consistent. Primary alcoholics possess a character trait, or attitude, which makes them believe that it is not possible to be cared for and nurtured in a consistent manner. (See "The Differential Diagnosis of Alcoholism," this issue.) They try to prove that they are right by testing the counselor's limits, which can be extremely frustrating for the counselor. If the counselor does not prepare for such a maneuver beforehand, failure to rehabilitate the patient is inevitable.

For an alcoholic, alcohol is usually the single most important thing in life. It is a combination of mother, lover, best friend, spouse. The counselor who attempts to come between the alcoholic and alcohol poses a paramount threat to the alcoholic's perceived source of love. As a result, the alcoholic resists with every ounce of strength the counselor's attempts to help him or her stop drinking. The only way counselors can successfully rehabilitate the patient is to counteract with equal strength.

Stresses from dealing with alcoholics sometimes result in professionals developing the "burnout" syndrome. This syndrome occurs when a counselor enters alcoholic patient rehabilitation enthusiastically, but in a relatively short period of time feels hopeless, and becomes depressed and frustrated—even angry—and retreats. Counselors can, and must, counteract the stresses and prevent their own burnout. They have their own needs and lives, and must maintain themselves or lose the caring energy necessary for treating patients.

THE NEED FOR REGENERATION

Maintaining self can be thought of in terms of regenerating emotional resources. Without regeneration counselors eventually crumble. The particular strain caused by counseling alcoholics makes it absolutely necessary for professionals to "get away from it all" periodically. Engaging in recreational activities such as skiing is fun and helps regenerate counselors. Attending conferences that

---

Without regeneration of emotional resources, counselors eventually crumble. The particular strain caused by counseling alcoholics makes it absolutely necessary for professionals to "get away from it all" periodically.

---

educate while providing reasonable and legitimate excuses for getting away also helps regenerate.

Counseling alcoholics is too important a task to lose people who truly care. Concerned counselors must be careful that their concern does not consume them and that their lives provide sources for renewing inner strength. Professionals on call 24 hours a day, seven days a week for years at a time are in great danger of "burning out" and having their personal lives suffer considerably as a result. Counselors are experts at designing lifestyles for rehabilitated alcoholics, but the same counselors do not think often enough about their own lifestyles—lifestyles that should sustain, nurture and regenerate them.

Counselors lacking fulfillment in their private lives are unable to realize their own potential in helping others. This is especially evident to the alcoholic client who is clever, sensitive and mentally attuned to those things that show the counselor to be inconsistent. Alcoholic clients often strive to protect their relationships with alcohol, and use any sign of inconsistency to prove the counselor incapable of providing consistent care and nurturance, therefore justifying continuance of the relationship with the substance.

AVOIDING BURNOUT

Paradoxically, the very characteristics necessary to be good counselors can cause counselors to burnout. The more caring and involved the professionals are, the less likely they are to think about themselves. To avoid burnout, professionals have to know when to stop getting involved; they have to know when they have given enough.

OBTAINING NURTURING

Professionals who treat alcoholics recognize that these clients need people who can be trusted and relied upon for nurturing. Alcoholics Anonymous (AA) and other alcoholic treatment programs provide such nurturing individuals. Who sees to the same needs of counselors? Trusting, nurturing, dependable colleagues are necessary for preventing burnout of counselors.

Through Working Conditions

Professionals must strive to prevent burnout under many types of working conditions. The best work situation for the alcohol counselor is a program with a large staff; the worst is a one-person practice. The more counselors in a program, the better professionals can fill in for one another and offer each other support and fresh perspective.

Colleague support is extremely important. It would be a grave mistake for counselors to use clients for regenerating. Instead they should depend on other staff members and peers. Counselor regeneration occurs when staff members socialize with each other. Such socializing can release tensions and engender good feelings.

Alcoholic treatment programs may encourage counselor regeneration in a number of ways. Staff meetings, specifically organized for professionals to get together and talk about feelings or problems in the program, may be a highly

180   effective tool for developing counselor cohesiveness. For example, a few years ago, a military alcoholic treatment center held such a meeting in a cabin high in the mountains in which the author observed the following: that subsurface rivalries were revealed among the counselors on several levels—north versus south, enlisted versus officer, men versus women, black versus white. By sharing their thoughts, group members were able to exorcise some of the biases they brought to the meeting and emerge with a more caring and nurturing attitude toward one another. This should in turn enable them to more successfully treat their alcoholic clients.

Via Other Means

Counselors isolated from a caring, nurturing staff could attend AA for help in regeneration. Alcoholics Anonymous is available to professionals whether they are alcoholics or not.

Counselors who need but do not have an AA program readily available to them should explore other areas of help. What kind of nurturing people are there in their lives? Who are they? Rather than trying to help themselves, can these counselors find the caring they need in religious affiliations, in friends or associates with similar interests or in their own family circles?

DEFINING ROLES AND EXPECTATIONS

Another important element in preventing counselor burnout is the awareness of

Professionals should think of themselves as providers of "psychic bandaids." The professional offers a nurturing environment, but it is up to the client to do the healing.

exactly what the counselor's role is in treatment. Professionals do not cure or save anybody, and those who think they do may have problems treating clients. Professionals should think of themselves as providers of "psychic bandaids." The bandaid offers protection while the body heals. In treating the alcoholic, the professional offers a nurturing environment, but it is up to the client to do the healing. Even when counselors do their best their clients may not succeed.

ACCEPTING LIMITATIONS: A CASE STUDY

Recognizing limitations in treating alcoholics helps prevent counselor burnout. Consider the case of Mr. B, an alcoholic in a treatment program. Mr. B had been in counseling for three years yet he was getting drunk every day. The counselor reported that although the client had discussed all sorts of things, such as masturbatory fantasies, early childhood experiences, bad relationships in school and his criminal record, in his three years of treatment he had frequently missed appointments, manipulated the counselor into helping him obtain various kinds of social assistance and made no progress with his drinking problem. The counselor, whom Mr. B made very uncomfortable, was actually glad when the patient failed to show up. The counselor was in over his head. Although unsuccessful in establishing the client's sobriety, the counselor continued to attempt "therapy" but was chronically frustrated, and the patient did not improve.

A short talk with Mr. B confirmed that an ultimatum of some kind would be necessary if Mr. B (who professed to enjoy the counseling) was to be allowed to remain in the program. Offered the choice to continue the counseling if he gave up getting drunk every day, Mr. B *decided that drinking was more important* and ended treatment. Mr. B was told that he could return to treatment, but only when he was willing to stop drinking.

It is very important for clients to know that the door to treatment is always open. But when clients first enter treatment, counselors must establish the conditions of treatment from the outset, and insist that clients abide by them.

OBTAINING THERAPY

When counselors do all they can to avoid burnout—get out once in a while for renewal, recreate, obtain nurturing, surround themselves with caring people, recognize treatment program involvement and limitations—and still burnout, they need therapy. The best programs provide opportunities for counselor therapy by the counselor's supervisor or other treatment professionals.

Program administrators are responsible for determining counselor qualifications and for monitoring which counselors are burning out, identifying them before it happens and instituting remedies. Administrators may have to compel people to take advantage of training opportunities, conferences or trips and establish staff groups to avoid losing valuable, caring workers. Counselors who are not appropriate for treating alcoholics should be encouraged to find jobs in other fields.

All counselors should be supervised. Good supervisors can monitor counselor needs and confront counselors if they overreact or become too involved in treatment. As humans, counselors can develop emotional and psychiatric disorders. Supervisors can help recognize and treat these disorders. Many recovering or recovered alcoholics and drug or pill abusers work in the counseling field. Supervisors can also recognize these people and can help them deal with the stresses of counseling.

Providing Adequate Training

The possibility of burnout increases if counselors are not trained adequately to cope with a variety of alcoholic patients. A counselor who is a recovered alcoholic with only a high school education, for example, may have great difficulty counseling a drinking schizophrenic, and may experience the frustration that often leads to burnout.

In-house training and training in conferences are important deterrents to

182 burnout. Counselors who constantly increase knowledge and sharpen their skills become more effective and therefore more comfortable with their work.

Alcoholism counselors can only try to do their best. By recognizing their limitations and being aware of their own needs, counselors will be able to avoid burnout and will benefit more alcoholic patients.

REFERENCES

1. Hall, L. C. *Facts about Alcohol and Alcoholism* (Rockville, Md.: National Institute on Alcohol Abuse and Alcoholism 1976) p. 5.

2. Knauert, A. "The Treatment of Alcoholism in a Community Setting." *Family and Community Health* 2:1 (May 1979) p. 91–102.

Perspectives in Clinical Research: Relative Effectiveness of Alcohol Abuse Treatment

Chad D. Emrick, Ph.D.
Psychologist
Alcohol Treatment Program
Veterans Administration Medical
  Center
Denver, Colorado

THIS ARTICLE addresses the issue of whether alcohol abusers increase their chances of improving to any extent by having one treatment rather than another. Randomized controlled trials reported in the English treatment evaluation literature from 1952 to 1978 (Emrick, 1974, 1975) are analyzed. Only randomized controlled trials are considered because if any evidence exists for the relative effectiveness of different treatment approaches, it can best be found in these studies. They yield interpretable data on treatment effects inasmuch as they control a powerful determinant of outcome, viz., patient-characterizing variables. Any observed differences can probably be attributed to divergent approaches as applied by the therapeutic agents involved.

This article was prepared for HEW's Alcohol Program and Policy Review Project at the request of the Secretary of HEW, Joseph Califano, under the direction of Dr. Gerald Klerman and Ms. Laura Miller.

184   PROCEDURE

Ninety studies were reviewed which randomly assigned patients to two or more treatments. Included among these investigations were those which used a crossover technique to evaluate drug treatments (Carlsson & Fasth, 1976; Ditman, Mooney, & Cohen, 1964; Gelder & Edwards, 1968). Also included were projects that used sequential groups for whom the order of presentation of two types of experimental interventions was counterbalanced (Alterman, Gottheil, Skoloda, & Grasberger, 1974; Alterman, Gottheil, Skoloda, & Thornton, 1977; Gallen, Williams, Cleveland, O'Connell, & Sands, 1973; Levinson & Sereny, 1969; Reed, Van Lewen, & Williams, 1972; Scherer & Freedberg, 1976). This body of research was screened for all outcome differences significant at the .05 level or better, using two-tailed tests. Two-tailed tests were used since the operating hypothesis of this analysis was that no treatment outcome differences would be observed. In studies where just some groups were randomly assigned, only the results for these groups were considered (Bowen, Soskin, & Chotlos, 1970; Charnoff, 1967; Charnoff, Kissin, & Reed, 1963; Clancy, Vanderhoof, & Campbell, 1967; Ditman & Crawford, 1966; Ditman, Crawford, Forgy, Moskowitz, & MacAndrew, 1967; Ends & Page, 1959; Gerrein, Rosenberg, & Manohar, 1973; Hallam, Rachman, & Falkowski, 1972; Kissin & Charnoff, 1965; Kissin, Charnoff, & Rosenblatt, 1968; Kissin & Gross, 1968; Kissin, Platz, & Su, 1970, 1971; Kissin, Rosenblatt, & Machover, 1968; Lanyon, Primo, Terrell, & Wener,

1972; McCance & McCance, 1969; Miller, in press; Schaefer, Sobell, & Mills, 1971; Schaefer, Sobell, & Sobell, 1972; Storm & Cutler, 1968; Tomsovic & Edwards, 1970; Vogler, Lunde, Johnson, & Martin, 1970; Wedel, 1965). Some studies were excluded because allocation of patients to groups was not clearly random (Caddy & Lovibond, 1976; Ends & Page, 1957; Whyte & O'Brien, 1974); randomization was admittedly broken for all groups involved (Passini, Watson, Dehnel, Herder, & Watkins, 1977) or patients were found to be similar or comparable on certain characteristics rather than being randomly allocated (Baekeland & Kissin, 1973; Baekeland, Lundwall, Kissin, & Shanahan, 1971; Blake, 1965, 1966, 1967; Ends & Page, 1957; Hoff, 1967; Lal, 1969; Miller, Hersen, Eisler, & Hemphill, 1973; Robson, Paulus, & Clarke, 1965; Soskin, 1970; Van Dusen, Wilson, Miners, & Hook, 1967).

When specific results and the methods used to obtain them were reported, the former were checked wherever possible for accuracy, the latter for appropriateness. Computational errors were found in two reports (Lanyon et al., 1972; Reed et al., 1972). In several other cases inappropriate methods were detected such as not using Fisher's exact method for computing p values when the data required it (Swinson, 1971; Gallant, Faulkner, Stoy, Bishop, & Langdon, 1968) and applying Yates' correction when the data did not (Kurland, Savage, Pahnke, Grof, & Olsson, 1971; Pahnke, Kurland, Unger, Savage, & Grof, 1970). In three cases (Ashem & Donner, 1968; Kurland et al., 1971; McClelland, 1977; Pahnke et al.,

1970) a one-tailed test was performed. In these studies the significance level was redetermined using a two-tailed test. In another project (Lovibond & Caddy, 1970, 1971) early dropouts were not properly excluded from the calculation of outcome rates, and in still another (Swinson, 1971) a single patient was inappropriately excluded from one group before determining rates. Finally, the study of Vogler et al. (1970) was excluded because patients in a nonrandomly assigned group were inappropriately combined with those in a randomly assigned group before comparing the latter with another properly formed group.

Greater weight regarding relative treatment effects is given to those long-term differences found more than six months after the start of treatment or after the termination of intensive therapy, depending on the evaluation procedure used in a project. This policy was adopted because several studies found significant outcome differences at evaluations covering six months or less, but no such results at later follow-ups (Hollister, Shelton, & Krieger, 1969; Kurland et al., 1971; Laverty, 1966; Ludwig, Levine, & Stark, 1970; Ludwig, Levine, Stark, & Lazar, 1969; Madill, Campbell, Laverty, Sanderson, & Vandewater, 1966; Pahnke et al., 1970). Apparently the initial benefits of one approach are wiped out, ultimately leaving patients having that treatment no better off than other patients. In a previous work Emrick (1975) considered as long-term differences only those found more than six months after termination of *all* treatment by at least 50 percent of patients in all comparison groups. The definition of long-term effects adopted

for this analysis more accurately reflects the reality of treatment. As Edwards, Orford, Egert, Guthrie, Hawker, Hensman, Mitcheson, Oppenheimer, and Taylor (1977, p. 1019) recently stated, "for many patients it would be artificial and against normal clinical practice to suppose that the treatment process is abruptly terminated after a certain number of months, or at the moment of inpatient discharge."

RESULTS AND DISCUSSION

Results of the randomized controlled trials were catalogued according to the following treatment aspects: locus of therapy (inpatient versus outpatient), nature of admission (compulsory versus voluntary), therapy involvement techniques, amount of nonbehavioral treatment, traditional outpatient psychotherapy, drugs, nonbehavioral and nondrug interventions in inpatient treatment, and behavioral approaches. Within each category (except therapy involvement techniques) the findings were further catalogued according to those showing (1) no differences between interventions, (2) short-term differences (i.e., covering six months or less after the start of treatment or termination of intensive therapy) and (3) long-term differential effects (i.e., covering more than six months after the start of treatment or termination of intensive therapy).

Locus of Treatment (Inpatient versus Outpatient)

No Differences. One month of coerced inpatient treatment followed by five months of coerced outpatient treatment

186 resulted in no differences on a variety of outcome dimensions when compared with six months of coerced outpatient treatment (Gallant, 1971). In this study of chronic municipal court offenders, an advantage not reflected in outcome was noticed for inpatient treatment in the form of medical attention that was given the 44 percent of inpatients who were found to have serious physical problems.

Short-Term Differences. Two weeks of intensive inpatient treatment followed by outpatient group therapy was found to be more effective with respect to drinking and nondrinking indices 90 to 100 days after intake than was at least three in-community treatment sessions followed by outpatient group therapy (Wanberg, Horn, & Fairchild, 1974). The patients treated in this project were a moderately socially intact group, with 51 percent of the evaluated patients being married.

Long-Term Differences. An average of 7.7 weeks of "intensive care" on an outpatient basis followed by outpatient aftercare was found to be more effective with regard to global ratings over 12 months following intensive treatment than was an average of 8.9 weeks of inpatient treatment followed by outpatient aftercare (Edwards, 1970; Edwards & Guthrie, 1966, 1967). Eighty percent of the outpatients were married and 70 percent were middle class and above. Sixty percent of the inpatients were married and 75 percent were middle class and above.

Discussion. For socially deteriorated alcoholics, one month of inpatient treatment was no different from outpatient treatment with respect to post-treatment functioning. Yet inpatient treatment does appear to result in such alcoholics receiving better medical attention. For more socially integrated alcohol abusers, evidence regarding the relative effectiveness of inpatient versus outpatient treatment is inconsistent. While results of the Wanberg et al. (1974) and Edwards (1970), Edwards and Guthrie (1966, 1967) studies appear to be contradictory, it should be observed that the length of both intensive treatment and evaluation differed considerably for the two projects, being several times longer in the latter study. The effects found by Wanberg et al. (1974) were only short term. Perhaps with longer evaluation they would have washed out or even reversed direction. Consistent with this point, the differences found between experimental groups in the Edwards (1970) and Edwards and Guthrie (1966, 1967) studies did not begin to emerge until five months after intensive treatment, and they did not reach statistical significance until the second six months of evaluation. At present, little is known about the relative effectiveness of inpatient versus outpatient therapy for alcohol abusers.

Nature of Admission (Compulsory versus Voluntary)

No Differences. No differential therapy effects were found comparing (1) compulsory outpatient "group therapy" alone, "group therapy" plus disulfiram, or disulfiram alone versus voluntary outpatient therapy (Gallant, Bishop, Faulkner, Simpson, Cooper, Lathrop, Brisolara, & Bossetta, 1968) and (2) compulsory outpatient "psychiatrically oriented" clinic treatment or Alcoholics Anonymous versus no treatment (Ditman & Crawford, 1966; Ditman et al., 1967). In both of these projects patients were chronic municipal court offenders. Failure to comply with compulsory treatment resulted in legal consequences of $25 fine or a maximum of five days in jail (Ditman & Crawford, 1966; Ditman et al., 1967) or a minimum 60-day jail sentence (Gallant, Bishop, Faulkner, Simpson, Cooper, Lathrop, Brisolara, & Bossetta, 1968).

Short-Term Differences. One month of coerced inpatient treatment followed by five months of coerced outpatient therapy was found to be more effective with respect to drinking and nondrinking variables six months after intake than was six months of voluntary outpatient treatment (Gallant, 1971). In this study of chronic municipal court offenders, improvement rates following six months of coerced outpatient treatment fell between the other two groups. Failure to follow through with involuntary treatment resulted in a 90-day jail sentence.

Long-Term Differences. A minimum of six months of coerced outpatient therapy was observed to be more effective with respect to drinking and nondrinking variables one year after intake than was six months of voluntary outpatient treatment (Gallant, Faulkner et al., 1968). The patients in this experiment were state penitentiary parolees who faced a return to prison for many months or years if they were coerced into treatment and failed to comply.

Discussion. Compulsory outpatient treatment for chronic municipal court offenders has not been found to be more effective than voluntary outpatient therapy or no treatment. The lack of positive findings appears to be due, in part, to inadequate strength of the negative consequences for failure to comply with treatment (Gallant, Faulkner et al., 1968). A combination of enforced inpatient treatment followed by outpatient work may, on the other hand, be more effective than voluntary outpatient care. This may be a function, at least partially, of the medical attention given the municipal court offender during the inpatient stay. The 44 percent of the municipal court offenders who were inpatients in the Gallant (1971) project were found to have serious physical problems for which they were treated.

For state prison parolees who faced a severe penalty for not complying with treatment, compulsory outpatient treatment was shown to be more effective than voluntary outpatient therapy.

Therapy Involvement Techniques

Several randomized controlled trials of alcoholism treatment found differential effects with regard to involving patients in therapy. The findings are summarized here in order to identify those involvement methods which are most successful. While the findings do not indicate whether or not patients receive any benefit from the greater amount of therapy received as a function of these methods, knowledge of the most successful approaches might prove useful in our efforts to "hook" patients into the best of treatments.

188   The relatively effective involvement techniques were found to be (1) audiotape feedback of outpatient group counseling sessions versus the same feedback but of individual sessions (Davis, 1972); (2) no videotape playback of drinking sessions while in inpatient treatment versus five and 30 minutes of playback (Schaefer et al., 1971, 1972); (3) contingent shocking of drinking behavior while in outpatient treatment versus noncontingent shocking (Lovibond & Caddy, 1970, 1971); (4) contingent shocking of drinking behavior while in inpatient treatment versus noncontingent shocking or no shocking while attached to electrical aversion equipment (Vogler et al., 1970); (5) special assistance from a social worker during two to four weeks of outpatient evaluation versus no special assistance (Wedel, 1965); (6) compulsory outpatient treatment for state penitentiary parolees versus voluntary treatment (Gallant, Faulkner et al., 1968); (7) taped relaxation therapy while in inpatient treatment versus no relaxation treatment (Reed et al., 1972); (8) disulfiram as an adjunct to inpatient milieu treatment versus milieu therapy only (Wallerstein, 1957); (9) twice a week outpatient treatment including disulfiram versus once a week treatment with or without disulfiram or twice a week treatment without disulfiram (Gerrein et al., 1973); (10) chlordiazepoxide versus placebo or vitamins (Rosenberg, 1974); (11) chlordiazepoxide versus diazepam (Ditman et al., 1964) and (12) a combination of meprobamate and promazine hydrochloride versus placebo (Charnoff et al.,

1963; Kissin, Charnoff et al., 1968, Kissin & Gross, 1968).

Discussion. These data suggest that alcohol abusers can be helped to become involved in treatment by (1) reducing anxiety, through such means as tranquilizers and relaxation training, (2) giving extra help in the form of frequent meetings, special assistance by a care giver or group counseling and (3) following an avoidance paradigm using such interventions as disulfiram and compulsory treatment with severe consequences for failure to cooperate with therapy. Alcoholics, on the other hand, can be driven away from treatment by employing such aversive techniques as noncontingent or sham electrical aversive conditioning and videotape playback of drunken comportment without counseling. Techniques such as those revealed here should be used to get alcoholics into the most effective interventions. Those procedures that drive patients away from therapy should be avoided.

Amount of Nonbehavioral Treatment

No Differences. No differential effects were observed on drinking and nondrinking measures comparing (1) at three months after admission, a mean of 9.31 days of inpatient detoxification versus a mean of 30.45 inpatient days including detoxification (Newton & Stein, 1973; Stein, Newton, & Bowman, 1975), (2) at two years after inpatient discharge, 20 days of inpatient treatment followed by two years of outpatient psychotherapy versus 82 days of inpatient treatment followed by two years of outpatient treatment (Willems, Letemendia, & Arroyave, 1973a, 1973b), (3) at six months after inpatient discharge, nine days of inpatient treatment versus 30 days of inpatient treatment (Mosher, Davis, Mulligan, & Iber, 1975), (4) at a median of 13.2 months after inpatient discharge, three to seven days of inpatient detoxification versus three to six weeks of inpatient treatment, including detoxification, plus aftercare (Boggs, 1967), (5) at two months after intake, "intensive" inpatient social therapy versus "routine" inpatient treatment (Waters, Cochrane, & Collins, 1972), (6) at one year after discharge, six weeks of "regular psychiatrically oriented" inpatient treatment versus six weeks of inpatient treatment during which all formal aspects of the program were discontinued (Levinson & Sereny, 1969), (7) at more than two years after termination of therapy, a mean of ten outpatient disulfiram treatment sessions versus a mean of 32 sessions which included group psychotherapy in addition to disulfiram (Bruun, 1963), (8) at one year after intake, (a) an initial assessment and counseling session; a mean of 5.2 days of inpatient treatment and 4.7 hours of contact with a social worker and no contact with a psychiatrist versus (b) an initial assessment plus counseling session plus a mean of 23.9 inpatient days, a mean of 18.3 hours of contact with a social worker and a mean of 9.7 outpatient visits with a psychiatrist (Edwards et al., 1977), and (9) at an average of 20 months after intake, outpatient treatment versus outpatient treatment plus special assistance from a social worker during two to four weeks of evaluation (Wedel, 1965).

Patient groups were varied across the studies. For example, more than four-fifths of the alcoholics in one project were Class IV or V on Hollingshead's Index of Social Position (Newton & Stein, 1973; Stein et al., 1975) whereas less than one-quarter of the patients in another project were of the same lower class levels (Willems et al., 1973a, 1973b). Also, 100 percent of alcohol abusers in one investigation were married (Edwards et al., 1977) compared to only 24.3 percent in another project (Boggs, 1967).

Short-Term Differences. Outcome at six months after intake for patients who had an average of 10.9 outpatient visits plus monthly face-to-face evaluation interviews surpassed outcome for patients who had either an average of 5.9 outpatient visits plus a telephone or mail contact upon failure to continue with treatment or a mean of 4.8 visits plus no further contact other than six months after intake (Harris & Walter, 1976). The group receiving the longer treatment plus more intensive evaluation of progress had fewer days when more than "six standard drinks" were consumed, fewer residential moves and less time spent in jail or a hospital. No differences were observed for arrests, "general satisfaction with life situations," and total abstinence from alcohol. The alcohol abusers in this study were, as a group, fairly socially disintegrated. Of the 65 patients, only 29.2 percent were employed and 32.3 percent were married.

Long-Term Differences. One year after inpatient discharge, alcohol abusers given 20 days of inpatient treatment differed on a global rating of adjustment from those treated for 82 inpatient days, but the nature of the difference does not clearly suggest that one treatment was more effective than the other (Willems et al., 1973a, 1973b). Furthermore, as reported above, no intergroup differences were observed two years after discharge.

At a median of 12.9 months after inpatient discharge, two differences were observed comparing seven to ten days of inpatient treatment versus three to six weeks of inpatient therapy followed by aftercare (Pittman & Tate, 1969, 1972). More of the patients who received the longer term treatment were socially stable (i.e., had held a job for three years or more, lived either in own home or that of relative or friends, and were married and living with spouse) and more had moved during the year. No differences were found with respect to such indices as drinking behavior, being arrested, having a place to stay and health. The patients in this study were fairly socially disintegrated. Only 23 percent were married and at least 50 percent had a pretreatment history of legal arrests.

Discussion. The evidence with respect to amount of nonbehavioral inpatient treatment strongly suggests that outcome is not improved by extending therapy beyond several days (i.e., two to three weeks). Only three differences were found between groups receiving variable amounts of inpatient treatment, and the nature of two of the three does not clearly reflect superiority of one approach over

the other. The one meaningful finding, viz., greater social stability for the more heavily treated group in the Pittman and Tate (1969, 1972) study, seems on first blush to support the value of longer inpatient treatment plus aftercare for fairly socially disintegrated alcoholics. However Boggs (1967) found no differences in favor of an identical amount of treatment (versus detoxification only) for an apparently similar sample of alcohol abusers. A clear implication of these findings is that *our limited human and financial resources should be spent on no more than very brief nonbehavioral inpatient treatment (under three weeks), at least when applied indiscriminately to alcoholic patients.* Some patients may benefit from a longer nonbehavioral inpatient experience, but until or unless these types are identified through research efforts, inpatient programs should offer only brief treatment.

With respect to amount of nonbehavioral outpatient treatment, the evidence again supports very brief intervention. Only one study found a relationship between amount of treatment and outcome (Harris & Walter, 1976) and this relationship was confounded with the variable of amount of evaluation. Patients who had the most treatment were the only ones who received monthly face-to-face evaluation interviews, plus less frequent checks of blood alcohol levels and telephone interviews with collaterals. Within the context of other data on the amount of outpatient treatment, the Harris and Walter (1976) finding seems to support the value of intense follow-up work rather than of greater amounts of outpatient treatment. In any event an implication of the data as a whole is that, as with inpatient treatment, *our limited human and financial resources should be spent on no more than very brief nonbehavioral outpatient treatment (under three months) at least when it is applied indiscriminately to alcohol abusers.* Until or unless research efforts identify those patients who can benefit from longer term nonbehavioral outpatient therapy, ongoing programs should offer only brief treatment.

Traditional Outpatient Psychotherapy

No Differences. No treatment effects were observed comparing (1) "psychotherapy" versus hypnosis (Jacobson & Silfverskiold, 1973), (2) compulsory "group therapy" alone versus "group therapy" plus disulfiram versus disulfiram alone (Gallant, Bishop, Faulkner et al., 1968), (3) compulsory "psychiatrically oriented" clinic treatment versus Alcoholics Anonymous (Ditman & Crawford, 1966; Ditman et al., 1967), (4) "psychotherapy" plus "pharmacologic therapy" versus "pharmacologic therapy" alone (Kissin et al., 1970, 1971; Kissin, Rosenblatt et al., 1968), (5) "insight therapy" versus systematic desensitization or covert sensitization (Piorkowski & Mann, 1975), and (6) "individual counselling and psychotherapy" versus systematic desensitization (Storm & Cutler, 1968).

Short-Term Differences—none.

Long-Term Differences—none.

Discussion. At present, no evidence exists which suggests that traditional outpatient psychotherapy is more or less effective than comparison outpatient interventions.

Drugs

Antidipsotropics. With one exception, no meaningful beneficial effects were observed for disulfiram, metronidazole, apomorphine, or citrated calcium cyanamide. Wilson, Davidson and White (1976) reported that patients who received a disulfiram implant were more often abstinent for the 90 days preceding follow-up than those given a sham operation.

Hallucinogens. Many short-term beneficial effects were observed following lysergide treatment, but they tended to disappear by six months or more after intensive treatment (Hollister et al., 1969; Johnson, 1969, 1970; Kurland et al., 1971; Ludwig et al., 1969, 1970; Pahnke et al., 1970). The only observed long-term effect, favoring LSD over being denied an LSD experience or being given a placebo (Tomsovic & Edwards, 1970), appears to have been a function of the control subjects responding negatively to the disappointment of being in the control rather than experimental group (Emrick, 1975).

Psychotropics. Many short-term positive effects were observed for a variety of psychotropic drugs (i.e., diazepam, LA-I, propranolol, benzoctamine, amitriptyline hydrochloride, mesoridazine, chlordiazepoxide, hydroxyzine, nialamide), yet the importance of these findings is questionable since no differences were noted for such relevant variables as drinking behav-

192 ior and work, family and social adjustment. Only one long-term difference was reported. Reynolds, Merry, and Coppen (1977) found that over a mean of about 40 weeks after the start of treatment, depressed alcoholics who were given lithium functioned better in their drinking behavior than those treated with placebo.

Discussion. Only two drug treatments were shown to have long-term effectiveness relative to comparison interventions: lithium (versus placebo) for depressed alcoholics and disulfiram implant (versus sham implant). Further controlled experimentation with these promising drug treatments seems to be advisable.

Nonbehavioral and Nondrug Interventions in Inpatient Treatment

No Differences. No between-treatment differences were found in experiments of Power Motivation Training (Cutter, Boyatzis, & Clancy, 1977; McClelland, 1977), individual psychotherapy (Newton & Stein, 1973, 1974), group hypnotherapy (Wallerstein, 1957) and individual hypnosis when combined with lysergide (Edwards, 1966).

Short-Term Differences. Group therapy (Ends & Page, 1959; McGinnis, 1963), as well as hypnosis combined with lysergide (Ludwig et al., 1969, 1970), resulted in demonstrable short-term benefits. However the relative effectiveness of hypnosis plus lysergide was found to have washed out at follow-up more than three months after inpatient discharge, and the group therapy effects were limited to psychological functioning.

Long-Term Differences—none.

Discussion. The addition of nonbehavioral and nondrug interventions to ongoing inpatient programs appears to be of little value, at least insofar as their application to heterogeneous groups of patients is concerned.

Behavioral Approaches

No Differences. Several behavioral interventions have failed to produce meaningful beneficial effects relative to other approaches: Systematic desensitization (Hedberg & Campbell, 1974; Piorkowski & Mann, 1975; Storm & Cutler, 1968), covert sensitization (Ashem & Donner, 1968; Hedberg & Campbell, 1974; Piorkowski & Mann, 1975), emetic aversion (Wallerstein, 1957) and implosive therapy (Newton & Stein, 1973, 1974).

Short-Term Differences. Benefits of limited scope and duration have been demonstrated for relaxation therapy (Reed et al., 1972), assertion training (Hirsch, von Rosenberg, Phelan, & Dudley, 1978), aversion by apneic paralysis (Laverty, 1966; Madill et al., 1966), and electrical aversion (Hallam et al., 1972). However, for aversion by apneic paralysis (Clancy et al., 1967) and for electrical aversion (Marlatt, 1973; McCance & McCance, 1969) other research has failed to find even short-term benefits relative to comparison approaches.

Though evaluated in studies using only short-term follow-up, additional behavioral treatments which show relative effectiveness seem more significant because of the apparent robustness of their effects. In one project Miller (1975) placed Skid Row alcoholics on a contingency management program in which the receipt of goods and services was contingent upon maintaining a blood alcohol concentration of 10 mg/100 ml of blood volume or less. At two months follow-up, subjects on the program had been arrested less and employed more than those not on any program. Unfortunately no further follow-up was conducted because the investigator moved from the area. Alterman et al. (1974, 1977) studied the effects of giving patients a chance to drink alcohol during the middle four weeks of a six-week inpatient program. Patients who were urged to refuse the alcohol were less often intoxicated during six months after discharge than were those who were urged to drink. Faillace, Flamer, Imber, and Ward (1972) evaluated the relative effectiveness of having patients drink on a fixed schedule while in an inpatient program. Those alcohol abusers who were given the experience of regulated drinking versus those who were not, had better residential adjustment and better overall adjustment six months after inpatient discharge. In two projects (Azrin, 1976; Hunt & Azrin, 1973), a community reinforcement procedure was studied. The major objective was to help alcoholics develop social, family, work and recreational satisfactions which interfere with drinking. Six months after hospital discharge, patients receiving this treatment, both while in the hospital and during aftercare, functioned better than did those who received the "standard hospital treatment." Better outcome was found for amount of drinking, time employed, time spent at home and time institutionalized. Unfortunately only the experimental group was followed up beyond six months with the result that no data exist on the long-term relative effectiveness of this approach. Taken alone it appears to produce durable benefits. In the second project (Azrin, 1976), the community reinforcement group was found to have abstained from drinking at least 90 percent of the time for two years after inpatient discharge.

Long-Term Differences. Two projects found long-term differences which appear to have been a function of one treatment being particularly unsuccessful, rather than of one having unusually beneficial effects (Emrick, 1975). One of these studies (Hedberg & Campbell, 1974) found results favoring both behavioral family counseling and systematic desensitization over electrical aversion. The other (Vogler et al., 1970) showed favorable results for contingent shocking in aversive conditioning versus sham conditioning and noncontingent shocking.

Three other studies reported differences which more clearly pinpoint relatively successful treatments. Inpatient treatment (skill-training) designed to teach patients nondrinking responses to situations which elicited drinking in the past was found to be more effective than either a general discussion group of how to respond to such situations or "regular" inpatient treatment (Chaney, 1976). At 12 months after intensive therapy, the skill-training patients (compared to the other groups) had had less alcohol, shorter drinking relapses and fewer days of alcohol-induced incapacitation. Vogler, Compton, and Weissbach (1975) and

194 Vogler, Weissbach, and Compton (1977), in other studies of inpatient behavioral treatment, found an intergroup difference at 12 months' follow-up. Patients treated with videotape self-confrontation of drunken behavior, discrimination training for blood alcohol concentration, aversion training for overconsumption, discriminated avoidance practice, alcohol education, alternatives training, and behavioral counseling drank less during follow-up than those who received just the last three techniques. Finally, Sobell and Sobell (1972, 1973a, 1973b, 1976) and Caddy, Addington, and Perkins (1978) reported a favorable difference in inpatient behavioral treatment versus the regular inpatient program. In the third year of follow-up after inpatient discharge it was found that patients trained to regulate drinking behavior with controlled drinking as the goal had functioned well for longer periods, had a lower percentage of drunk days, had better vocational status, had more success combining three outcome indices and better scores on a general index of outcome than those in a nonbehavioral control group. Behaviorally treated patients with abstinence as the goal of treatment also had better vocational status and occupational status than those in a nonbehavioral control group.

Discussion. Several behavioral approaches have been demonstrated to have long-term beneficial effects and others show promise of having durable relative effectiveness. A remarkable aspect of these interventions is that at least some of them appear to help alcohol abusers more by reducing problem drinking than by stopping drinking altogether. Patients who receive these treatments seem to be as likely to return to some drinking as do those who receive comparison approaches, but the nature of the drinking creates fewer problems with resultant improvement in other areas of functioning. More research should be conducted toward refinement of these behavioral treatments which help alcohol abusers reduce drinking and related problems.

CONCLUDING COMMENTS

The most salient findings of this review appear to be twofold: (1) the effectiveness of nonbehavioral treatments is not increased by giving more than very brief care when such therapy is applied to heterogeneous groups of alcohol abusers and (2) some behavioral approaches have been found to be relatively effective in reducing problem drinking.

Further research using recent advances in treatment evaluation methodology (Harris & Walter, 1976; Sobell, L. C., 1978) should be directed toward (1) refinement of those behavioral methods which have been found to be effective in reducing drinking problems and (2) further identification of optimal patient–treatment interactions (see, e.g., Smart, 1978).

In line with this second endeavor, efforts have been made toward discovering *general* prognostic indicators among patient characteristics, but this work has been disappointing (see, e.g., Gibbs & Flanagan, 1977).

Attempts to isolate patient characteristics which are *specific* indicators may be more fruitful. The potential productiveness of this approach is exemplified by findings from a post-hoc analysis of data in the Edwards et al. (1977) study (Orford, Oppenheimer, & Edwards, 1976). For patients taken as a whole in this project, no differences were observed between those who received minimal treatment and those who got considerably more. By itself this finding suggests that treatment should be kept to a minimum. However Orford et al. (1976) found that Gamma alcoholics responded well to the greater amount of treatment but were not helped by minimal therapy (69 percent were rated as having "good" outcome versus 0 percent respectively). Non-Gamma alcoholics, on the other hand, responded better to minimal amounts of treatment (46 percent with "good" outcome versus 29 percent). Thus more than minimal treatment of the sort investigated in this study appears to be helpful to some types of alcohol abusers and may

be unhelpful, and perhaps even harmful, to other types. If substantiated by prospective research, findings such as this can give treatment personnel guidelines for delivering individualized, and therefore potentially more effective, treatment.

Just as with nonbehavioral approaches, behavioral interventions may actually harm some patients and help others. Further research is needed, for example, to identify those patients who can benefit from treatment designed to teach controlled drinking behavior and those who might be harmed by having this type of treatment (see Sobell, M. B., 1978).

An impressive array of controlled experimentation has been done in the alcoholism field toward finding the most effective treatment approaches. It is hoped that future research will continue to advance our knowledge of those methods which have the best chance of helping each individual alcohol abuser.

REFERENCES

Alterman, A. I., Gottheil, E., Skoloda, T. E., & Grasberger, J. C. Social modification of drinking by alcoholics. *Quarterly Journal of Studies on Alcohol*, 1974, *35*, 917–924.

Alterman, A. I., Gottheil, E., Skoloda, T. E., & Thornton, C. C. Consequences of social modification of drinking behavior. *Quarterly Journal of Studies on Alcohol*, 1977, *38*, 1032–1035.

Ashem, B., & Donner, L. Covert sensitization with alcoholics: A controlled replication. *Behaviour Research and Therapy*, 1968, *6*, 7–12.

Azrin, N. H. Improvements in the community-reinforcement approach to alcoholism. *Behaviour Research and Therapy*, 1976, *14*, 339–348.

Baekeland, F., & Kissin, B. The clinical use of disulfiram in the treatment of chronic alcoholism. In M. E. Chafetz (Ed.), *Proceedings of the 1st annual alcoholism conference of the National Institute on Alcohol*

Abuse and Alcoholism: Research on alcoholism: Clinical problems and special populations, Washington, D. C., June 25–26, 1971. Rockville, Md.: National Institute on Alcohol Abuse and Alcoholism, 1973.

Baekeland, F., Lundwall, L., Kissin, B., & Shanahan, T. Correlates of outcome in disulfiram treatment of alcoholism. *Journal of Nervous and Mental Disease*, 1971, *153*, 1–9.

Bartholomew, A. A. An assessment of the therapeutic efficacy of "Trepidone". *Medical Journal of Australia*, 1963, *50*, 150–151.

Blake, B. G. The application of behaviour therapy to the treatment of alcoholism. *Behaviour Research and Therapy*, 1965, *3*, 75–85.

Blake, B. G. Alcoholism: Special techniques of therapy. *Discovery*, 1966, *27*, 44–47.

Blake, B. G. A follow-up of alcoholics treated by behav-

196

iour therapy. *Behaviour Research and Therapy*, 1967, *5*, 89–94.

Boggs, S. L. Measures of treatment outcome for alcoholics: A model of analysis. In D. J. Pittman (Ed.), *Alcoholism*. New York: Harper & Row, 1967.

Bowen, W. T., Soskin, R. A., & Chotlos, J. W. Lysergic acid diethylamide as a variable in the hospital treatment of alcoholism: A follow-up study. *Journal of Nervous and Mental Disease*, 1970, *150*, 111–118.

Bruun, K. Outcome of different types of treatment of alcoholics. *Quarterly Journal of Studies on Alcohol*, 1963, *24*, 280–288.

Caddy, G. R., Addington, H. J., Jr., & Perkins, D. Individualized behavior therapy for alcoholics: A third year independent double-blind follow-up. *Behaviour Research and Therapy*, 1978, *16*, 345–362.

Caddy, G. R., & Lovibond, S. H. Self-regulation and discriminated aversive conditioning in the modification of alcoholics' drinking behavior. *Behavior Therapy*, 1976 *7*, 223–230.

Carlsson, C., & Fasth, B. - G. A comparison of the effects of propranolol and diazepam in alcoholics. *British Journal of Addiction*, 1976, *71*, 321–326.

Chaney, E. F. Skill training with alcoholics. Unpublished doctoral dissertation, University of Washington, 1976.

Charnoff, S. M. Long-term treatment of alcoholism with amitriptyline and emylcamate: A double-blind evaluation. *Quarterly Journal of Studies on Alcohol*, 1967, *28*, 289–294.

Charnoff, S. M., Kissin, B., & Reed, J. I. An evaluation of various psychotherapeutic agents in the long term treatment of chronic alcoholism: Results of a double blind study. *American Journal of the Medical Sciences*, 1963, *246*, 172–179.

Clancy, J., Vanderhoof, E., & Campbell, P. Evaluation of an aversive technique as a treatment for alcoholism: Controlled trial with succinylcholine-induced apnea. *Quarterly Journal of Studies on Alcohol*, 1967, *28*, 476–485.

Costello, R. M. Alcoholism treatment and evaluation: In search of methods. *International Journal of the Addictions*, 1975, *10*, 251–275.

Cutter, H. S. G., Boyatzis, R. E., & Clancy, D. D. Effectiveness of power motivation training in rehabilitating alcoholics. *Journal of Studies on Alcohol*, 1977, *38*, 131–141.

Davis, M. A self-confrontation technique in alcoholism treatment. *Quarterly Journal of Studies on Alcohol*, 1972, *33*, 191–192.

Denson, R., & Sydiaha, D. A controlled study of LSD treatment in alcoholism and neurosis. *British Journal of Psychiatry*, 1970, *116*, 443–445.

Devenyi, P., & Sereny, G. Aversion treatment with electroconditioning for alcoholism. *British Journal of Addiction*, 1970, *65*, 289–292.

Ditman, K. S., & Crawford, G. G. The use of court probation in the management of the alcohol addict. *American Journal of Psychiatry*, 1966, *122*, 757–762.

Ditman, K. S., Crawford, G. G., Forgy, E. W., Moskowitz, H., & MacAndrew, C. A controlled experiment on the use of court probation for drunk arrests. *American Journal of Psychiatry*, 1967, *124*, 160–163.

Ditman, K. S., Mooney, H. B., & Cohen, S. New drugs in the treatment of alcoholism. In P. B. Bradley, F. Flugel, & P. H. Hoch (Eds.), *Neuropsychopharmacology*, Vol. 3. New York: Elsevier, 1964.

Edwards, G. Hypnosis in treatment of alcohol addiction: Controlled trial, with analysis of factors affecting outcome. *Quarterly Journal of Studies on Alcohol*, 1966, *27*, 221–241.

Edwards, G. Alcoholism: The analysis of treatment. In R. E. Popham (Ed.), *Alcohol and alcoholism*. Toronto: University of Toronto Press, 1970.

Edwards, G., & Guthrie, S. A comparison of inpatient and outpatient treatment of alcohol dependence. *Lancet*, 1966, *1*, 467–468.

Edwards, G., & Guthrie, S. A controlled trial of inpatient and outpatient treatment of alcohol dependency. *Lancet*, 1967, *1*, 555–559.

Edwards, G., Orford, J., Egert, S., Guthrie, S., Hawker, A., Hensman, C., Mitcheson, M., Oppenheimer, E., & Taylor, C. Alcoholism: A controlled trial of "treatment" and "advice." *Quarterly Journal of Studies on Alcohol*, 1977, *38*, 1004–1031.

Egan, W. P., & Goetz, R. Effect of metronidazole on drinking by alcoholics. *Quarterly Journal of Studies on Alcohol*, 1968, *29*, 899–902.

Emrick, C. D. A review of psychologically oriented treatment of alcoholism. I. The use and interrelationships of outcome criteria and drinking behavior following treatment. *Quarterly Journal of Studies on Alcohol*, 1974, *35*, 523–549.

Emrick, C. D. A review of psychologically oriented treatment of alcoholism. II. The relative effectiveness of different treatment approaches and the effectiveness of treatment versus no treatment. *Quarterly Journal of Studies on Alcohol*, 1975, *36*, 88–108.

Ends, E. J., & Page, C. W. A study of three types of group psychotherapy with hospitalized male inebriates. *Quarterly Journal of Studies on Alcohol*, 1957, *18*, 263–277.

Ends, E. J., & Page, C. W. Group psychotherapy and concomitant psychological change. *Psychological Monographs*, 1959, *73*, (10 whole No. 480).

Faillace, L. A., Flamer, R. N., Imber, S. D., & Ward, R.

F. Giving alcohol to alcoholics: An evaluation. *Quarterly Journal of Studies on Alcohol*, 1972, *33*, 85–90.

Gallant, D. M. Evaluation of compulsory treatment of the alcoholic municipal court offender. In N. K. Mello & J. H. Mendelson (Eds.), *Recent advances in studies of alcoholism: An interdisciplinary symposium, Washington, D. C., June 25–27, 1970*. Rockville, Md.: National Institute on Alcohol Abuse and Alcoholism, 1971.

Gallant, D. M., Bishop, M. P., Camp, E., & Tisdale, C. A six-month controlled evaluation of metronidazole (Flagyl) in chronic alcoholic patients. *Current Therapeutic Research*, 1968, *10*, 82–87.

Gallant, D. M., Bishop, M. P., Faulkner, M. A., Simpson, L., Cooper, A., Lathrop, D., Brisolara, A. M., & Bossetta, J. R. A comparative evaluation of compulsory (group therapy and/or Antabuse) and voluntary treatment of the chronic alcoholic municipal court offender. *Psychosomatics*, 1968, *9*, 306–310.

Gallant, D. M., Faulkner, M., Stoy, B., Bishop, M. P., & Langdon, D. Enforced clinic treatment of paroled criminal alcoholics: A pilot evaluation. *Quarterly Journal of Studies on Alcohol*, 1968, *29*, 77–83.

Gallant, D. M., Swanson, W. C., & Guerrero - Figueroa, R. A controlled evaluation of propranolol in chronic alcoholic patients presenting the symptomatology of anxiety and tension. *Journal of Clinical Pharmacology*, 1973, *13*, 41–43.

Gallen, M., Williams, B., Cleveland, S. E., O'Connell, W. E., & Sands, P. M. A short term follow-up of two contrasting alcoholic treatment programs: A preliminary report. *Newsletter for Research in Psychology*, 1973, *15*, 36–37.

Gelder, M. G., & Edwards, G. Metronidazole in the treatment of alcohol addiction: A controlled trial. *British Journal of Psychiatry*, 1968, *114*, 473–475.

Gerrein, J. R., Rosenberg, C. M., & Manohar, V. Disulfiram maintenance in outpatient treatment of alcoholism. *Archives of General Psychiatry*, 1973, *28*, 798–802.

Gibbs, L., & Flanagan, J. Prognostic indicators of alcoholism treatment outcome. *International Journal of the Addictions*, 1977, *12*, 1097–1147.

Gillmer, R. E. Benzoctamine and oxazepam in the management of alcohol withdrawal states: Comparison by double-blind trial. *South African Medical Journal*, 1973, *47*, 2267–2268.

Haden, H. H. Experiences with a tranquilizing agent in the treatment of chronic alcoholism. *Psychosomatics*, 1961, *2*, 279–282.

Hallam, R., Rachman, S., & Falkowski, W. Subjective, attitudinal and physiological effects of electrical aversion therapy. *Behaviour Research and Therapy*, 1972, *10*, 1–13.

Harris, R. N., & Walter, J. Outcome, reliability and validity issues of alcoholism follow-up. Paper presented at the meeting of the Alcohol and Drug Problems Association of North America, New Orleans, September 1976.

Hedberg, A. G., & Campbell, L. A comparison of four behavioral treatments of alcoholism. *Journal of Behavior Therapy and Experimental Psychiatry*, 1974, *5*, 251–256.

Hirsch, S. M., von Rosenberg, R., Phelan, C., & Dudley, H. K., Jr. Effectiveness of assertiveness training with alcoholics. *Quarterly Journal of Studies on Alcohol*, 1978, *39*, 89–97.

Hoff, E. C. Pharmacologic and metabolic adjuncts. In R. J. Cantanzaro (Ed.), *Alcoholism: The total treatment approach*. Springfield, Ill.: Charles C Thomas, 1967.

Hoffer, A. A program for the treatment of alcoholism: LSD, malvaria, and nicotinic acid. In H. A. Abramson (Ed.), *The use of LSD in psychotherapy and alcoholism*. New York: Bobbs-Merrill, 1967.

Hollister, L. E., Shelton, J., & Krieger, G. A controlled comparison of lysergic acid diethylamide (LSD) and dextroamphetamine in alcoholics. *American Journal of Psychiatry*, 1969, *125*, 1352–1357.

Hunt, G. M., & Azrin, N. H. A community-reinforcement approach to alcoholism. *Behaviour Research and Therapy*, 1973, *11*, 91–104.

Jacobson, N. O., & Silfverskiold, N. P. A controlled study of a hypnotic method in the treatment of alcoholism, with evaluation by objective criteria. *British Journal of Addiction*, 1973, *68*, 25–31.

Jensen, S. B., Christoffersen, C. B., & Noerregaard, A. Apomorphine in out-patient treatment of alcohol intoxication and abstinence: A double-blind study. *British Journal of Addiction*, 1977, *72*, 325–330.

Johnson, F. G. LSD in the treatment of alcoholism. *American Journal of Psychiatry*, 1969, *126*, 481–487.

Johnson, F. G. A comparison of short-term treatment effects of intravenous sodium amytal-methedrine and LSD in the alcoholic. *Canadian Psychiatric Association Journal*, 1970, *15*, 493–497.

Kaplan, R., Blume, S., Rosenberg, S., Pitrelli, J., & Turner, W. J. Phenytoin, metronidazole and multivitamins in the treatment of alcoholism. *Quarterly Journal of Studies on Alcohol*, 1972, *33*, 97–104.

Kissin, B., & Charnoff, S. M. Clinical evaluation of tranquilizers and antidepressant drugs in the long term treatment of chronic alcoholism. In B. Kissin (Ed.), *Evaluation of present day treatment modalities in the long term rehabilitation of alcoholics: A clinical symposium, Atlantic City, N. J., September 19, 1965.*

198

Washington, D. C.: North American Association of Alcoholism Programs, 1965.

Kissin, B., Charnoff, S. M., & Rosenblatt, S. M. Drug and placebo responses in chronic alcoholics. *Psychiatric Research Reports*, 1968, *24*, 44–60.

Kissin, B., & Gross, M. M. Drug therapy in alcoholism. *American Journal of Psychiatry*, 1968, *125*, 31–41.

Kissin, B., Platz, A., & Su, W. H. Social and psychological factors in the treatment of chronic alcoholism. *Journal of Psychiatric Research*, 1970, *8*, 13–27.

Kissin, B., Platz, A., & Su, W. H. Selective factors in treatment choice and outcome in alcoholics. In N. K. Mello and J. H. Mendelson (Eds.), *Recent advances in studies of alcoholism: An interdisciplinary symposium, Washington, D. C., June 25–27, 1970*. Rockville, Md.: National Institute on Alcohol Abuse and Alcoholism, 1971.

Kissin, B., Rosenblatt, S. M., & Machover, S. Prognostic factors in alcoholism. *Psychiatric Research Reports*, 1968, *24*, 22–43.

Knott, D. H., & Beard, J. D. A study of drugs in the management of chronic alcoholism. *GP, Kansas City*, 1967, *36*, 118–123.

Kurland, A., Savage, C., Pahnke, W. N., Grof, S., & Olsson, J. E. LSD in the treatment of alcoholics. *Pharmakopsychiatrie-Neuro-Psychopharmakologie*, 1971, *4*, 83–94.

Lader, M. H. Alcohol reactions after single and multiple doses of calcium cyanamide. *Quarterly Journal of Studies on Alcohol*, 1967, *28*, 468–475.

Lal, S. Metronidazole in the treatment of alcoholism: A clinical trial and review of the literature. *Quarterly Journal of Studies on Alcohol*, 1969, *30*, 140–151.

Lanyon, R. I., Primo, R. B., Terrell, F., & Wener, A. An aversion desensitization treatment for alcoholism. *Journal of Consulting and Clinical Psychology*, 1972, *38*, 394–398.

Laverty, S. G. Aversion therapies in the treatment of alcoholism. *Psychosomatic Medicine*, 1966, *28*, 651–666.

Levinson, T., & Sereny, G. An experimental evaluation of "insight therapy" for the chronic alcoholic. *Canadian Psychiatric Association Journal*, 1969, *14*, 143–146.

Lovibond, S. H., & Caddy, G. Discriminated aversive control in the moderation of alcoholics' drinking behavior. *Behavior Therapy*, 1970, *1*, 437–444.

Lovibond, S. H., & Caddy, G. The reduction of alcohol consumption by aversive procedures. In L. G. Kiloh (Ed.), *29th international congress on alcoholism and drug dependence*. Australia: Butterworths, 1971.

Ludwig, A. M., Levine, J., & Stark, L. H. *LSD and alcoholism: A clinical study of treatment efficacy*. Springfield, Ill.: Charles C Thomas, 1970.

Ludwig, A., Levine, J., Stark, L., & Lazar, R. A clinical study of LSD treatment in alcoholism. *American Journal of Psychiatry*, 1969, *126*, 59–69.

Madill, M. F., Campbell, D., Laverty, S. G., Sanderson, R. E., & Vandewater, S. L. Aversion treatment of alcoholics by succinylcholine-induced apneic paralysis: An analysis of early changes in drinking behavior. *Quarterly Journal of Studies on Alcohol*, 1966, *27*, 483–509.

Marlatt, G. A. A comparison of aversive conditioning procedures in the treatment of alcoholism. Paper presented at the meeting of the Western Psychological Association, Anaheim, California, April 1973.

McCance, C., & McCance, P. F. Alcoholism in North-East Scotland: Its treatment and outcome. *British Journal of Psychiatry*, 1969, *115*, 189–198.

McClelland, D. C. The impact of power motivation training on alcoholics. *Quarterly Journal of Studies on Alcohol*, 1977, *38*, 142–144.

McGinnis, C. A. The effect of group-therapy on the ego-strength scale scores of alcoholic patients. *Journal of Clinical Psychology*, 1963, *19*, 346–347.

Miller, P. M. A behavioral intervention program for chronic public drunkenness offenders. *Archives of General Psychiatry*, 1975, *32*, 915–918.

Miller, P. M., Hersen, M., Eisler, R. M., & Hemphill, D. P. Electrical aversion therapy with alcoholics: An analogue study. *Behaviour Research and Therapy*, 1973, *11*, 491–497.

Miller, W. R. Behavioral treatment of problem drinkers: A comparative outcome study of three controlled drinking therapies. *Journal of Consulting and Clinical Psychology*, in press.

Mosher, V., Davis, J., Mulligan, D., & Iber, F. L. Comparison of outcome in a 9-day and 30-day alcoholism treatment program. *Quarterly Journal of Studies on Alcohol*, 1975, *36*, 1277–1281.

Mottin, J. L. Drug-induced attenuation of alcohol consumption: A review and evaluation of claimed, potential or current therapies. *Quarterly Journal of Studies on Alcohol*, 1973, *34*, 444–472.

Newton, J. R., & Stein, L. I. Implosive therapy, duration of hospitalization, and degree of coordination of after-care services with alcoholics. In M. E. Chafetz (Ed.), *Proceedings of the 1st annual alcoholism conference of the National Institute on Alcohol Abuse and Alcoholism: Research on alcoholism: Clinical problems and special populations, Washington, D. C., June 25–26, 1971*. Rockville, Md.: National Institute on Alcohol Abuse and Alcoholism, 1973.

Newton, J. R., & Stein, L. I. Implosive therapy in alcoholism: Comparison with brief psychotherapy. *Quarterly Journal of Studies on Alcohol*, 1974, *35*, 1256–1265.

Orford, J., Oppenheimer, E., & Edwards, G. Abstinence or control: The outcome of excessive drinking two years after consultation. *Behaviour Research and Therapy*, 1976, *14*, 409–418.

Overall, J. E., Brown, D., Williams, J. D., & Neill, L. T. Drug treatment of anxiety and depression in detoxified alcoholic patients. *Archives of General Psychiatry*, 1973, *29*, 218–221.

Pahnke, W. N., Kurland, A. A., Unger, S., Savage, C., & Grof, S. The experimental use of psychedelic (LSD) psychotherapy. *Journal of the American Medical Association*, 1970, *212*, 1856–1863.

Paredes, A., Gregory, D., & Jones, B. M. Induced drinking and social adjustment in alcoholics: Development of a therapeutic model. *Quarterly Journal of Studies on Alcohol*, 1974, *35*, 1279–1293.

Passini, F. T., Watson, C. G., Dehnel, L., Herder, J., & Watkins, B. Alpha wave biofeedback training therapy in alcoholics. *Journal of Clinical Psychology*, 1977, *33*, 292–299.

Penick, S. B., Carrier, R. N., & Sheldon, J. B. Metronidazole in the treatment of alcoholism. *American Journal of Psychiatry*, 1969, *125*, 1063–1066.

Penick, S. B., Sheldon, J. B., Templer, D. I., & Carrier, R. N. Four year follow-up of metronidazole treatment program for alcoholism. *Industrial Medicine and Surgery*, 1971, *40*, 30–32.

Piorkowski, G. K., & Mann, E. T. Issues in treatment efficacy research with alcoholics. *Perceptual and Motor Skills*, 1975, *41*, 695–700.

Pittman, D. J., & Tate, R. L. A comparison of two treatment programs for alcoholics. *Quarterly Journal of Studies on Alcohol*, 1969, *30*, 888–889.

Pittman, D. J., & Tate, R. L. A comparison of two treatment programs for alcoholics. *International Journal of Social Psychiatry*, 1972, *18*, 183–193.

Reed, A. C., Van Lewen, A., & Williams, J. H. Effects of progressive relaxation on alcoholic patients. *Quarterly Journal of the Florida Academy of Sciences*, 1972, *34*, 213–222.

Reinert, R. E. A comparison of reserpine and disulfiram in the treatment of alcoholism. *Quarterly Journal of Studies on Alcohol*, 1958, *19*, 617–622.

Reynolds, C. M., Merry, J., & Coppen, A. Prophylactic treatment of alcoholism by lithium carbonate: An initial report. Alcoholism: *Clinical and Experimental Research*, 1977, *1*, 109–111.

Robson, R. A. H., Paulus, I., & Clarke, G. G. An evaluation of the effect of a clinic treatment program on the rehabilitation of alcoholic patients. *Quarterly Journal of Studies on Alcohol*, 1965, *26*, 264–278.

Rosenberg, C. M. Drug maintenance in the outpatient treatment of chronic alcoholism. *Archives of General Psychiatry*, 1974, *30*, 373–377.

Rothstein, E., & Clancy, D. D. Combined use of disulfiram and metronidazole in treatment of alcoholism. *Quarterly Journal of Studies on Alcohol*, 1970, *31*, 446–447.

Schaefer, H. H., Sobell, M. B., & Mills, K. C. Some sobering data on the use of self-confrontation with alcoholics. *Behavior Therapy*, 1971, *2*, 28–39.

Schaefer, H. H., Sobell, M. B., & Sobell, L. C. Twelve month follow-up of hospitalized alcoholics given self-confrontation experiences by videotape. *Behavior Therapy*, 1972, *3*, 283–285.

Shaffer, J. W., Freinek, W. R., Wolf, S., Foxwell, N. H., & Kurland, A. A. A controlled evaluation of chlordiazepoxide (Librium) in the treatment of convalescing alcoholics. *Journal of Nervous and Mental Disease*, 1963, *137*, 494–507.

Shaffer, J. W., Freinek, W. R., Wolf, S., Foxwell, N. H., & Kurland, A. A. Replication of a study of nialamide in the treatment of convalescing alcoholics with emphasis on prediction of response. *Current Therapeutic Research*, 1964, *6*, 521–530.

Shaffer, J. W., Hanlon, T. E., Wolf, S., Foxwell, N. H., & Kurland, A. A. Nialamide in the treatment of alcoholism. *Journal of Nervous and Mental Disease*, *1962*, *135*, 222–232.

Scherer, S. E., & Freedberg, E. J. Effects of group videotape feedback on development of assertiveness skills in alcoholics: A follow-up study. *Psychological Reports*, 1976, *39*, 983–992.

Schlatter, E. K. E., & Lal, S. Treatment of alcoholism with Dent's oral apomorphine method. *Quarterly Journal of Studies on Alcohol*, 1972, *33*, 430–436.

Smart, R. G. Do some alcoholics do better in some types of treatment than others? *Drug and Alcohol Dependence*, 1978, *3*, 65–75.

Smart, R. G., Storm, T., Baker, E. F. W., & Solursh, L. A controlled study of lysergide in the treatment of alcoholism. I. The effects on drinking behavior. *Quarterly Journal of Studies on Alcohol*, 1966, *27*, 469–482.

Smart, R. G., Storm, T., Baker, E. F. W., & Solursh, L. *Lysergic acid diethylamide (LSD) in the treatment of alcoholism: An investigation of its effects on drinking behavior, personality structure, and social functioning.* (Brookside Monograph, No. 6) Toronto: University of Toronto Press, 1967.

Sobell, L. C. Alcohol treatment outcome evaluation: Contributions from behavioral research. In P. E. Nathan & G. A. Marlatt (Eds.), *Experimental and behavioral approaches to alcoholism*. New York: Plenum Press, 1978, in press.

Sobell, M. B. Alternatives to abstinence: Evidence, issues and some proposals. In P. E. Nathan & G. A. Marlatt

200

(Eds.), *Experimental and behavioral approaches to alcoholism.* New York: Plenum Press, 1978, in press.

Sobell, M. B., & Sobell, L. C. Individualized behavior therapy for alcoholics: Rationale, procedures, preliminary results and appendix. *California Mental Health Research Monograph* No. 13. Sacramento: California Department of Mental Hygiene, 1972.

Sobell, M. B., & Sobell, L. C. Alcoholics treated by individualized behavior therapy: One year treatment outcome. *Behaviour Research and Therapy,* 1973, *11,* 599–618. (a)

Sobell, M. B., & Sobell, L. C. Individualized behavior therapy for alcoholics. *Behavior Therapy,* 1973, *4,* 49–72. (b)

Sobell, M. B., & Sobell, L. C. Second year treatment outcome of alcoholics treated by individualized behavior therapy: Results. *Behaviour Research and Therapy,* 1976, *14,* 195–215.

Soskin, R. A. Personality and attitude change after two alcoholism treatment programs: Comparative contributions of lysergide and human relations training. *Quarterly Journal of Studies on Alcohol,* 1970, *31,* 920–931.

Stein, L. I., Newton, J. R., & Bowman, R. S. Duration of hospitalization for alcoholism. *Archives of General Psychiatry,* 1975, *32,* 247–252.

Storm, T., & Cutler, R. E. Systematic desensitization in the treatment of alcoholics: An experimental trial. Unpublished manuscript, Alcoholism Foundation of British Columbia, 1968.

Swinson, R. P. Long term trial of metronidazole in male alcoholics. *British Journal of Psychiatry,* 1971, *119,* 85–89.

Tomsovic, M., & Edwards, R. V. Lysergide treatment of schizophrenic and nonschizophrenic alcoholics: A controlled evaluation. *Quarterly Journal of Studies on Alcohol,* 1970, *31,* 932–949.

Turek, I. S., Ota, K., Brown, C., Massari, F., & Kurland, A. A. Tiotixene and thioridazine in alcoholism treatment. *Quarterly Journal of Studies on Alcohol,* 1973, *34,* 853–859.

Tyndel, M., Fraser, J. G., & Hartleib, C. J. Metronidazole as an adjuvant in the treatment of alcoholism. *British Journal of Addiction,* 1969, *64,* 57–61.

Van Dusen, W., Wilson, W., Miners, W., & Hook, H. Treatment of alcoholism with lysergide. *Quarterly Journal of Studies on Alcohol,* 1967, *28,* 295–304.

Vogler, R. E., Compton, J. V., & Weissbach, T. A. Integrated behavior change techniques for alcoholics. *Journal of Consulting and Clinical Psychology,* 1975, *43,* 233–243.

Vogler, R. E., Lunde, S. E., Johnson, G. R., & Martin, P. L. Electrical aversion conditioning with chronic alcoholics. *Journal of Consulting and Clinical Psychology,* 1970, *34,* 302–307.

Vogler, R. E., Weissbach, T. A., & Compton, J. V. Learning techniques for alcohol abuse. *Behaviour Research and Therapy,* 1977, *15,* 31–38.

Wallerstein, R. S. *Hospital treatment of alcoholism: A comparative experimental study.* (Menninger Clinic Monograph Series, No. 11) New York: Basic Books, 1957.

Wanberg, K. W., Horn, J. L., & Fairchild, D. Hospital versus community treatment of alcoholism problems. *International Journal of Mental Health,* 1974, *3,* 160–176.

Waters, W. E., Cochrane, A. L., & Collins, J. Evaluation of social therapy in chronic alcoholism. *British Journal of Preventive and Social Medicine,* 1972, *26,* 57–58.

Wedel, H. L. Involving alcoholics in treatment. *Quarterly Journal of Studies on Alcohol,* 1965, *26,* 468–479.

Whyte, C. R., & O'Brien, P. M. J. Disulfiram implant: A controlled trial. *British Journal of Psychiatry,* 1974, *124,* 42–44.

Willems, P. J. A., Letemendia, F. J. J., & Arroyave, F. A categorization for the assessment of prognosis and outcome in the treatment of alcoholism. *British Journal of Psychiatry,* 1973, *122,* 649–654. (a)

Willems, P. J. A., Letemendia, F. J. J., & Arroyave, F. A two-year follow-up study comparing short with long stay in-patient treatment of alcoholics. *British Journal of Psychiatry,* 1973, *122,* 637–648. (b)

Wilson, A., Davidson, W. J., & White, J. Disulfiram implantation: Placebo, psychological deterrent, and pharmacological deterrent effects. *British Journal of Psychiatry,* 1976, *129,* 277–280.